Mothering Rhetorics

Once only a topic among women in the private sphere, motherhood and mothering have become important intellectual topics across academic disciplines. Even so, no book has yet devoted a sustained look at how exploring mothering rhetorics – the *rhetorics of reproduction* (rhetorics about the reproductive function of women/mothers) and *reproducing rhetorics* (the rhetorical reproduction of ideological systems and logics of contemporary culture) expand our understanding of mothering, motherhood, communication, and gender.

Mothering Rhetorics begins to fill this gap for scholars and teachers interested in the study of mothering rhetorics in their historical and contemporary permutations. The contributions explore the racialized rhetorical contexts of maternity; how fixing food is thought to fix families, while also regulating maternal activities and identity; how Black female breastfeeding activists resisted the exploitation of African-American mothers in Detroit; how women in pink-collar occupations both adhere to and challenge maternity leave discourses by rhetorically positioning their leaves as time off and (dis)ability; identifying verbal and nonverbal shaming practices related to unwed motherhood during the mid-twentieth century; and redefining alternative postpartum placenta practices.

This book was originally published as a special issue of *Women's Studies in Communication*.

Lynn O'Brien Hallstein is Associate Professor of Rhetoric in the College of General Studies and an Affiliated Faculty of the Women's, Gender & Sexuality Studies Program at Boston University, USA. She is the author or editor of four books, multiple book chapters, and has been published in a variety of feminist and communication journals.

Mothering Rhetorics

Edited by
Lynn O'Brien Hallstein

LONDON AND NEW YORK

First published 2019
by Routledge
2 Park Square, Milton Park, Abingdon, Oxon, OX14 4RN, UK

and by Routledge
711 Third Avenue, New York, NY 10017, USA

Routledge is an imprint of the Taylor & Francis Group, an informa business

© 2019 The Organization for Research on Women and Communication.

All rights reserved. No part of this book may be reprinted or reproduced or utilised in any form or by any electronic, mechanical, or other means, now known or hereafter invented, including photocopying and recording, or in any information storage or retrieval system, without permission in writing from the publishers.

Trademark notice: Product or corporate names may be trademarks or registered trademarks, and are used only for identification and explanation without intent to infringe.

British Library Cataloguing-in-Publication Data
A catalogue record for this book is available from the British Library

ISBN13: 978-1-138-60045-4

Typeset in Minion Pro
by codeMantra

Publisher's Note
The publisher accepts responsibility for any inconsistencies that may have arisen during the conversion of this book from journal articles to book chapters, namely the possible inclusion of journal terminology.

Disclaimer
Every effort has been made to contact copyright holders for their permission to reprint material in this book. The publishers would be grateful to hear from any copyright holder who is not here acknowledged and will undertake to rectify any errors or omissions in future editions of this book.

Contents

Citation Information		vi
Notes on Contributors		viii
	Introduction: Mothering Rhetorics *D. Lynn O'Brien Hallstein*	1
1	Michelle Obama, Mom-in-Chief: The Racialized Rhetorical Contexts of Maternity *Sara Hayden*	11
2	Fixing Food to Fix Families: Feeding Risk Discourse and the Family Meal *Amber E. Kinser*	29
3	#SpoiledMilk: Blacktavists, Visibility, and the Exploitation of the Black Breast *Megan Elizabeth Morrissey and Karen Y. Kimball*	48
4	Standpoints of Maternity Leave: Discourses of Temporality and Ability *Patrice M. Buzzanell, Robyn V. Remke, Rebecca Meisenbach, Meina Liu, Venessa Bowers, and Cindy Conn*	67
5	Rhetorics of Unwed Motherhood and Shame *Heather Brook Adams*	91
6	Empowering Disgust: Redefining Alternative Postpartum Placenta Practices *Elizabeth Dickinson, Karen Foss, and Charlotte Kroløkke*	111
	Index	129

Citation Information

The chapters in this book were originally published in the Journal *Women's Studies in Communication* volume 40, issue 1 (February 2017). When citing this material, please use the original page numbering for each article, as follows:

Introduction
Introduction: Mothering Rhetorics
D. Lynn O'Brien Hallstein
Women's Studies in Communication, volume 40, issue 1 (February 2017) pp. 1–10

Chapter 1
Michelle Obama, Mom-in-Chief: The Racialized Rhetorical Contexts of Maternity
Sara Hayden
Women's Studies in Communication, volume 40, issue 1 (February 2017) pp. 11–28

Chapter 2
Fixing Food to Fix Families: Feeding Risk Discourse and the Family Meal
Amber E. Kinser
Women's Studies in Communication, volume 40, issue 1 (February 2017) pp. 29–47

Chapter 3
#SpoiledMilk: Blacktavists, Visibility, and the Exploitation of the Black Breast
Megan Elizabeth Morrissey and Karen Y. Kimball
Women's Studies in Communication, volume 40, issue 1 (February 2017) pp. 48–66

Chapter 4
Standpoints of Maternity Leave: Discourses of Temporality and Ability
Patrice M. Buzzanell, Robyn V. Remke, Rebecca Meisenbach, Meina Liu, Venessa Bowers, and Cindy Conn
Women's Studies in Communication, volume 40, issue 1 (February 2017) pp. 67–90

Chapter 5
Rhetorics of Unwed Motherhood and Shame
Heather Brook Adams
Women's Studies in Communication, volume 40, issue 1 (February 2017) pp. 91–110

CITATION INFORMATION

Chapter 6

Empowering Disgust: Redefining Alternative Postpartum Placenta Practices
Elizabeth Dickinson, Karen Foss, and Charlotte Kr?kke
Women's Studies in Communication, volume 40, issue 1 (February 2017) pp. 111-128

For any permission-related enquiries please visit:
http://www.tandfonline.com/page/help/permissions

Notes on Contributors

Venessa Bowers is Clinical Social Worker Specialist for Eastern Shore Psychological Services, USA.

Heather Brook Adams is Assistant Professor in the Department of English at the University of North Carolina at Greensboro, USA.

Patrice M. Buzzanell is Chair and Professor of the Department of Communication at the University of South Florida and Endowed Visiting Professor for the School of Media and Design at Shanghai Jiaotong University.

Cindy Conn is Assistant Professor in the Department of Management in the Love School of Business at Elon University, USA.

Elizabeth Dickinson is Clinical Associate Professor of Management and Corporate Communication in the Kenan-Flagler Business School at the University of North Carolina at Chapel Hill, USA. She also is an affiliated Faculty Member in the Curriculum for the Environment and Ecology in the College of Arts & Sciences.

Karen Foss is Professor Emeritus, Regents Professor, Presidential Teaching Fellow, and former Chair of the Department of Communication & Journalism at the University of New Mexico, Albuquerque, USA.

Lynn O'Brien Hallstein is Associate Professor of Rhetoric in the College of General Studies and an Affiliated Faculty of the Women's, Gender & Sexuality Studies Program at Boston University, USA. She is the author or editor of four books, multiple book chapters, and has been published in a variety of feminist and communication journals.

Sara Hayden is Professor in the Department of Communication Studies at the University of Montana, Missoula, USA.

Karen Y. Kimball is an Adjunct Instructor in the Department of Communication Studies at the University of North Texas, Denton, USA.

Amber E. Kinser is Professor of Communication and Women's Studies and Chair of the Department of Communication at East Tennessee State University, Johnson City, USA.

Charlotte Krol\u00f8kke is Professor in the Department for the Study of Culture at the University of Southern Denmark, Odense, Denmark.

Meina Liu is Associate Professor of Communication and Director of the MA Program in Communication Management at George Washington University, Washington, D.C., USA.

NOTES ON CONTRIBUTORS

Rebecca Meisenbach is Associate Professor of Organizational Communication at the University of Missouri, Columbia, USA.

Megan Elizabeth Morrissey is Assistant Professor in the Department of Communication Studies at the University of North Texas, Denton, USA.

Robyn V. Remke is Lecturer in the Department of Leadership and Management at Lancaster University Management School, UK.

INTRODUCTION

Introduction: Mothering Rhetorics

D. Lynn O'Brien Hallstein

Once only a topic among women in the private sphere, motherhood and mothering have become important intellectual topics across academic disciplines, including communication studies. Indeed, books (Hayden and O'Brien Hallstein's *Contemplating Maternity in an Era of Choice*; Hundley and Hayden's *Mediated Moms*; Buchanan's *Rhetorics of Motherhood*; Demo, Borda, and Kr"lokke's *The Motherhood Business*; Seigel's *The Rhetoric of Pregnancy*; O'Brien Hallstein's *White Feminists and Contemporary Maternity*), essays in communication journals, such as the *Quarterly Journal of Speech* (Tonn; Foss and Domenici; Hayden, "Family Metaphors"; Schely-Newman), the *Rhetoric Review* (Enoch), and even past issues of *Women's Studies in Communication* (Foster; Gilbert; Harris; Hayden, "Constituting Savvy"; O'Brien Hallstein, "She Gives Birth"; Peeples and DeLuca; Sotirin; Waggoner) have all shown the newfound importance of motherhood and mothering as both intellectual and communication topics.

Communication scholars, for example, have explored motherhood as a site of cultural and political struggle and as an important place to examine political, social, environmental, and/or reproductive justice (de Onís; Fabj; Fixmer-Oraiz; Foss and Domenici; Hayden, "Revitalizing the Debate"; Reid-Brinkley). Considering how mothers have used the ethos of maternal identity to build grassroots movements and to speak against various forms of injustice has also been a fruitful focus for communication scholars interested in motherhood (Di Chiro; Peeples and DeLuca; Hayden, "Family Metaphors"; Murray). Moreover, a variety of communication scholars have investigated the discourses of motherhood and care, how those discourses impact mothers, and women's experiences of mothering and the languages of motherhood (Arnold and Doran; Bochantin and Cowan; Dorgan, Hutson, Duvall, Kinser, and Hall; Foster; Gilbert and von Wallmenich; Townsley and Broadfoot; Kinser, "Mosaic," "If I Could"; Lockridge and Lockridge; Sotirin; Varallo).

Equally important, rhetoricians and scholars employing rhetorical approaches and working in communication have also examined the various rhetorical dimensions of motherhood and mothering (Buchanan; Dubriwny and Ramadurai; Foss and Domenici; Demo, Borda, and Krølokke; Flores; Gilbert; Gilbert and von Wallmenich; Harris; Hayden, "Constituting"; Hayden and O'Brien Hallstein; O'Brien Hallstein, "She Gives Birth," *Bikini-Ready Moms*; Kinser, *Mothering in the Third Wave*; Mack, "The Self-Made Mom"). This work has revealed that motherhood has rhetorical force: Motherhood functions, as Lindal Buchanan argues, drawing on Richard Weaver, as a "god term" in culture, shaping positive connotations, assumptions, and ideals about women, family, and society (8). Moreover, as

Buchanan also contends, motherhood and mothering are rhetorical topoi: locations or spaces in art where speakers can look for "available means of persuasion" (3).

Even though motherhood and mothering are clearly now important intellectual topics within communication generally and within rhetorical studies specifically, no communication journal has yet offered a sustained look at how exploring mothering rhetorics expands our understanding of communication studies and rhetoric, nor how rhetorical methods or concepts can also help us better understand mothering, motherhood, communication, and gender. Thus, this special issue on mothering rhetorics—the rhetorics of reproduction (rhetorics about the reproductive function of women/mothers) and reproducing rhetorics (the rhetorical reproduction of ideological systems and logics of contemporary culture)[1]—seeks to begin to fill this gap for scholars and educators interested in the study of mothering rhetorics in their historical and contemporary permutations, while also enabling *Women's Studies in Communication* to break new ground and further advance the intellectual agenda for exploring mothering rhetorics in communication studies generally and women's studies in communication specifically.

Intellectual context

While this is the first issue devoted to mothering rhetorics, contemporary work on motherhood and mothering has begun to develop some key foundational tenets that are germane to the essays in this special issue. Each of the essays here assumes and is grounded in a key distinction that Adrienne Rich first detailed in her landmark book, *Of Woman Born: Motherhood as Experience and Institution*. In the book, Rich made an all-important distinction between the institution of motherhood and the potential empowered relations in mothering. In viewing motherhood as a complex site of women's oppression and as a potential location of women's creativity and joy, Rich argued, "I try to distinguish two meanings of motherhood, one superimposed on the other: the *potential relationship* of any woman to her powers of reproduction and to children; and the *institution*, which aims at ensuring that that potential—and all women—shall remain under male control" (13; italics in original). Based on this groundbreaking distinction, Rich viewed the institution of motherhood as male defined, male controlled, and deeply oppressive to women, while she viewed the experience of mothering as a potentially empowering relationship for both women and children. All essays here explore the institution of motherhood or what contemporary scholars now, often, refer to as *institutionalized motherhood*.

Today, institutionalized motherhood is premised on the contemporary hegemonic ideology of "good mothering," what Sharon Hays first named *intensive mothering*, Andrea O'Reilly calls *patriarchal mothering,* and what Susan J. Douglas and Meredith Michaels call *the new momism*. While each of these three labels takes a slightly different focus—Douglas and Michaels, for example, explore how the new momism emerged via mediated representations of motherhood—all agree that this "good mothering" ideology emerged in the 1980s and continues to be in full force today, albeit in new and even more intensive ways (O'Brien Hallstein, *Bikini-Ready Moms*). Drawing on Sharon Hays' work, Douglas and Michaels argue that this "good mothering" ideology rests on three core beliefs and values: "the insistence that no woman is truly complete or fulfilled unless she has kids, that women remain the best primary caretakers of children, and that to be a remotely decent mother, a woman has to devote her entire physical, psychological, emotional, and intellectual being,

24/7, to her children" (4). These three core principles also mean that the new momism requires mothers to develop professional-level skills, such as therapist, pediatrician, consumer products safety instructor, and teacher, to meet and treat the needs of children (Douglas and Michaels 6). In addition to creating impossible ideals of mothering, the new momism also defines women first and foremost in relation to their children and encourages women to believe that mothering is the most important job for women, regardless of any professional or educational success a woman might have had prior to motherhood. Consequently, Douglas and Michaels suggest the new momism no longer makes women subservient to men and instead makes mothers subservient "to children" (299).

Moreover, as I have argued elsewhere ("Public Choices"; *Bikini-Ready Moms*), the new momism is a post–second wave backlash ideology, because it both acknowledges and integrates second wave feminist rhetoric and ideas, while also continuing to reinforce childrearing and child care as mothers' responsibilities. Indeed, the post–second wave middle-class premise that contemporary women now have the choice to "have it all" is entrenched in the new momism. Specifically, first young girls and then young women are taught that they live at a time when women can "do it all": have an education, a career, and a family as long as they make good choices. As Douglas and Michaels put it, embedded in the new momism is the idea that women:

> have their own ambitions and money, raise kids on their own, or freely choose to stay at home with kids rather than being forced to … . Central to the new momism, in fact, is the feminist insistence that woman [*sic*] have choices, that they are active agents in control of their own destiny, that they have autonomy. (5)

In short, institutionalized motherhood today simultaneously acknowledges the large-scale changes brought about by second wave feminisms, while also being a backlash ideology that keeps mothers primarily responsible, still, for childrearing and family-life management. Thus, as I have argued elsewhere (*Bikini-Ready Moms*), this also means that intensive mothering acknowledges that gender roles and expectations have changed in the public sphere without significantly changing in terms of ongoing gender-based assumptions and expectations that mothers are still primarily responsible for childrearing and caregiving in the private sphere.

Acknowledging the various forms of privilege that are intertwined and reinforced by intensive mothering in all of its permutations is crucial to any analysis of mothering rhetorics. Doing so is important because intersectional theorists (Chávez and Griffin; Collins; Crenshaw; Reid-Brinkley) have shown that women's lives are shaped differently based on intersecting factors of race, class, and sexuality; the same is true both for mothers generally and specifically for how mothers are positioned in relation to institutionalized motherhood because intensive mothering is thoroughly ensconced in economic, racial, cisgender, and heterosexual privilege. In fact, today, this "good mothering" ideology assumes and promotes privileged motherhood, primarily by reinforcing White, at least middle-class, cisgender, heterosexual privilege, and an even more intensive ideology of good mothering, and any mother who "fails" to meet the standards of intensive mothering is policed and labeled a "bad mother." Or, as Shanara Reid-Brinkley puts it, "The Good White Mother in the U.S. social imagination stands as an idealized standard for femininity that constrains all women across various intersections, although in markedly different ways" (46).

Consequently, as Natalie Fixmer-Oraiz suggested recently in this journal, "the capacity to be valued and publicly lauded for motherhood remains a privilege of Whiteness, wealth, and heteronuclear family formation" (131).

The essays here all acknowledge these facts, and all contributors have situated their specific work in mothering rhetorics intersectionally. In the context of this special issue, this means that all contributors have heeded Karma Chávez and Cindy Griffin's call for communication scholars to recognize and acknowledge that both scholars themselves and their intellectual projects are shaped by social location. As Griffin and Chávez suggest in the introduction to *Standing in the Intersection*, "Integrating an intersectional approach to the study of communication requires that scholars recognize that each individual stands and swims in the intersections of race/gender/sex/sexuality/ability/economic means and more" (19). Situating this imperative explicitly within the context of mothering rhetorics, Reid-Brinkley argues that in the United States "motherhood has various symbolic associations, particularly when intersected by race, class, sexuality, nationality, and religion. Not all women have equal access to the rhetorical saliency of the motherhood frame" (46).

As a result, a focus on mothering rhetorics requires communication scholars to recognize the "rhetorical saliency" of motherhood, as Amber E. Kinser does when she situates her interviewees in relation to their class position vis-à-vis education and the discourse of food; as Megan Elizabeth Morrissey and Karen Y. Kimball do by exploring the complex, overlapping, and nuanced manner in which power circulates to place Black mothers within the U.S. social hierarchy to reveal how Black breastfeeding activists assert agency within the complex power relations in which they are positioned; as does Sara Hayden by situating Michelle Obama within the complex and dynamic contextual field in which Obama circulates in order to situate and explain the divergent responses of Black and White scholars to Obama; as do Elizabeth Dickinson, Karen Foss, and Charlotte Kroløkke when they situate postpartum placenta practices as primarily middle- to upper-class, college-educated, heterosexual, White mothers' practices; as does Heather Brook Adams when she situates the narratives of 1960s once-unwed mothers within the unspoken raced and classed purity practice of hiding unwed pregnancy; and, finally, as do Patrice M. Buzzanell, Robyn V. Remke, Rebecca Meisenbach, Meina Liu, Venessa Bowers, and Cindy Conn when they argue that it is imperative that we both recognize and study the different experiences "pink-collar" mothers face in terms of access to maternity leave.

Moreover, distinguishing the rhetorical saliency of motherhood also means recognizing that institutionalized motherhood denies and/or fails to recognize Black mothering practices and Black mothers, the subjects of two essays here. Contemporary feminist scholars (Collins; Edwards; O'Reilly; James; Thomas) have shown decisively that Black mothers and Black feminists have had a very different relationship to both institutionalized motherhood and mothering, including within the context of second wave feminisms. Indeed, bell hooks suggests that during the second wave "had black women voiced their views on motherhood, it would not have been named a serious obstacle to our freedom as women. Racism, availability of jobs, lack of skills or education ... would have been at the top of the list—but not motherhood" (133). In addition, Black feminist scholars (Collins; Edwards; James; Thomas) have resolutely shown that African American mothers have traditionally used and continue to use mothering practices that are nonnormative within institutionalized motherhood because they engage in othermothering—the practice of accepting responsibility for a child that is not one's own, in an arrangement that may or may not be formal—and community mothering—the practice of supporting and sustaining the larger community (James). Unfortunately, however, the practices of othermothering and community mothering are often viewed by dominant culture as "inappropriate" maternal practices because they deviate from the institutionalized White intensive ideology of mothering, even though many feminist maternal scholars (Collins; Edwards; James; O'Reilly; Thomas) view othermothering and community mothering as empowering for Black mothers—an important point that Hayden also notes in her essay. Moreover, as Morrissey and Kimball argue here, mothering rhetorics that reinforce hierarchal distinctions between Black and White mothers also continue to play into narratives that make Black motherhood and mothers suspect or even "bad." Thus, these hierarchal distinctions must be resisted and challenged in the study of mothering rhetorics.

This special issue on mothering rhetorics, then, takes as its foundation these key intellectual issues, implicitly or explicitly, because each contributor recognizes institutionalized motherhood, the ways that White intensive mothering privileges some mothers over others, while also heeding the call to situate their work intersectionally. In doing so, all of the essays in this special issue also take a critical rhetorical orientation to analysis in that the authors explore how cultural practices, discourses, and/or texts reproduce and/or challenge the reproductive function of mothers and/or the rhetorical reproduction of ideological systems and logics of contemporary motherhood.

The essays

Sara Hayden's essay, "Michelle Obama, Mom-in-Chief: The Racialized Rhetorical Contexts of Maternity," in fact, explores the divergent responses of Black and White scholars to Michelle Obama's self-professed mantel of "Mom-in-Chief" by considering the complex, dynamic, and paradoxical rhetorical contexts of maternity within which Obama's performances circulate and participate. As Obama participates in this complex and dynamic contextual field, Hayden maintains that Obama constructs a polysemous set of texts that are read differently by her Black and White audiences and that function simultaneously to reinforce and resist sexist and racist norms. Hayden ultimately argues that Obama's rhetorical performances, and the conflicting responses to them, can be understood as invoking the varied traditions of dominant White mothering ideologies, the denigration of Black motherhood in mainstream, White culture, and the African American tradition of othermothering.

In "Fixing Food to Fix Families: Feeding Risk Discourse and the Family Meal," Amber E. Kinser focuses on the ways that family meal discourse has emerged in contemporary culture as an ideological system that is working to shape and reproduce particular understandings of "good" motherhood. Exploring the influence of neoliberal thought, its relationship to constructions of family risk and well-being, and its focus on familializing risk, particularly feeding risk, Kinser reveals that the family meal discourse works as a reproducing mothering rhetoric that moralizes maternal feeding work and encourages mother blame, or the assignment of culpability for child outcomes to mothers. Kinser also concludes that family meal discourse is problematic because it obscures the ways in which it is mother-targeted and mother-blaming, suppresses maternal voice and misrepresents family food labor, and regulates maternal activity, delimiting maternal identity.

Scrutinizing the response to Medolac Laboratories' announced initiative to purchase pumped breast milk from African American mothers in Detroit, Michigan, in

"#SpoiledMilk: Blacktavists, Visibility, and the Exploitation of the Black Breast," Megan Elizabeth Morrissey and Karen Y. Kimball shift our attention to a community of Black female breastfeeding activists, or Blacktavists, who swiftly took to blogs, Twitter, and Facebook to express their concerns about the initiative. Also analyzing the valuable, problematic, and complex characteristics of Blacktavists' advocacy, Morrissey and Kimball argue that Blacktavists (working on, against, and through the Black breastfeeding body) constructed a persuasive narrative about Medolac's campaign that made visible (1) the historical legacy of Black labor for White interests, (2) the economic value of that labor, and (3) Whiteness as a racial category. They conclude that future successful advocacy must continue to challenge normative mothering rhetorics to bring about impactful social change.

By asking what maternity leave might look like if considered through the standpoints of mothers employed in pink-collar occupations, Patrice M. Buzzanell, Robyn V. Remke, Rebecca Meisenbach, Meina Liu, Venessa Bowers, and Cindy Conn expand our understanding of maternity leave by exploring how twenty-one women in pink-collar occupations both adhere to and challenge maternity leave discourses by rhetorically positioning their leaves as time off and (dis)ability in "Standpoints of Maternity Leave: Discourses of Temporality and Ability." Employing a feminist standpoint approach, Buzzanell and colleagues find that the women they interviewed both reproduce and contest contemporary mothering rhetorics by both acknowledging the advantages of and resisting discourses of time and (dis)ability by constructing complicated, contradictory, and ironic knowledge such that language both secures their leaves and revokes their images as competent workers. Buzzanell et al. conclude that, by using standpoint analyses, changes in organizational policy and workplace practices for mothers working in pink-collar occupations can be made based on common knowledge and differences in local-specific experiences.

In a diachronic study of mothering rhetorics that queers the recent history of motherhood, Heather Brook Adams, in the "Rhetorics of Unwed Motherhood and Shame," examines published and unpublished personal narratives of once-unwed and pregnant women of the 1960s who gave up or were forced to give up their children for adoption. Adams finds that all accounts cite shame as a primary factor shaping once-unwed mothers' "decisions" to surrender their children for adoption. Adams argues that, as rhetorics of reproduction, these stories account for an unspoken raced and classed purity practice of hiding unwed pregnancy and erasing an illicit mother identity because of the threat of communicable shame. Adams concludes, as reproducing rhetorics of shame, the narratives demarcate the pure from the impure and serve as a mechanism through which unwed pregnancy could be figured as proof of what she calls *ontological failure*. Adams also concludes that these histories enhance the study of mothering rhetorics because they populate a partial and secreted portion of the recent history of motherhood in the United States and demonstrate how motherhood was, paradoxically, an identity that was rhetorically foreclosed and factually true for these women, while the rhetorics of shame also functioned to maintain an ideal of morally pure motherhood recognized within the context of marriage.

Elizabeth Dickinson, Karen Foss, and Charlotte Krotøkke, in "Empowering Disgust: Redefining Alternative Postpartum Placenta Practices," examine communication practices surrounding the unconventional yet emerging trend of postpartum placenta use (e.g., eating, encapsulating, or burying the human placenta). Through interviews with both supporters and nonsupporters of postpartum placenta practices, Dickinson, Foss, and Kroløkke explore conceptualizations of placenta consumption and burial within larger mothering, childbirth, and postpartum rhetorics. They argue that alternative placenta practices function rhetorically within a core frame of disgust, which supporters and non-supporters initially use to respond to alternative placenta use. Yet Dickinson, Foss, and Kroløkke also argue that supporters move from a literal reading of disgust to create an empowering frame from which to view not only placenta use but also mainstream Western medicine. In effect, supporters reframe the meaning of disgust toward the medicalization of birth to position placenta practices and natural childbirth as empowering practices for mothers.

Taken as a whole, this issue reveals that communication studies generally and women's studies in communication specifically have much to offer the ongoing and growing work on and about motherhood. While exploring mothering rhetorics, these essays continue important conversations about key rhetorical concepts and methods—rhetorical contexts and polysemy (Hayden); historiography and rhetorical shaming (Adams); discourse analyses and food (Kinser); feminist standpoint theory (Buzzanell et. al); the rhetoric of disgust and reframing meaning as rhetorical strategies (Dickinson, Foss, and Kroløkke), and visibility as a rhetorical strategy in advocacy (Morrissey and Kimball). Thus, while the contributors continue to expand our understanding of how mothering rhetorics work as rhetorics of reproduction and reproducing rhetorics, they also offer important and exciting insights about how rhetorical methods and concepts can also help us better understand mothering, motherhood, communication, and gender.

Note

1. I am indebted to Ashley Mack's work in her dissertation, "Disciplining Mommy: Rhetorics of Reproduction in Contemporary Maternity Culture," for this definition of *mothering rhetorics*.

Works cited

Adams, Heather Brook. "Rhetorics of Unwed Motherhood and Shame." *Women's Studies in Communication* 40.1 (2017): 91–110. Print.
Arnold, Leslie B., and E. Doran. "Stop Before You Hurt the Kids: Communicating Self-Control and Self-Negation in Femininity, Mothering, and Eating Disorders." *Women's Studies in Communication* 30.3 (2007): 310–39. Print.
Bochantin, Jamie E., and Renee L. Cowan. "Total Motherhood and Having It All: Reproduction, Maternity, and Discourses of Choice among Female Police Officers." *Contemplating Maternity in an Era of Choice: Explorations into Discourses of Reproduction*. Ed. Sara Hayden and D. Lynn O'Brien Hallstein. Lanham, MD: Lexington Books, 2010. 247–66. Print.
Borda, Jennifer. "Lean in or Leave Before You Leave? False Dichotomies of Choice and Blame in Public Debates about Working Motherhood." *The Mother Blame-Game*. Ed. Vanessa Reimer and Sarah Sahagian. Toronto, Canada: Demeter Press, 2015. 219–36. Print.
Buchanan, Lindal. *Rhetorics of Motherhood*. Carbondale: Southern Illinois UP, 2013. Print.
Buzzanell, Patrice M., Robyn V. Remke, Rebecca Meisenbach, Meina Liu, Venessa Bowers, and Cindy Conn. "Standpoints of Maternity Leave: Discourses of Temporality and Ability." *Women's Studies in Communication* 40.1 (2017): 67–90. Print.
Chávez, Karma, and Cindy Griffin eds. *Standing in the Intersection: Feminist Voices, Feminist Practices in Communication Studies*. Albany: State U of New York P, 2012. Print.

Collins, Patricia H. "The Meaning of Motherhood in Black Culture and Black Mother/Daughter Relationships." *Double Stitch: Black Women Write about Mothers and Daughters.* Ed. Patricia Bell-Scott Beverly Guy-Sheftall Jacqueline Jones Royster Janet Sims-Wood, Miriam DeCosta-Willis and Lucie Fultz. Boston: Beacon Press, 1991. 42–60. Print.

Crenshaw, Kimberle. "Mapping the Margins: Intersectionality, Identity Politics, and Violence against Women of Color." *Stanford Law Review* 43.6 (1991): 1241–1299. Print.

Demo, Anne Teresa, Jennifer Borda, and Charlotte Kroløkke eds. *The Motherhood Business: Consumption, Communication, and Privilege.* Tuscaloosa: U of Alabama P, 2015. Print.

de Onís, Kathleen M. "Lost in Translation: Challenging (White, Monolingual Feminism's) <Choice> with *Justicia Reproductiva*." *Women's Studies in Communication* 38.1 (2015): 1–19. Print.

Di Chiro, Giovanna. "Local Actions, Global Visions: Remaking Environmental Expertise." *Frontiers: A Journal of Women Studies* 18.2 (1997): 203–31. Print.

Dickinson, Elizabeth, Karen Foss, and Charlotte Kroløkke. "Empowering Disgust: Redefining Alernative Postpartum Placenta Practices." *Women's Studies in Communication* 40.1 (2017): 111–128. Print.

Dorgan, Kellie A., Sadie P. Hutson, Kathryn L. Duvall, Amber E. Kinser, and Joanne M. Hall. "Connecting Place to Disease and Gender: Cohabitating Morbidities in Narratives of Women Cancer Survivors in Southern Central Appalachia." *Women's Studies in Communication* 37.3 (2014): 292–312. Print.

Douglas, Susan J., and Meredith Michaels. *The Mommy Myth: The Idealization of Motherhood and How It Has Undermined Women.* New York: Free Press, 2004. Print.

Dubriwny, Tasha, and Vandhana Ramadurai. "Framing Birth: Postfeminism in the Delivery Room." *Women's Studies in Communication* 36.3 (2013): 243–66. Print.

Edwards, Arlene. "Community Mothering: The Relationship between Mothering and the Community Work of Black Women." *Mother Outlaws: Theories and Practices of Empowered Mothering.* Ed. Andrea O'Reilly. Toronto, Canada: Women's Press, 2004. 203–14. Print.

Enoch, Jessica. "There's No Place Like the Childcare Center: A Feminist Analysis of in the World War II Era." *Rhetoric Review* 31.4 (2012): 422–42. Print.

Fabj, Valerie. "Motherhood as Political Voice: The Rhetoric of the Mothers of Plaza de Mayo." *Communication Studies* 44.1 (1993): 1–8. Print.

Fixmer-Oraiz, Natalie. "Contemplating Homeland Maternity." *Women's Studies in Communication* 38.2 (2015): 129–34. Print.

Flores, Lisa. "Choosing to Consume: Race, Education, and the School Voucher Debate." *The Motherhood Business: Consumption, Communication, and Privilege.* Ed. Anne Teresa Demo, Jennifer Borda and Charlotte Kroløkke. Tuscaloosa: U of Alabama P, 2015. 243–67. Print.

Foss, Karen A., and Kathy L. Domenici. "Haunting Argentina: Synecdoche in the Protests of the Mothers of the Plaza de Mayo." *Quarterly Journal of Speech* 87.3 (2001): 237–58. Print.

Foster, Elissa. "Desiring Dialectical Discourse: A Feminist Ponders the Transition to Motherhood." *Women's Studies in Communication* 28.1 (2005): 57–83.

Gilbert, Joanne. "Why I Feel Guilty All the Time: Performing Academic Motherhood." *Women's Studies in Communication* 31.2 (2008): 203–08. Print.

Gilbert, Joanne, and Laura von Wallmenich. "When Words Fail Us: Mother Time, Relational Attention, and the Rhetorics of Focus and Balance." *Women's Studies in Communication* 37.1 (2014): 66–89. Print.

Griffin, Cindy, and Karma Chávez. "Introduction: Standing at the Intersections of Feminisms, Intersectionality, and Communication Studies." *Standing in the Intersection: Feminist Voices, Feminist Practices in Communication Studies.* Ed. Karma Chávez and Cindy Griffin. Albany: State U of New York P, 2012. 1–34. Print.

Harris, Leslie J. "Motherhood, Race, and Gender: The Rhetoric of Women's Antislavery Activism in the *Liberty Bell* Gift Books." *Women's Studies in Communication* 32.3 (2009): 293–319. Print.

Hayden, Sara. "Constituting Savvy Aunties: From Childless Women to Child-Focused Consumers." *Women's Studies in Communication* 34.1 (2011): 1–19. Print.

———. "Family Metaphors and the Nation: Promoting a Politics of Care Through the Million Moms March." *Quarterly Journal of Speech* 89.3 (2003): 196–215. Print.

———. "Michelle Obama, Mom-in-Chief: The Racialized Rhetorical Contexts of Maternity." *Women's Studies in Communication* 40.1 (2017): 11–28. Print.

———. "Revitalizing the Debate between <Life> and <Choice>: The 2004 March for Women's Lives." *Communication and Critical/Cultural Studies* 6.2 (2009): 111–31. Print.

Hayden, Sara, and Lynn O'Brien Hallstein eds. *Contemplating Maternity in an Era of Choice: Explorations into Discourses of Choice.* Lanham, MD: Lexington Books, 2010. Print.

hooks, bell. *Feminist Theory: From Margin to Center.* Boston: South End Press, 1984. Print.

Hundley, Heather, and Sara E. Hayden. *Mediated Moms: Contemporary Challenges to the Motherhood Myth.* New York: Peter Lang, 2016. Print.

James, Stanlie. "Mothering: A Possible Black Feminist Link to Social Transformation?" *Theorizing Black Feminisms: The Visionary Pragmatism of Black Women.* Ed. Stanlie M. James and Abena P. A. Busia. New York: Routledge Press, 1993. 44–54. Print.

Kinser, Amber. "Fixing Food to Fix Families: Feeding Risk Discourse and the Family Meal." *Women's Studies in Communication* 40.1 (2017): 29–47. Print.

———. "If I Could Give a Yopp: Confronting Sex, Talk, & Parenting." *Performing Motherhood: Artist, Activist, & Everyday Enactments.* Ed. Amber E. Kinser Kryn Freehling-Burton and Terri Hawkes. Bradford, ON: Demeter Press. 2014. 121–31. Print.

———. "A Mosaic of Pregnancy Expertise." *Mother Knows Best: Talking Back to the Experts.* Ed. Jessica Nathanson and Laurie Camille Tuley. Toronto: Demeter Press, 2009. 25–33. Print.

———, ed. *Mothering in the Third Wave.* Toronto: Demeter Press, 2008. Print.

———. "Public Choices, Private Control: How Mediated Mom Labels Work Rhetorically to Dismantle the Politics of Choice and White Second Wave Feminist Successes." *Contemplating Maternity in an Era of Choice: Explorations of Discourses of Reproduction.* Ed. Sara Hayden and D. Lynn O'Brien Hallstein. Lanham, MD: Lexington Books, 2010. 5–26. Print.

Lockridge, Rebecca B., and Sarah Lockridge. "Mother Care/Daughter Care: The Bridge That Is My Back." *Mothers, & Daughters: Complicated Connections across Cultures.* Ed. Alice H. Deakins Rebecca B. Lockridge, and Helen M. Sterk. Lanham, MD: UP of America. 2012. 105–20. Print.

Mack, Ashley N. "Disciplining Mommy: Rhetorics of Reproduction in Contemporary Maternity Culture." Diss. U of Texas at Austin, 2013. Web. <http://repositories.lib.utexas.edu/bitstream/handle/2152/21299/MACK-DISSERTATION-2013.pdf?sequence=1>.

———. "The Self-Made Mom: Neoliberalism and Masochistic Motherhood in Home-Birth Videos on YouTube." *Women's Studies in Communication* 39.1 (2016): 47–68. Print.

Marquez, Loren. "Narrating Our Lives: Retelling Mothering and Professional Work in Composition Studies." *Composition Studies* 39.1 (2011): 73–85. Print.

Morrissey, Megan Elizabeth, and Karen Y. Kimball. "#SpoiledMilk: Blacktavists, Visibility, and the Exploitation of the Black Breast." *Women's Studies in Communication* 40.1 (2017): 48–66. Print.

Murray, Billie. "For What Noble Cause: Cindy Sheehan and the Politics of Grief in Public Spheres of Argument." *Argumentation and Advocacy* 49 (2012): 1–15. Print.

O'Brien Hallstein, D. Lynn. *Bikini-Ready Moms: Celebrity Profiles, Motherhood, and the Body.* Albany: State U of New York P, 2015. Print.

———. "She Gives Birth, She's Wearing a Bikini: Mobilizing the Postpregnant Celebrity Mom Body to Manage the Post–Second Wave Crisis in Femininity." *Women's Studies in Communication* 34.2 (2011): 111–38.

———. *White Feminists and Contemporary Maternity: Purging Matrophobia.* New York: Palgrave Macmillan, 2010. Print.

O'Reilly, Andrea. *Mother Outlaws: Theories and Practices of Empowered Mothering.* Toronto: Women's Press, 2004. Print.

Peeples, Jennifer A., and Kevin DeLuca. "The Truth of the Matter: Motherhood, Community, and Environmental Justice." *Women's Studies in Communication* 29.1 (2006): 59–87. Print.

Reid-Brinkley, Shanara Rose. "Mammies and Matriarchs: Feminine Style and Signifyin(g) in Carol Moseley Braun's 2003–2004 Campaign for the Presidency." *Standing in the Intersection: Feminist Voices, Feminist Practices in Communication Studies.* Ed. Karma Chávez and Cindy Griffin. Albany: State U of New York P, 2012. 35–58. Print.

Rich, Adrienne. *Of Woman Born: Motherhood as Experience & Institution, 2nd ed.* New York: W. W. Norton, 1986. Print.

Schely-Newman, Esther. "Mothers Know Best: Constructing Meaning in a Narrative Event." *Quarterly Journal of Speech* 87.5 (1999): 285–302. Print.

Seigel, Marika. *The Rhetoric of Pregnancy.* Chicago: U of Chicago P, 2013. Print.

Sotirin, Patty. "Academic Momhood: In for the Long Haul." *Women's Studies in Communication* 31.2 (2008): 258–67. Print.

Thomas, Trudelle. "'You'll Become a Lioness': African-American Women Talk about Mothering." *Mother Outlaws: Theories and Practices of Empowered Mothering.* Ed. Andrea O'Reilly. Toronto, Canada: Women's Press, 2004. 215–28.

Tonn, Mari Boor. "Militant Motherhood: Labor's Mary Harris 'Mother' Jones." *Quarterly Journal of Speech* 82.1 (2001): 237–58. Print.

Townsley, Nikki C., and Kirsten Broadfoot. "Care, Career, and Academe: Heeding the Calls of a New Professoriate." *Women's Studies in Communication* 31.2 (2008): 133–42. Print.

Varallo, Sharon. "Mother Work in Academe: Intensive Caring for the Millennial Student." *Women's Studies in Communication* 31.2 (2008): 151–57. Print.

Waggoner, Catherine Egley. "Academic Adultery: Surreptitious Performances of the Professor/Mother." *Women's Studies in Communication* 31.2 (2008): 209–12. Print.

Michelle Obama, Mom-in-Chief: The Racialized Rhetorical Contexts of Maternity

Sara Hayden

ABSTRACT
Directly following her husband's 2008 election, Michelle Obama assumed the moniker "mom-in-chief," and in her tenure as first lady she has extended this role to "mother" the children of the nation through her policy choices. Noting her Ivy League education and her prior work as a high-powered attorney, many White feminists decried Obama's maternal focus. Black feminists, however, rejected those critiques, pointing to the progressive potential of Obama's maternal persona. In this article, I explain these divergent perspectives by examining Obama's maternal first lady rhetoric through an expansive understanding of context. Specifically, I argue that the varied readings of Obama's maternal performances reflect the racialized rhetorical contexts within which she was acting and through which audience members understood her. This analysis points to the importance of investigating the rhetorical contexts within which both audience members *and* rhetors circulate and participate.

First ladies of the United States occupy a role that is complex, heterogeneous, and paradoxical (Anderson, 2004; Wertheimer, 2004). Robert Watson (2000) lists 11 duties first ladies are expected to perform, and perhaps none is as challenging as the requirement to serve as the "symbol of American womanhood" when assumptions about what an "ideal woman" entails are in constant flux (Campbell, 1996; Wertheimer, 2004). Yet if all first ladies must negotiate a complex and demanding job, Michelle Obama, the first African American woman to step into this role in the United States, has faced even greater challenges. In speaking broadly of the position, Karrin Vasby Anderson (2004) noted that "first ladies have functioned as 'symbols' of traditional *white* middle- to upper-class femininity in America" (p. 18; emphasis added). Attending to Obama specifically, Patricia J. Williams (2009) wrote, "Even when she [was] holding court at the head of the White House dinner table, she [was] a 'black woman' performing a 'white lady' role." Obama's assumption of the first lady role thus brought to the forefront the intersections of gender, race, and class (also see McAlister, 2009).[1]

It is particularly noteworthy, then, that Michelle Obama has been popular throughout her tenure as first lady. According to a 2014 Gallup poll, "sixty-six percent of Americans [had] a favorable opinion of the first lady, unchanged from a year and a half [prior] and on par with her ratings since her husband's inauguration in January 2009" (Brown, 2014).

Indeed, Michelle Obama's popularity outpaced the president's, whose favorability ratings concurrently hovered around 52% (Brown, 2014).

Of course, while serving as first lady, Michelle Obama had her critics, and one thread of criticism came from what at first glance was an unexpected source: feminist pundits, many of whom were White.[2] Noting Obama's Ivy League education, her previous work as an attorney, and her position as vice president of University of Chicago hospitals, what bothered many of these pundits was Obama's choice to prioritize her maternity. For example, shortly after Barack Obama's election to the presidency, Rebecca Traister (2008) lamented "the momification of Michelle Obama" in an article published in *Salon*. In response to Obama's assumption of the moniker "mom-in-chief," Lonnae O'Neal Parker (2013) reported that "many feminists decried her decision to give up her career and said she had been victimized by her husband's choices." Following her speech at the 2012 Democratic National Convention when Obama affirmed, "[Y]ou see, at the end of the day, my most important title is still 'mom-in-chief,'" Jessica Valenti tweeted, "I long for the day when powerful women don't need to assure Americans that they're moms above all else" (Winfrey Harris, 2012).

White feminist responses to Obama can be understood as part of a broader critique of dominant ideologies that posit maternity as a woman's first and most important role (Douglas & Michaels, 2004; Hays, 1996; O'Brien Hallstein, 2010, 2011), yet when discussing Obama, many Black women rejected these critiques, pointing to the progressive potential of Obama's maternal persona. As Tami Winfrey Harris (2012) pointed out, Black women in the United States have rarely had the opportunity to prioritize motherhood; moreover, positive images of Black mothers are largely absent in popular culture, media, and politics. Deborah K. King (2010) agreed that White pundits misinterpret what mothering means for Michelle Obama, arguing that Obama's actions must be understood within the African American context of othermothering.

In this article, I seek to explain the divergent responses of Black and White scholars and pundits through a consideration of the complex, dynamic, paradoxical, and racialized rhetorical contexts of maternity within which Obama's first lady performances circulated and participated. Building on the work of James Jasinski (1997), Kristan Poirot (2014) writes:

> A rhetorical context is not merely an aggregate of immediate variables (e.g., audience, rhetor, medium, topic obstacles, setting, etc.), nor is it exclusively the producer of pressing exigencies. Rather, context saturates public discourse, comprising both itself and rhetorical acts as amalgamations and orchestrations of various traditions. These traditions are more enduring than any immediate political scene, and they in turn comprise and are constituted by a multitude of rhetorical acts. (p. 10)

In what follows, I argue that Obama's first lady rhetorical performances and the conflicting responses to them can be understood as invoking the varied traditions of dominant White mothering ideologies, the denigration of Black motherhood in mainstream, White culture, and the African American tradition of othermothering. As Obama participated in this complex and dynamic contextual field, I maintain that she constructed a polysemous set of texts that were read differently by her Black and White audiences and that functioned simultaneously to reinforce and resist sexist and racist norms. This article thus contributes to both an understanding of maternal appeals and discussions of polysemy.

The article proceeds as follows: I begin with a review of scholarship that explores the function of maternal appeals on the public stage followed by an overview of literature that addresses polysemy. I then turn to a discussion of White feminist critiques of the institution of motherhood and ways in which Obama's maternal first lady performances could be understood to reinforce those institutions. Next, I offer a discussion of dominant images of African American maternity in juxtaposition to African American maternal practices and Obama's mothering specifically. Then, I provide an analysis of some of Obama's actions and words in light of the African American tradition of othermothering. I conclude by discussing the implications of understanding mothering rhetorics within a multifaceted and fluid rhetorical context.

Polysemous maternity

Rhetorics of maternity

The varied reactions pundits offered in response to Michelle Obama's maternal first lady performances echoed similarly divergent responses found in scholarship that explores the uses of maternal appeals on the public stage. Some scholars see a liberatory potential when women claim maternity as the grounds for their authority. Jennifer A. Peeples and Kevin M. DeLuca (2006), for example, explore how a group of women use motherhood to promote environmental justice in their communities. Isaac West (2007) considers how the maternal pacifist group La WISP reconstituted the meanings of war and peace through the writing and selling of cookbooks to support their cause. Mari Boor Tonn (1996) argues that "symbolic motherhood" was a particularly potent rhetorical strategy in the hands of Mary Harris "Mother" Jones. And Valeria Fabj (1993) praises the use of maternal appeals by the Mothers of the Plaza de Mayo, arguing that these mothers were able to demand information about the children who disappeared during the Argentine military dictatorship of 1976 to 1983 because they cloaked the political aspects of their critique in motherhood.

Yet not all scholars offer positive assessments of maternal appeals. Like Fabj (1993), Karen A. Foss and Kathy L. Domenici (2001) explore the rhetoric of the Mothers of the Plaza de Mayo; however, Foss and Domenici suggest that the maternal appeals Fabj celebrates led to the dismissal of the mothers' protests as irrational. Lynn Stearney (1994) similarly questions the value of maternal appeals in ecofeminist activism, arguing that such appeals reinforce an association of women with reproduction while also implying that caretaking activities are women's responsibilities. In a slightly different vein, Katie L. Gibson and Amy L. Heyse (2010) question the progressive potential of maternal appeals through an examination of Sarah Palin's rhetoric during the 2008 presidential campaign. Palin, these authors maintain, enacted "a persona of motherhood by employing domestic examples, maternal appeals, and a feminine discursive style" while also "joining the RNC's [Republican National Convention's] celebration of hegemonic masculinity" (p. 239).

Elsewhere I explain the varied assessments of maternal appeals' utility and function through reference to the metaphorical family structures within which they are embedded (Hayden, 2003). Turning to George Lakoff's (1996) discussion of the nation-as-family metaphor, I argue that when embedded in the "nurturant family" metaphorical structure, maternal appeals have the potential to function progressively. However, when embedded in the "strict father" metaphorical structure, maternal appeals are likely to promote a conservative, nonliberatory rhetoric. Yet this explanation does not shed light on the differing responses to Obama's maternal performances. It is not that the metaphorical structure of Obama's maternal performances shift; rather, different pundits offered conflicting readings in response to the same texts, suggesting that these pundits are responding to the same metaphorical structure in varied ways. To explain these discrepant interpretations and reactions, then, I suggest that Obama's maternal appeals be considered within an expansive understanding of rhetorical context and the concept of polysemy.

Polysemy in rhetorical studies

Polysemy—the idea that audiences receive different meanings from the same texts—has been widely discussed in rhetorical and media studies, yet, according to Robin E. Jensen (2008), the term was not commonly used until the 1980s, when scholars such as John Fiske and Stuart Hall sought to offer an understanding of an audience's active and subversive relationships to media texts. Unlike neo-Marxists, Fiske, Hall, and others argue that although media promote dominant, oppressive messages, audience members have the ability to resist those messages and the power relations entailed therein (e.g., see Bielby & Harrington, 1994; Fiske, 1986, 1991, 2006; Hall, 1994, 1996; Lewis, 1991; Press & Cole, 1994; Yousman, 2013). Moreover, scholars in this tradition attribute the impetus to resist dominant meaning to the subject positions of audience members; the polysemy of a text, Fiske (1986) maintains, lies "in the ways that different socially located *viewers* will activate its meaning potential differently" (p. 394; emphasis added).

Leah Ceccarelli (1998) offers a typology of polysemy as employed by rhetorical critics. Noting that scholars use the term to reference different things, she urges writers to be more specific, suggesting polysemy can be broken down into at least three types. She defines *resistive reading* as a practice wherein audience members read against rhetors' intended meanings, a form of polysemy most closely aligned with scholars working in the tradition of Fiske and Hall. *Strategic ambiguity*, in turn, involves rhetors purposefully inviting multiple meanings from audiences, and *hermeneutic depth* references the practice whereby critics uncover the multiple extant meanings a text might invite.

Ceccarelli's (1998) typology has been used frequently by rhetorical scholars (e.g., see Asen, 2010; Endres, 2012; Meyer, 2003; Perks, 2010; Rockler, 2001; Schutten, 2006; Terrill, 2000; Waisanen, 2013); it is not surprising, then, that it offers a productive framework for understanding *some* of the divergent responses to Obama's rhetoric. For example, as I argue in the sections that follow, there are moments when Obama seems to utilize strategic ambiguity to couch her more pointed critiques of U.S. culture and politics; moreover, building on the work of Reid-Brinkley (2011), I suggest these moments can be understood as instances of "signifying," a language strategy that emerges from African American traditions.

Resistive reading, however, is a less useful concept when it comes to understanding audience responses to Obama. Again, Ceccarelli (1998) argues that resistive reading occurs when audience members read a meaning other than that intended by the rhetor. To illustrate this concept, Ceccarelli discusses the varied ways Northern and Southern newspapers depicted Abraham Lincoln's second inaugural address. She references "Lincoln's own description of the message" (p. 400) to elucidate what he intended, concluding that

Northern papers "read the message as it was designed by Lincoln" (p. 402), whereas Southern papers "misread him" (p. 410). Thus Ceccarelli points to the potential for readers to discern nonintended meanings from texts activated as a result of audience members' social context.

What Ceccarelli (1998) pays less attention to, however, are the social and rhetorical contexts within which the rhetor is circulating. Indeed, there is an element of instrumentalism in her discussion as she reads Lincoln's second inaugural as "a manifestation of the author's conscious design" (Jasinski, 1997, p. 196). Jasinski (1997) rejects this approach to criticism, insisting:

> Texts do not emerge from the inspiration or genius of the author. Invention is a social process in that the words employed by any author are always already part of a performative tradition in which the author is situated and from which the author draws. Textual production or rhetorical invention is also not a process of following rules or precepts … Traditions enable and constrain practice but do not dictate or proscribe. *Attention to performative traditions leads to a conceptualization of invention as the discursive management of multiple traditions.* (p. 214; emphasis added)

Thus Jasinski (1997) challenges critics to read texts as emerging from multifaceted and shifting contexts that rhetors negotiate. Such a critical practice will not assume situational stability, nor will it assume that a rhetor's intent is unambiguous and fully capable of directing textual production. Finally, such a critical practice will not assume that rhetorical performances are coherent or that their meanings are singular. Following Jasinski (1997), I suggest that to understand audience responses to Obama's maternal performances, attention must be paid to the multiple, shifting, and paradoxical contexts within which *both* audience members *and* Obama are situated.

As I have already noted, during her tenure as first lady, Obama has occupied a unique position. Firmly embedded in norms associated with White, middle- to upper-class femininity, the first lady role conferred on Obama a distinctive influence, visibility, and power (albeit a very constrained kind of power). However, as a Black woman, Obama was marginalized. Thus, as I argue in the following sections, when Obama spoke as a mother she drew (intentionally or not) from multiple maternal contexts, including (White) intensive mothering, the denigration of Black mothers in dominant discourse, and the African American tradition of othermothering. When Black and White audiences read Obama's maternal performances differently, there was no error in either set of interpretations, nor was it the case that one group of audience members read her as intended while the other read her resistively. Rather, the different interpretations Black and White audiences brought to Obama's maternal rhetoric reflected the various and paradoxical racialized rhetorical contexts through which both audience members and Obama circulated and participated.

Motherhood in Black and White

Michelle Obama, an "intensive mom"

White pundits who lamented Obama's choice to highlight her maternity over her professional accomplishments echoed a long history of White feminist critiques of the institution of motherhood.[3] First articulated by Adrienne Rich (1976) in *Of Woman*

Born: Motherhood as Experience and Institution, White feminist scholars have productively explored the ways institutions of and ideologies surrounding dominant motherhood are profoundly oppressive to many women with children. Referred to variously as "intensive mothering" (Hays, 1996), "the mommy myth" (Douglas & Michaels, 2004), or "patriarchal mothering" (O'Reilly, 2006), the assumptions underlying the contemporary ideology of (White) mothering include:

> 1) children can only be properly cared for by the biological mother; 2) this mothering must be provided 24/7; 3) the mother must always put children's needs before her own; 4) mothers must turn to the experts for instruction; 5) the mother is fully satisfied, fulfilled, completed, and composed in motherhood; and finally, 6) mothers must lavish excessive amounts of time, energy, and money in the rearing of their children. (O'Reilly, 2006, p. 43)

These assumptions leave little room for women to focus on careers; indeed, intensive mothering leaves practically no space for activities or commitments outside of maternity.

It is easy to hear reverberations of intensive mothering in Obama's first lady rhetoric; also present are the challenges that face any woman who seeks to enact this all-consuming role. For example, in an interview with *Vogue* magazine shortly before Barack Obama's first inauguration, Michelle Obama noted that prior to occupying the White House the family moved into a D.C.-area hotel so that her daughters could start the school semester with the rest of their classmates. She asserted:

> I'm going to try to take [daughters Sasha and Malia] to school every morning—as much as I can. But there's also a measure of independence. And obviously there will be times I won't be able to drop them off at all. I like to be a presence in my kids' school. I want to know the teachers; I want to know the other parents. (Talley, 2009)

Obama (NPR, 2008) similarly called on the tenets of intensive mothering in her 2008 speech to the Democratic National Convention when she said, "I come here as a mom whose girls are the heart of my heart and the center of my world—they're the first thing I think about when I wake up in the morning, and the last thing I think about when I go to bed at night." Intensive mothering also can be seen in Obama's signature "Let's Move" campaign. Rolled out in February 2010, Obama made clear that her concern about childhood obesity began when their pediatrician brought her daughter's weight to her attention; her passion for the topic, she regularly told audiences, stemmed not just from her role as first lady but also from her role "as a mom" (The White House, 2010).[4]

A critique of intensive mothering and its subsequent denial of the importance of career and other, nonmaternal activities also can be found in White feminist pundits' lamentations regarding Obama's maternal performances. In "Dispatches from the Democratic National Convention," Emily Bazelon (2012) wrote, "The words *family* and *sacrifice* showed up over and over again in Michelle's text. The words *career* and *breadwinner* didn't" (emphasis in original). In response to her "televised workouts and kid-show cameos and 'mom-dancing' with Jimmy Fallon," Linda Hirshman insisted, "After the feminist revolution, you don't envision a brilliantly educated, well-connected grown woman doing that kind of thing" (qtd. in Cottle, 2013).

In part, then, Michelle Obama's maternal first lady performances participated in and reinforced the problematic discourse of intensive mothering. She, like other intensive mothers, claimed to prioritize her children over all other aspects of her life, offering a public image that highlighted her maternal role while obscuring her professional and other nonmaternal activities and successes. Nonetheless, it is important to recognize that while Obama may have participated in and reinforced intensive mothering, she did so with a twist. Intensive mothering disciplines all women; however, it is also an ideology that is raced and classed. Like the role of the first lady, intensive mothering assumes a femininity that is both White and middle to upper class (Douglas & Michaels, 2004; O'Brien Hallstein, 2011; O'Reilly, 2006). Conversely, images of African American maternity in the dominant public imagination have been largely negative. Indeed, according to Douglas and Michaels (2004), Black women's role in intensive mothering is to serve as the stigmatized other—the mother who fails to enact intensive mothering and hence functions as a cautionary tale.

As I argue next, then, although it is possible to understand Obama's maternal first lady performances as enactments of intensive mothering, those same performances simultaneously and paradoxically can be understood as challenges to the negative stereotypes of Black maternity.

African American motherhood: Public images versus private enactments

Numerous myths shape public perceptions of Black motherhood. From slavery emerged the "mammy" image, the "faithful, obedient domestic servant" who cares for her "'White children' and 'family' better than her own" (Collins, 2009, p. 80). Patricia Hill Collins (2009) argues that the mammy "symbolize[s] the dominant group's perceptions of the ideal Black female relationship to elite White male power" (p. 80). In contrast to the mammy is the matriarch. Widely disseminated through a 1965 government report authored by Daniel Patrick Moynihan, the matriarch is understood to be the domineering African American mother whose failure to enact appropriate femininity both emasculates African American men and is at the root of the social ills that plague African American communities (Collins, 2009; Roberts, 1997). Finally, the "welfare queen," frequently trotted out during the Reagan administration as justification for cutting social programs, is seen as the lazy, morally deviant, and conniving African American mother dependent on the public dime (Collins, 2009; Douglas & Michaels, 2004; Roberts, 1997).

Negative images of African American maternity continue to shape dominant beliefs about Black mothers in U.S. public culture. As Dorothy Roberts (1997) asserts, "Black motherhood has borne the weight of centuries of disgrace manufactured in both popular culture and academic circles. A lurid mythology of Black mothers' unfitness, along with a science devoted to proving Black biological inferiority, cast Black childbearing as a dangerous activity" (p. 21). Thus again, while serving as first lady Michelle Obama may have performed intensive mothering, but in doing so she simultaneously challenged negative stereotypes and myths. She positioned herself as a Black woman who was also a "good mother" according to dominant (White) norms.

Yet Obama did not enact *only* intensive mothering; a closer look at her maternal performances suggests that she sometimes strayed from intensive mothering's norms, building on elements of maternity that are embedded in African American communities. For example, like many African American mothers, Michelle Obama served as her family's disciplinarian. When the Obamas first moved into the White House, Michelle Obama insisted that the girls' bedtime remain 8:00 p.m.; the girls were required to set their own alarm clocks, get themselves up for school, clean their own rooms, and make their own beds (Swarns, 2009). In an ABC News interview, Obama recounted a conversation she had with the

White House staff: "Don't make their beds. Make mine. Skip the kids. They have to learn these things" (Swarns, 2009).

Over time, the White House rules became more stringent. When Sasha and Malia took a trip they were required to write a report—whether their schools asked this of them or not. Screen time was limited to the weekends; during the week, the girls could watch television or use the computer only if they were needed for homework. Obama was strict about the girls' nutrition and exercise. They were required to eat healthfully and to participate in two sports—one of their choosing and one Obama chose for them. "I want them to understand what it feels like to do something you don't like and to improve," Obama explained (Kantor, 2012). Indeed, Obama's reputation for discipline was so strong that "some staff members even joke[d] that they wish they could send their own children to Mrs. Obama's boot camp for training" (Kantor, 2012).

African American women grow up in a culture that continually devalues them; for an African American woman to be healthy and whole she needs to develop a strong sense of self-reliance and self-respect (Collins, 2009; King, 2010; O'Reilly, 2006). These attributes are not learned from a parent who coddles; they are not learned from traditionally performed intensive mothering. Collins (2009) writes:

> Understanding this goal of balancing the need for the physical survival of their daughters with the vision of encouraging them to transcend the boundaries of the sexual politics of Black womanhood explains many apparent contradictions in Black mother-daughter relationships. U.S. Black mothers are often described as strong disciplinarians and overly protective; yet these same women manage to raise daughters who are self-reliant and assertive. (p. 200)

Thus Obama's performances of maternal discipline can be seen as stemming from a cultural tradition aimed at providing African American women with the skills and fortitude they need to survive in a racist and sexist world.

Again, though, Obama was not just any (African American) mother prioritizing the well-being of her daughters; she was the first lady of the United States. The juxtaposition of this high-profile position with the enduring presence of the mammy myth and the denigration of Black maternity heightened the impact of Obama's maternal performances. If the mammy is beloved by White families because she tends to and loves her White "children" better than her own, Obama could be seen as publicly rejecting this stance. She illustrated to the nation that her most important responsibility was to raise and care for her African American daughters. By prioritizing her daughters, she disavowed dominant beliefs about Black motherhood while also exalting the value of Black girls. This is something many African American pundits understood and articulated. Renee Martin (2013), for example, insisted that "by simply continuing to be a positive role model as a wife and mother, Michelle Obama is doing wonders for black women and girls across the globe. It may not be what mainstream feminists have in mind, but choice is about having the freedom to chart our own path in life" (qtd. in Gandy, 2013; also see Harris-Perry, 2013).

White feminist criticism of Obama's mom-in-chief role came to a head following her 2012 speech at the Democratic National Convention. In particular, White feminists seemed irked at where Obama's "mom-in-chief" assertion appeared. Nearing the climax of her address Obama said:

> If farmers and blacksmiths could win independence from an empire ... if immigrants could leave behind everything they knew for a better life on our shores ... if women could be dragged to jail for seeking the vote ... if a generation could defeat a depression, and define greatness for

all time ... if a young preacher could lift us to the mountaintop with his righteous dream ... and if proud Americans can be who they are and boldly stand at the altar with who they love ... then surely, surely we can give everyone in this country a fair chance at the great American Dream ... . And I say all of this tonight not just as First Lady ... and not just as a wife. You see, at the end of the day my most important title is still "mom-in-chief." (NPR, 2012)

The trajectory of this line led Irin Carmon (2012) to write, "If you feel let down by an arc that begins with anti-colonialism, immigration and women being dragged to jail, but returns to the cult of motherhood, you're not alone." Hanna Rosin similarly tweeted, "ok 'mom in chief' is not where I thought that sentence was headed. It was so soaring just before that" (qtd. in Winfrey Harris, 2012).

Considered in terms of White intensive motherhood, these responses make sense. From the perspective of intensive mothering, children are first and foremost in a woman's life; seemingly rejecting the hard-won advances of (White) feminist activism, an intensive mother sublimates her own desires, ambitions, and abilities to her children's perceived needs. Considered in light of the mammy myth and the broader denigration of Black motherhood and Black children, however, Michelle Obama's line does indeed soar. To proudly prioritize the well-being of Black daughters in a racist, sexist society stands firmly in line with women's suffrage, civil rights, marriage equality, and other social justice efforts. Thus the meaning of Obama's assertion is multifaceted and paradoxical. Understood within a polygonal maternal rhetorical context, it, like other aspects of Obama's maternal performances, functioned both to reinforce and challenge sexist and racist norms.

Michelle Obama: Othermother-in-chief

In addition to the rhetorical contexts of intensive mothering and the denigration of African American maternity, Obama's maternal first lady performances also circulated within the African American tradition of othermothering. Andrea O'Reilly (2006) defines othermothering as the "acceptance of responsibility for a child not one's own, in an arrangement that may or may not be formal" (p. 210). In African American communities this broader base of care is understood as a boon to the community's children:

> African and African-American communities have ... recognized that vesting one person with full responsibility for mothering a child may not be wise or possible. As a result, othermothers—women who assist bloodmothers by sharing mothering responsibilities— traditionally have been central to the institution of Black motherhood. (Collins, 2009, p. 192)

Thus, African American children typically grow up in communities that function as extended families.

African American women who serve as bloodmothers and othermothers understand their roles not solely in relation to the community's children; they understand their work in relation to the welfare of the community as a whole. As O'Reilly (2006) maintains, "[T]he practice of othermothering ... is regarded as essential for the survival of black people" (p. 111). Othermothering and bloodmothering have several distinct functions, and one of those functions is to preserve and celebrate the unique aspects of African American culture. Collins (1998) writes:

> Since women typically carry the burden of care responsibilities within African-American households, conceptualizing family as intricately linked with both community

and nation effectively joins women's activity in socializing the young in individual households to that of transmitting the symbols, meanings, and culture of the Black nation itself. (pp. 171–172)

Moreover, by creating a nurturing and loving family and community, bloodmothers and othermothers provide refuge; home is a place where African American men, women, and children can flourish and grow. Indeed, bell hooks (1990) writes:

> Historically, African-American people believed that the construction of a homeplace, however fragile and tenuous (the slave hut, the wooden shack), had a radical political dimension. Despite the brutal reality of racial apartheid, of domination, one's homeplace was one site where one could freely confront the issue of humanization, where one could resist. Black women resisted by making homes where all black people could strive to be subjects, not objects, where one could be affirmed in our minds and hearts despite poverty, hardship, and deprivation, where we could restore to ourselves the dignity denied to us on the outside in the public world. (p. 42)

Finally, the practices of bloodmothering and othermothering have led many African American women into community service, or what Collins refers to as community othermothering. Referencing a study by sociologist Nancy Naples, Collins (2009) writes, "[F]or Black women ... what began as the daily expression of their obligations to their children and as community othermothers often developed into full-fledged actions as community leaders" (p. 207).

Given the significant role the family and the community play in African American lives, and given the prominent roles mothers play in those institutions, it is not surprising that Black women who serve as bloodmothers, othermothers, and community othermothers are highly respected. Collins (1991) writes:

> [M]otherhood, whether bloodmother, othermother, or community othermother, can be invoked by Black women as a symbol of power. A substantial portion of Black women's status in African American communities stems not only from their roles as mothers in their own families but from their contributions as community othermothers to Black community development as well. (p. 51; also see King, 2010; O'Reilly, 2006)

An understanding of the roles bloodmothers, othermothers, and community other-mothers play in African American lives offers yet another context through which Michelle Obama's maternal first lady performances may be understood. Within the context of bloodmothering and othermothering, Obama's maternal posture can be seen as a means of garnering respect while also serving her community at large. Moreover, because othermothering is not a familiar practice or concept in dominant White culture, it is possible to read Obama's othermothering activities as "signifyin[g] practices." Following Henry Louis Gates Jr., Shanara Rose Reid-Brinkley (2011) argues that African Americans have developed coded communication strategies that *appear* to conform to White dominant norms while also conveying information and messages that White audiences will not receive. Reid-Brinkley writes, "Although white audience members may often read the rhetoric of black people literally, black discourse can function to produce underlying messages designed to be heard by members of the discourse community, but also misdirect non-members from interpreting or attaching significance to the message" (p. 39). In Ceccarelli's (1998) terminology, to signify is to partake in strategic ambiguity.

In her 1985 undergraduate thesis, *Princeton-Educated Blacks and the Black Community*, Obama (née Robinson) addressed the divergent aspects of Black and White communities:

> There is a distinctive Black culture very different from White culture. Elements of Black culture which make it unique from White culture such as its music, its language, the struggles and a "consciousness" shared by its people may be attributed to the injustices and oppressions suffered by this race of people which are not comparable to the experiences of any other race of people through this country's history. (p. 54)

Moreover, Obama illustrated that she understood the resistive, protective function the family plays for African Americans. Her thesis involved a qualitative study of African Americans' experiences at Princeton, a White-dominated institution. In it she wrote:

> During Pre-Princeton, if respondents became frustrated or discouraged as a result of their experiences in a predominantly White academic environment the respondents could always escape from these frustrations when they left these environments to go home. Thus, respondents' families and home lives provided relief from any problems or tensions encountered in predominately White environments. (pp. 61–62)

King (2010) maintains that Obama's "family and church raised her with expectations that [*sic*] what a Black woman ought to be and to do: specifically the expectation to strive for excellence was conjoined with the imperative to remain responsive to the needs of that community" (p. 97). In her thesis, Obama (1985) acknowledged her commitment to give back to her community, and she suggested that commitment was heightened as a result of her Princeton experiences:

> Earlier in my college career, there was no doubt in my mind that as a member of the Black community I was somehow obligated to this community and would utilize all of my present and future resources to benefit this community first and foremost. My experiences at Princeton have made me far more aware of my "Blackness" than ever before ... This realization has presently made my goals to actively utilize my resources to benefit the Black community more desirable. (pp. 2–3)

It would be unfair, of course, to assume that Obama continued to hold *all* of the views she expressed in her undergraduate thesis when serving as first lady. Nonetheless, the passages noted here make clear that Obama recognized the African American community as distinct from dominant White culture; she saw it as a place where African Americans could seek refuge from the racism they experience elsewhere; and she expressed her commitment to contributing to her community. The views articulated in Obama's thesis, then, support a reading of her actions as first lady through the lens of othermothering as a signifyin[g] practice. As I discuss next, when Obama extended her mothering practices to the Black and Brown children of the nation, White pundits and audience members may have seen a bland set of policies; viewed as a set of signifyin[g] practices, however, Obama's maternal performances functioned to critique dominant White culture and to work for the good of African American communities without drawing unwanted [White] attention to these efforts.

Mothering the (Black and Brown) children of the nation

I have offered evidence of the young Michelle Obama's commitment to give back to her community. This is a commitment she reiterated in 2008 when talking to CBS reporter Steve Kroft:

> I, both Barack and I, believe that we can have an impact in the D.C. area. You know, in terms of making sure we're contributing to the community that we immediately live in. That's always been something that we try to do. Whether it's in our own neighborhoods or in the schools that we've attended. (qtd. in King, 2010, p. 78)

Obama has also acknowledged the link between her community service and her maternity. In a 2010 interview, she affirmed: "If I'm giving those experiences to Malia and Sasha, and I think it's important to them, then I can't pretend it's not important for everyone" (King, 2010, p. 110).

In line with community othermothering practices, First Lady Obama provided celebrations of African American history and culture for her daughters and the nation's children. For example, in 2009, Obama hosted an event in honor of African American history month for young people; Sasha and Malia had front row seats. Accompanied by the African American vocal ensemble Sweet Honey in the Rock, Obama led her young audience through a history lesson, pointing out, among other things, that African American slaves helped build the White House (Brown, 2009). On the surface, a celebration of (African) American history and culture for an audience of children appears to be an example of the somewhat pedestrian activities expected of first ladies. In a country in which the first museum dedicated to the history of slavery opened only in December 2014 (Amsden, 2015), however, this reference to slavery spoken by the first African American first lady turned an otherwise innocuous public relations event into an opportunity to cast a critical eye on the history of the United States.

In the same year, Obama hosted another event designed to promote greater awareness about the roles of African Americans in U.S. history: the unveiling of the Sojourner Truth bust in the U.S. Capitol. Truth, of course, was the 19th-century woman born into slavery who became an outspoken advocate for abolition and women's rights. In her remarks, Obama (The White House, 2009) identified herself as "a descendent of slaves" and expressed pleasure at the fact that "now many young boys and girls, like my own daughters, will come to Emancipation Hall and see the face of a woman who looks like them." Thus, as she did when she referenced the slaves who helped build the White House, Obama turned an otherwise placid affair into one with a political edge. By calling attention to the lasting legacies of slavery that mark her own background and by noting that only with Truth's bust can Black and Brown children see a face that looks like theirs, Obama implicitly criticized the lack of diversity in Emancipation Hall and, by extension, the seeming unwillingness in official quarters to attend to the troubling past of the United States. However, because she couched her critique in the pabulum of a first lady's daily activities, she was able to avoid garnering negative attention from mainstream White pundits or press.

In addition to veiling her critiques of U.S. racism through traditional first lady activities, Obama framed her policy initiatives in terms of her concern for the nation's children. Nonetheless, the majority of the projects Obama championed held special salience for children of color. For example, at the "Let's Move" campaign launch Obama was surrounded by D.C.-area children, the vast majority of whom were Black and Brown (The White House, 2010). Significantly, one of the four goals of the campaign—the elimination of food deserts (see American Nutrition Association, 2010)—has specific relevance to poor neighborhoods, many of which are home to African Americans and other people of color.

Later in her tenure Obama began an initiative aimed at increasing the number of low-income students who attend college—a program that was likely to benefit many students of color. Speaking to the Bell Multicultural High School in Washington about this initiative, Obama told the crowd: "I'm here today because I want you to know that my story can be your story…. The details might be a little different, but so many of the challenges and triumphs will be just the same" (Steinhauer, 2013).

From a dominant perspective, it is easy to read both the "Let's Move" campaign and the low-income student college initiative as traditional first lady fare that reinforces outmoded gendered norms. Similarly, the "my story can be your story" line can be heard as a mere cliché. And indeed, many White pundits critiqued Obama along these lines. Referencing Obama's "Let's Move" campaign, Leslie Morgan Steiner (2012) declared that she had "read enough bland dogma on home-grown vegetables and aerobic exercise to last me several lifetimes." Similarly, Michelle Cottle (2013) called Obama a "feminist nightmare" as a result of her priorities. In response, African American pundit and scholar Melissa Harris-Perry (2013) insisted that Cottle and other White pundits were "wrong to write off the first lady's priorities as fluff," insisting that Obama's "Let's Move" campaign and her low-income student college effort have the potential to make important changes in [Black and Brown] people's lives and in the country as a whole. Thus as is evident in Harris-Perry's response, while White pundits may have read Obama's actions as similar to the apolitical and unremarkable projects other first ladies have championed, those who read Obama's maternal performances as acts of signifyin[g] saw Obama playing a powerful role, offering both a critique of the racism extant in U.S. culture and working to advance the needs of people of color, many of whom are poor.

Multifaceted mothering contexts, polysemous texts

Given the racism that continues to haunt U.S. culture, it is not surprising that Obama turned to signifyin[g] when critiquing the United States or promoting policies that might aid communities of color. Indeed, early in Barack Obama's first bid for the presidency, Michelle Obama became a target for racist commentary as media outlets questioned her patriotism and framed her through the "Angry Black Woman" trope (King, 2010). After her much maligned February 2008 assertion that "for the first time in my life I am proud of my country because it feels like hope is finally making a comeback" (Thomas, 2008), Obama stepped back from campaigning. When she did make public appearances, she was more careful about what she said (Cooper, 2010). Hortense Spillers (2010) both noticed and decried this change. Comparing a speech she saw Obama deliver during the primaries to Obama's 2008 Democratic National Convention address, Spillers (2010) lamented that "the 'handlers' had apparently moved in" and Obama's "discourse had lost its sparkle, its sting of engagement" (pp. 307–308).

Bonnie J. Dow (2014) offers a similar critique, noting that "the image problems that arose during the [2008] campaign prompted a media makeover to produce 'a new Michelle, carefully edited for public consumption' and as one Obama adviser remarked, designed to avoid controversy by emphasizing 'a much more traditional woman's role'" (p. 238). Dow suggests that this media makeover involved the embrace of a "nostalgic familialism" (p. 252) by both Obama and the press that reported on her. And while Dow states she is not sure that "the Obamas and their advisers had better rhetorical choices … to fall back on," she nonetheless suggests that Obama's mom-in-chief rhetoric has troubling consequences:

> Such discourses of familialism not only present "family" as a utopian sphere of safety and love, but also function to fundamentally restrict the range of subject positions available for the performance of citizenship. We have a long history of such restrictions on women's civic identities, a history that includes varied manifestations—from republican motherhood to "soccer mom" voters—of the notion that "women's political space is somehow different from men's." (Dow, 2014, p. 252)

In part, I agree with Dow's point; as argued previously, Obama's maternal first lady rhetoric reinforced intensive mothering, suggesting that a woman's first and foremost priority lies with her children. It would stand to reason, then, that the ideology of intensive mothering would prompt some mothers to view and enact their citizenship through the same child-focused lens. Where I disagree with Dow, however, is in her implication that at any one time familialism functions as a singular ideal. In this article, I have argued that Obama's familial rhetoric circulated through a multifaceted set of contexts and mothering rhetorics. These contexts included [White] intensive mothering, but they also included dominant White stereotypes surrounding Black mothering and the African American tradition of othermothering. To suggest that the familialism that marked Obama's first lady performance functioned *only* to restrict women (and others) to a limited form of citizenship ignores the complicated, messy, and multilayered contexts within which Obama's rhetoric circulated and participated.

I began this article by noting the divergent responses to Obama's maternal performances articulated by Black and White feminist pundits. I also maintained that neither position is "right" nor "wrong." And so I conclude: It is inaccurate to claim that Obama's assumption of the mom-in-chief moniker and her children-focused projects were *simply* acts of self-sacrifice at the altar of intensive motherhood. It is also inaccurate to suggest that Obama's maternal performances functioned *only* to rehabilitate dominant attitudes toward Black mothering, to garner status for Obama among African Americans, or to aid African American communities. Instead, Obama's rhetoric and actions must be understood as polysemous texts that drew on multifaceted maternal rhetorical contexts to do all of these things simultaneously, speaking variously to different audiences in different moments. What Obama's maternal performances and the receptions of them teach us about polysemy, then, is that it is important to take into account the context or social position of *both* rhetors *and* audience members. This analysis suggests that mothering rhetorics and practices are not monolithic but they are malleable. They can simultaneously exploit and empower; they can both oppress and enrich.

Acknowledgments

This essay was presented at the 2015 National Communication Association Convention in Las Vegas, Nevada. The author would like to thank D. Lynn O'Brien Hallstein, Joan McAlister, and the anonymous reviewers for their constructive and insightful feedback.

Notes

1. Although space prohibits me from addressing it, there is a large and varied body of literature that addresses first lady rhetoric. See, for example, Anderson, 2002; Blair, 2001; Burns, 2005;

Dubriwny, 2005; Erickson & Thomson, 2012; Hogan, 2013; Joseph, 2011; Maddux, 2008; Parry-Giles, 2000; Parry-Giles & Blair, 2002; Sheeler, 2013; Watts, 2010.

2. My use of the terms *White feminists* and *Black feminists* throughout the article is general and not absolute. In other words, I use these terms as shortcuts, recognizing that *most* of the criticism of Obama came from White feminists, but of course these critiques do not represent the views of *all* White feminists. Similarly, *most* of the challenges to these critiques came from Black feminists, but these challenges do not represent the views of *all* Black feminists.

3. See O'Brien Hallstein (2017) for an overview of feminist discussions of motherhood.

4. Obama frequently speaks on behalf of the "Let's Move" campaign, and in her speeches she consistently refers to herself as a "mom." Texts of Obama's speeches can be found on the White House website: http://www.whitehouse.gov.

References

American Nutrition Association. (2010). USDA defines food deserts. *Nutrition Digest, 38*(1). Retrieved from http://americannutritionassocation.org/newsletter/usda-defines-food-deserts

Amsden, D. (2015, February 26). Building the first slavery museum in America. *New York Times Magazine*. Retrieved from http://www.nytimes.com/2015/03/01/magazine/building-the-first-slave-museum-in-america.html?_r=0

Anderson, K. V. (2002). From spouses to candidates: Hillary Rodham Clinton, Elizabeth Dole, and the gendered office of U.S. president. *Rhetoric and Public Affairs, 5*, 105–132.

Anderson, K. V. (2004). A site of "American womanhood." In M. M. Wertheimer (Ed.), *Inventing a voice: The rhetoric of American first ladies of the twentieth century* (pp. 17–30). Lanham, MA: Rowman & Littlefield.

Asen, R. (2010). Reflections on the rule of rhetoric in public policy. *Rhetoric and Public Affairs, 13*, 121–144.

Bazelon, E. (2012, September 5). Dispatches from the Democratic National Convention. *Slate*. Retrieved from http://www.slate.com/articles/news_and_politics/the_breakfast_table/features/2012/_2012_democratic_national_convention/michelle_obama_s_speech_was_an_enormous_success_but_it_didn_t_say_enough_for_working_moms_.html

Bielby, D., & Harrington, C. L. (1994). Reach out and touch someone: Viewers, agency, and audiences in the televisual experience. In J. Cruz and J. Lewis (Eds.), *Viewing, reading, listening: Audiences and cultural reception* (pp. 81–100). Boulder, CO: Westview Press.

Blair, D. M. (2001). No ordinary time: Eleanor Roosevelt's address to the 1940 Democratic National Convention. *Rhetoric and Public Affairs, 4*, 203–222.

Brown, A. (2014, March 3). Michelle Obama maintains positive image: Average favorable ratings tops Hillary Clinton's as first lady. *Gallup*. Retrieved from http://www.gallup.com/poll/167696/michelle-obalam-maintains-positive-image.aspx

Brown, D. L. (2009, Feb. 18). First lady guides district children through a history lesson. *Washington Post*. Retrieved from http://voices.washingtonpost.com/44/2009/02/18/first_lady_guides_district_chi.html

Burns, L. M. (2005). Collective memory and the candidates' wives in the 2004 presidential campaign. *Rhetoric and Public Affairs, 8*, 684–688.

Campbell, K. K. (1996). The rhetorical presidency: A two person career. In M. J. Medhurst (Ed.), *Beyond the rhetorical presidency* (pp. 175–195). College Station, TX: Texas A&M.

Carmon, I. (2012, September 5). Michelle Obama: Beyond mom-in-chief. *Salon*. Retrieved from http://www.salon.com/2012/09/05/michelle-obama-not-just-mom-in-chief/

Ceccarelli, L. (1998). Polysemy: Multiple meanings in rhetorical criticism. *Quarterly Journal of Speech, 84*, 395–415.

Collins, P. H. (1991). The meaning of motherhood in Black culture and Black mother-daughter relationships. In P. Bell-Scott, B. Guy-Sheftall, J. J. Royster, J. Sims-Wood, M. DeCosta-Willis, & L. Fultz (Eds.) *Double stitch: Black women write about mothers and daughters* (pp. 42–60). Boston, MA: Beacon.

Collins, P. H. (1998). *Fighting words: Black women and the search for justice*. Minneapolis: University of Minnesota.

Collins, P. H. (2009). *Black feminist thought: Knowledge, consciousness, and the politics of empowerment*. New York, NY: Routledge.

Cottle, M. (2013, November 21). Leaning out. *Politico Magazine*. Retrieved from http://www.politico.com/magazine/story/2013/11/leaning-out-michelle-obama-100244

Cooper, B. (2010). A'n't I a lady?: Race women, Michelle Obama, and the ever-expanding democratic imagination. *MELUS, 35*, 39–57.

Douglas, S. J., & Michaels, M. W. (2004). *The mommy myth: The idealization of motherhood and how it has undermined women*. New York, NY: Free Press.

Dow, B. J. (2014). Michelle Obama, "mom-in-chief." In J. S. Vaughn and J. R. Mercieca (Eds.), *The rhetoric of heroic expectations: Establishing the Obama presidency* (pp. 235–256). College Station, TX: Texas A&M.

Dubriwny, T. N. (2005). First ladies and feminism: Laura Bush as advocate for women's and children's rights. *Women's Studies in Communication, 28*, 84–114.

Endres, D. (2012). Sacred land or national sacrifice zone: The role of values in the Yucca Mountain participation process. *Environmental Communication, 6*, 328–345.

Erickson, K. V., & Thomson, S. (2012). First lady international diplomacy: Performing gendered roles on the world stage. *Southern Communication Journal, 77*, 239–262.

Fabj, V. (1993). Motherhood as political voice: The rhetoric of the Mothers of Plaza de Mayo. *Communication Studies, 44*, 1–18.

Fiske, J. (1986). Television: Polysemy and popularity. *Critical Studies in Mass Communication, 3*, 391–408.

Fiske, J. (1991). For cultural interpretation: A study of the culture of homelessness. *Critical Studies in Mass Communication, 8*, 453–474.

Fiske, J. (2006). *Television culture* (2nd ed.). London, United Kingdom: Routledge.

Foss, K. A., & Domenici, K. L. (2001). Haunting Argentina: Synecdoche in the protests of the Mothers of the Plaza de Mayo. *Quarterly Journal of Speech, 87*, 237–258.

Gandy, I. (2013, November 24). Michelle Obama is not a feminist nightmare, so shut up already. Retrieved from http://angryblackladychronicles.com/2013/11/24/michelle-obama-is-not-a-feminist-nightmare-so-shut-up-already/

Gibson, K. L., & Heyse, A. L. (2010). "The difference between a hockey mom and a pit bull": Sarah Palin's faux maternal persona and performance of hegemonic masculinity at the 2008 Republican National Convention. *Communication Quarterly, 58*, 235–256.

Hall, S. (1994). Reflections upon the encoding/decoding model: An interview with Stuart Hall. In J. Cruz and J. Lewis (Eds.), *Viewing, reading, listening: Audiences and cultural reception* (pp. 253–274). Boulder, CO: Westview Press.

Hall, S. (1996). Encoding/decoding. In S. Hall, D. Hobson, A. Lowe, and P. Willis (Eds.), *Culture, media, language: Working papers in cultural studies, 1972–1979* (pp. 128–138). London, United Kingdom: Routledge.

Harris-Perry, M. (2013, December 1). Michelle Obama a "feminist nightmare"? Please. *MSNBC*. Retrieved from http://www.msnbc.com/melissa-harris-perry/michelle-obama-no-ones-feminist-nightmare

Hayden, S. (2003). Family metaphors and the nation: Promoting a politics of care through the Million Mom March. *Quarterly Journal of Speech, 89*, 196–215.

Hays, S. (1996). *The cultural contradictions of motherhood*. New Haven, CT: Yale University.

Hogan, L. S. (2013). Exposing Mary Lincoln: Elizabeth Keckley and the rhetoric of intimate disclosure. *Southern Communication Journal, 78*, 405–426.

hooks, b. (1990). *Yearning: Race, gender, and cultural politics*. Boston, MA: South End.

Jasinski, J. (1997). Instrumentalism, contextualism, and interpretation in rhetorical criticism. In A. G. Gross and W. M. Keith (Eds.), *Rhetorical hermeneutics: Invention and interpretation in the age of science* (pp. 195–224). Albany: State University of New York Press.

Jensen, R. E. (2008). Sexual polysemy: The discursive ground of talk about sex and education in U.S. history. *Communication, Culture, and Critique, 1*, 396–425.

Joseph, R. L. (2011). "Hope is finally making a comeback": First lady reframed. *Communication, Culture, and Critique, 4,* 56–77.

Kantor, J. (2012, September 6). Obama girls' role: Not to speak, but to be spoken of. *New York Times.* Retrieved from http://www.nytimes.com/2012/09/07/us/politics/obama-girls-though-unheard-figure-prominently-in-race.html?_r=0

King, D. K. (2010). Mom-in-chief: Community othermothering and Michelle Obama, the first lady of the people's house. *Research in Race and Ethnic Relations, 16,* 77–123.

Lakoff, G. (1996). *Moral politics: How liberals and conservatives think.* Chicago, IL: University of Chicago.

Lewis, J. (1991). *The ideological octopus: An exploration of television and its audience.* New York, NY: Routledge.

Maddux, K. (2008). Feminism and foreign policy: Public vocabularies and the conditions of emergence for First Lady Rosalynn Carter. *Women's Studies in Communication, 31,* 29–55.

McAlister, J. F. (2009). ___ Trash in the White House: Michelle Obama, post-racism, and the pre-class politics of domestic style. *Communication and Critical/Cultural Studies, 6,* 311–315.

Meyer, M. D. E. (2003). Utilizing mythic criticism in contemporary narrative culture: Examining the "present-absence" of shadow archetypes in *Spider-Man. Communication Quarterly, 51,* 518–529.

NPR. (2008, August 25). Transcript: Michelle Obama's convention speech. Retrieved from http://www.npr.org/templates/story/story.php?storyID=93963863

NPR. (2012, September 4). Transcript: Michelle Obama's convention speech. Retrieved from http://www.npr/org/2012/09/04/160578836/transcript-michelle-obamas-convention-speech

Obama, M. (1985). *Princeton-educated Blacks & the Black community* (Unpublished master's thesis). Princeton University, Princeton, NJ. Retrieved from http://www.politico.com/pdf/080222_MOPrincetonThesis_1-251.pdf

O'Brien Hallstein, D. L. (2010). Public choices, private control: How mediated mom labels work rhetorically to dismantle the politics of choice and White second-wave feminist successes. In S. Hayden and D. L. O'Brien Hallstein (Eds.), *Contemplating maternity in an era of choice: Explorations into discourses of reproduction* (pp. 5–26). Lanham, MA: Lexington.

O'Brien Hallstein, D. L. (2011). She gives birth, she's wearing a bikini: Mobilizing the post-pregnant celebrity mom body to manage the second-wave crisis in femininity. *Women's Studies in Communication, 34,* 111–138.

O'Brien Hallstein, D. L. (2017). Introduction to mothering rhetorics. *Women's Studies in Communication, 40,* 1–10.

O'Neal Parker, L. (2013, January 18). Four years later, feminists split by Michelle Obama's "work" as first lady. *Washington Post.* Retrieved from https://www.washingtonpost.com/lifestyle/style/feminists-split-by-michelle-obamas-work-as-first-lady/2013/01/18/be3d636e-5e5e-11e2-9940-6fc488f3fecd_story.html

O'Reilly, A. (2006). *Rocking the cradle: Thoughts on motherhood, feminism, and the possibility of empowered mothering.* Toronto, Canada: Demeter.

Parry-Giles, S. J. (2000). Mediating Hillary Rodham Clinton: Television news practices and image-making in the postmodern age. *Critical Studies in Media Communication, 17,* 205–226.

Parry-Giles, S. J., & Blair, D. M. (2002). The rise of the rhetorical first lady: Politics, gender ideology, and women's voice, 1789–2002. *Rhetoric and Public Affairs, 5,* 565–600.

Peeples, J. A., & DeLuca, K. M. (2006). The truth of the matter: Motherhood, community, and environmental justice. *Women's Studies in Communication, 29,* 59–87.

Perks, L. G. (2010). Polysemic scaffolding: Explicating discursive clashes in *Chappelle's Show. Communication, Culture, and Critique, 3,* 270–289.

Poirot, K. (2014). *A question of sex: Feminism, rhetoric, and differences that matter.* Boston: University of Massachusetts.

Press, A., & Cole, E. (1994). Women like us: Working-class women respond to television representations of abortion. In J. Cruz and J. Lewis (Eds.), *Viewing, reading, listening: Audiences and cultural reception* (pp. 55–80). Boulder, CO: Westview Press.

Reid-Brinkley, S. R. (2011). Mammies and matriarchs: Feminine style and signifyin(g) in Carol Moseley Braun's 2003–2004 campaign for the presidency. In K. R. Chavez and C. L. Griffin

(Eds.), *Standing in the intersection: Feminist voices, feminist practices in communication studies* (pp. 35–58). Albany: State University of New York Press.

Rich, A. (1976). *Of woman born: Motherhood as experience and institution.* New York, NY: Bantam.

Roberts, E. (1997). *Killing the Black body: Race, reproduction, and the meaning of liberty.* New York, NY: Pantheon.

Rockler, N. R. (2001). A wall on the lesbian continuum: Polysemy and *Fried Green Tomatoes. Women's Studies in Communication, 24,* 90–106.

Schutten, J. K. (2006). Invoking *Practical Magic*: New social movements, hidden populations, and the public screen. *Western Journal of Communication, 70,* 331–354.

Sheeler, K. H. (2013). Remembering the rhetorical first lady. *Rhetoric and Public Affairs, 16,* 767–781.

Spillers, H. (2010). Views of the East Wing: On Michelle Obama. *Communication and Critical/ Cultural Studies, 6,* 307–310.

Stearney, L. M. (1994). Feminism, ecofeminism, and the maternal archetype: Motherhood as feminine universal. *Communication Quarterly, 42,* 145–159.

Steiner, L. M. (2012). Michelle Obama: Powerful or just popular? *Modern Mom.* Retrieved from http://www.modernmom.com/47ebe4d2-3b36-11e3-be8a-bc764e04a41e.html

Steinhauer, J. (2013, November 11). Michelle Obama edges into a policy role on higher education. *New York Times.* Retrieved from http://www.nytimes.com/2013/11/12/us/michelle-obama-edges-into-a-policy-role-on-higher-education.html

Swarns, R. L. (2009, February 22). First chores? You bet. *New York Times.* Retrieved from http://www.nytimes.com/2009/02/22/fashion/22firstp.html

Talley, A. L. (2009, March 1). Michelle Obama: Leading lady. *Vogue.* Retrieved from http://www.vogue.com/3056753/michelle-obama-leading-lady/

Terrill, R. E. (2000). Spectacular repression: Sanitizing the Batman. *Critical Studies in Media Communication, 17,* 493–509.

Thomas, E. (2008, March 12). Michelle Obama's "proud" remarks. *Newsweek.* Retrieved from http://www.newsweek.com/michelle-obamas-proud-remarks-83559

Tonn, M. B. (1996). Militant motherhood: Labor's Mary Harris "Mother" Jones. *Quarterly Journal of Speech, 82,* 1–21.

Traister, R. (2008, November 12). The momification of Michelle Obama. *Salon.* Retrieved from http://www.salon.com/2008/11/12/michelle_obama_14/.

Waisanen, D. J. (2013). Hermeneutic range in church-state deliberation: Cross meanings in the Los Angeles County seal controversy. *Western Journal of Communication, 77,* 361–381.

Watson, R. P. (2000). *The presidents' wives: Reassessing the office of first lady.* Boulder, CO: Lynne Rienner.

Watts, L. (2010). Covering Eleanor Roosevelt: Associated Press reporter Bess Furman and four years with the first lady. *Journalism History, 36,* 45–54.

Wertheimer, M. M. (Ed.). (2004). *Inventing a voice: The rhetoric of American first ladies of the twentieth century.* Lanham, MA: Rowman & Littlefield.

West, I. (2007). Performing resistance in/from the kitchen: The practice of maternal pacifist politics and La WISP's cookbooks. *Women's Studies in Communication, 30,* 358–383.

The White House. (2009, April 28). Remarks by the first lady at the Sojourner Truth bust unveiling. Retrieved from http://www.whitehouse.gov/the-press-office/remarks-first-lady-sojourner-truth-bust-unveiling

The White House. (2010, February 9). "Let's Move" kick-off. Retrieved from https://www.youtube.com/watch?v=70H7m_CkwoU&feature=youtube_gdata

Williams, P. J. (2009, April 27). Mrs. Obama meets Mrs. Windsor. *The Nation,* 9.

Winfrey Harris, T. (2012, September 11). A Black mom-in-chief is revolutionary: What White feminists get wrong about Michelle Obama. *Clutch.* Retrieved from http://www.clutchmagonline.com/2012/09/a-black-mom-in-chief-is-revolutionary-what-white-feminist-get-wrong-about-michelle-obama/

Yousman, B. (2013). Revisiting Hall's encoding/decoding model: Ex-prisoners respond to television representations of incarceration. *The Review of Education, Pedagogy, and Cultural Studies, 35,* 197–216.

Fixing Food to Fix Families: Feeding Risk Discourse and the Family Meal

Amber E. Kinser

ABSTRACT

This article examines mothering rhetorics as they relate to feeding the family. The analysis is grounded in public, popular, and institutional texts about family meals and focus-group data from 31 mothers talking about their experiences and perceptions of family meals. The author demonstrates how family meal discourses work as a reproducing rhetoric that moralizes maternal feeding work. The author argues that family meal discourse is problematic because it obscures the ways in which it is mother-targeted and mother-blaming; suppresses maternal voice and misrepresents family food labor; and regulates maternal activity, and thus identity.

In the years surrounding the turn of the 21st century, health profession industries, news and educational media, academic research, and the general public developed an increased and intensified interest in food. Political and marketing discourses became, and continue to be, infused with the languages of food scarcity, ethics, and pyramids; food that is slow, processed, and ethical; meals that are delivered, swapped, and home-cooked; eating that is mindful and clean; portions and weights that are controlled; and parents who are controlling. A recurring thread in these languages is the ubiquity of food risk, or the dangers and hazards associated with "bad" food and/or problematic eating/feeding practices. Food risk is related not only to the impacts of clearly dangerous environmental chemicals (MacKendrick, 2014) and food industry practices, but also to part of a long cultural history of food fear in the United States (Levenstein, 2012). Academic and corporate research, popular narratives, and institutional policy abound with efforts to identify and quantify risks to health, safety, and well-being (see Mudry, 2009). Grounded in a neoliberal ethos, a sizable portion of the management of such risk—whether precipitated or alleviated by food—falls upon families. Family meals in particular, and the need to increase their frequency, have been the subject of much consideration, analysis, and media attention as a method for mitigating childhood risks. While research evidences some dispute about the exact nature of frequent family meal benefits, the subject of families sharing an evening meal has been a darling of public and policy discourse. Arguably, few phenomena of this century have been more lauded as a social curative, or more lamented as a lost art, than the family meal.

In this article, I interrogate the discourse on the family meal as it relates to mothering experience and identity. While some communication scholarship has focused on mothering and food (Arnold, 2008; Meyers, 2013), little is understood about the relationships between discourse, motherhood/mothering, and food, especially regarding how food discourse shapes cultural definitions of motherhood and perceptions and assessments of mothers. This study extends recent scholarship (Kinser & Denker, 2016) on mothers and family meals through a rhetorical exploration of how family meal (FM) discourse has emerged in contemporary culture as an ideological system that is working to shape and reproduce particular understandings of "good" motherhood. I explore the influence of neoliberal thought, its relationship to constructions of family risk and well-being, and its focus on familializing risk, particularly feeding risk. I illustrate that FM discourse works as a reproducing mothering rhetoric that moralizes maternal feeding work and encourages mother blame. Finally, I argue that FM discourse is problematic because it obscures the ways it is mother-targeted and mother-blaming; it suppresses maternal voice and misrepresents family food labor; and it regulates maternal activity, delimiting maternal identity.

I come to this work as a communication and motherhood studies scholar—a working-class-turned-upper-middle-class, White, heterosexual, able-bodied mother who was afforded opportunity for advanced degrees by way of enormous debt. In my working-class upbringing, FMs were a routine—almost daily—practice orchestrated from beginning to end by my mother. In my children's upper-middle-class upbringing, FM regularity has ebbed and flowed in response to the rhythms and ruptures of our family life and my professional life, as I assume primary responsibility for meal provision in my family. In the past several years, as my research interests have been piqued by FM discourse, my own meal provision activity, in which I had for many years been greatly invested, has rather fallen away. Perhaps I feel pulled toward this work to make sense of such a shift in investment. I conduct my research on motherhood and FMs funded by my midsized university in southern Appalachia, where gender-normative and heteronormative values tend to prevail and where family is a central part of the identities of a majority of people, women in particular.

Methodological approach

For purposes of this analysis, I construed FM discourse broadly, analyzing how it functions from several data points and across two phases of analysis. In the first phase, I read the public discourse rhetorically, focusing especially on how neoliberal sensibilities and feeding-risk concerns work together to insist upon a particular and narrowed view of family accountability, as well as how FM outcomes and labor are represented. In the second phase of analysis, I called on the experiences and perceptions of 31 mothers with whom I spoke across six focus groups regarding their experiences with and perspectives about FMs. I used their accounts to help make sense of how these discourses may shape mothering and motherhood while helping illuminate ways that mothering rhetorics about food could be informed by maternal experience.

I recruited participants using flyers distributed by the student child care center and K–12 public school on the university campus. Some were recruited through snowball sampling and a few through convenience sampling. Focus group participants did not represent widely diverse perspectives and experiences for several reasons. For example, while their children's ages ranged from 1 to 21 years, 60% of them had children between 1 and 5 years old. In addition, a majority of them experienced social privilege in some way. First, only two of the mothers were Black, two were Asian, and one was Hispanic, while the other 25 women were White. Second, all but four of the mothers were partnered. One of these was in a same-sex partnership, and the others lived with a male partner or spouse. Third, a majority of the mothers had some kind of tie with the university—current/former employees or their partners, current/former students or their partners, and mothers of adolescent students who attended the campus K–12 school. Finally, just over half of the mothers' household incomes were more than $60,000, and all of the mothers had at least some college education; more than half had a graduate degree.[1]

A focus group methodology fits well with the purposes of this study because it capitalizes on the ability of groups to "reveal unarticulated norms and normative assumptions" (Kamberelis & Dimitriadis, 2011, p. 559). DeVault (1991) argued that the work of bringing about FMs is "invisible" even to those who do it and that there is both a paucity of language for understanding this kind of work and a "pervasive trivialization" of it (pp. 55–57). It can be difficult, then, for women to see and name their own foodwork and to position it as a topic for examination. Exploring experiences of FMs in a group context allows participants' awareness of their foodwork to be triggered by the discussion and by other participants' insights. Further, mothering is intimately tied to the culturally loaded construct of the "good mother." Telling one's stories in a group context with others who may face similar struggles with the complexities of feeding work can then, as Kamberelis & Dimitriadis (2011) note about focus groups, help reduce participants' sense of vulnerability (p. 557).

Using the focus group data, I looked at mothers' narratives about FMs and compared their representations with those in the larger FM discourse to determine how its foundational assumptions play out in family life as described by participants. In particular, I examined the discourse's rhetoric about FM *labor* relative to mothers' narratives about it. I began with the assumption that FM laborers speak with greater authority about that labor than do FM discourse sources, given that the latter place low value on meal-provider perspectives, as evidenced by their failure to seek out and become informed by those perspectives. In addition to comparing representations of FM labor, I looked at the mothers' narratives to explore, following Harvey (2007), how discourse functions in situ for mothers and to identify the extent to which the broader FM discourse is grounded in the complexities of FM provision and how it may impact maternal activity and identity.

The focus group discussions were audiotaped and transcribed verbatim. Pseudonyms were used throughout the process. Guided by grounded theory techniques (Strauss & Corbin, 1998; Charmaz, 2006), I worked from participant perspectives as they took form in the transcripts, coding the data beginning with line-by-line and in vivo codes, and moving to focused coding, meeting with student research assistants routinely to check perceptions of the data. Multiple times throughout the process, as themes and categories surfaced, I returned to the transcripts to apply emerging coding schemes. In the excerpts featured here, I edited only if needed for clarity when reading them outside the focus group context; I did not modify the speech of my participant mothers to conform to academic conventions. Rather than support broad generalizations across a variety of mothers, the narratives of the women I talked with offer possibilities for considering how mothers may struggle with FM work. In particular, they point to some of the ways that mothers might engage this work within the context of a contemporary motherhood shaped in part by neoliberal logics and advancing a set of standards against which mothers in general are judged.

Mothering and the production and management of neoliberal risk

The discourses that direct 21st-century family life in general and U.S. cultural understandings of motherhood in particular are fortified by neoliberal thought (Cairns, Johnston, & MacKendrick, 2013). The primary discourse of neoliberalism, Giles (2012) argued, is the mechanism and production of risk. It is pervasive throughout "all forms of political, economic and social consciousness" (p. 112). As contemporary families are understood more in terms of what they do than what they look like (Cossman, 2002, p. 212), much discursive energy is directed at family member (especially adult) activity, with particular regard to familial culpability for socially desirable outcomes. Families are presumed responsible for managing much of the risk their members confront. Despite ubiquitous references to appropriate conduct for "families" and "parents" in organizational, institutional, mass mediated, and policy rhetoric, it is largely maternal labor that is implicated in family culpability claims. Familial rhetorics function by and large as mothering rhetorics.

The neoliberal practice of familializing risk (Fudge & Cossman, 2002) obscures the impact that its management has on mothers, given that it "allows systemic gender inequalities to disappear from view, emphasizing instead a gender-neutral model of familial responsibility," wherein inequities are seen as products of individual decision making (Cossman, 2002, p. 212). The proliferation of food languages highlighted at the opening of this article points to a fundamental category of familialized risk—food and feeding—which represents a substantial portion of family labor and a burden that women disproportionately bear (Bowen, Elliott, & Brenton, 2014; Coveney, 2002; DeVault, 1991; McIntosh et al., 2010). Mothers' feeding activities function as "key vectors" for children's well-being (MacKendrick, 2014, p. 720). Consistent with neoliberal discourses in general, feeding risk discourses are characterized by implicit links to morality (Burrows, 2009). As mothering rhetorics, they reproduce mothers as moral actors to the extent that they manage risk to their families according to the feeding risk discourses of the day.

Feeding-risk discourses take a number of forms, many of which both overcomplicate and oversimplify health and well-being outcomes as well as the food paths to them. The discourse on FMs functions as a feeding risk discourse that directs meal providers/mothers to mitigate the health and psychosocial well-being risks confronting children by increasing the number of times per week their families gather together to share a meal. Family meal discourse works from assumptions grounded in an idealized image and narrow prescription of how people in the West have fed themselves. The evocation of a nuclear family routinely assembling around a table to enjoy a home-cooked meal serves as the bedrock of FM discourse. Although the myth depicts families, to borrow from Coontz (1992), "the way [they] never were" and the way they are not now, the FM in the popular imaginary is iconic, a "hegemonic collective representation of an ideal form of social behavior" (Wilk, 2010, p. 434). Corporate, public health, education, and food industries employ this icon to generate and proliferate a narrative of FMs profuse with promises about how adolescent health, success, and well-being are within easy reach of all families. In what follows, I examine these pervasive, cross-institutional narratives to identify how FMs are constructed, how FM labor is represented, and how both of these may impact cultural understandings and individual enactments of motherhood.

Risk management and the miracle of family meals

Since the mid-1990s, Columbia University's National Center on Addiction and Substance Abuse (CASAColumbia) has collected annual data about teen substance use to identify factors impacting the abuse of alcohol, illegal drugs, and tobacco. In 2003, CASAColumbia issued a public report linking abuse of these substances to frequency of shared FMs, and reports that continue to make these links have been issued almost annually since (*The Importance of Family Dinners*). In related work, University of Minnesota's School of Public Health conducted large- scale research, beginning in the late 1990s, linking adolescent dietary patterns to later life obesity, eating disorders, and chronic illness. From this work—"Eating Among Teens" or Project EAT—researchers published results, some longitudinal, in nutrition, dietetic association, and medical journals between 2000 and 2011 (University of Minnesota Epidemiology and Community Health Research, 2016; University of Minnesota School of Public Health, 2016). These findings, too, correlated frequency of FMs with psychosocial and physiological well-being.

Motivated or informed in large part by this research, a profusion of scholarly work, public education, and media distribution followed, a majority of which directed and continues to direct "families" and "parents" to mediate risks to children's health and well-being through more frequent FMs. Frequent FMs, the research argues, *decrease* the likelihood of substance abuse (CASAColumbia, 2003, 2005–2007, 2009–2012), sexual activity risk (Fulkerson et al. 2006), overweight and disordered eating (Hammons & Fiese, 2011; Rockett, 2007), poor academic performance (CASAColumbia, 2003, 2005–2007, 2009, 2010; Hamilton & Hamilton Wilson, 2009), getting in fights and other disorderly behavior (Sen, 2010; Story & Neumark-Sztainer, 2005), and depression and suicidal ideation (Eisenberg, Olson, Neumark-Sztainer, Story, & Bearinger, 2004). Further, FMs have been shown to *increase* healthy food intake (Hammons & Fiese, 2011; Neumark-Sztainer, Larson, Fulkerson, Eisenberg, & Story, 2010), vocabulary growth (Fiese & Schwartz, 2008; Larson, Branscomb, & Wiley, 2006), and the likelihood of being able to handle cyberbullying (Elgar et al., 2014).

Food industries and other corporations enjoy equally robust participation in FM discourse. Here, interests of capital assume an authoritative voice that "pedagogizes" (Burrows, 2009) meal providers. Their informational/educational/consumption-encouraging practices promote a particular image of family connection and health over meals that may or may not suit family desire but surely suits corporate gain. That is, such practices promote an image of the "good neoliberal family embracing market choice [and] consumerism" (Burrows, 2009, p. 136), as well as self-governing and self-culpable conduct. Food industry forces also have colluded with those in the health industries to craft rhetorical strategies that capitalize on the power of FM discourse to regulate maternal activity, thus reproducing their own social and economic power. A campaign by the National Cattlemen's Beef Association (2015), for instance, targets mothers explicitly through its "leading experts" who "speak on cutting-edge issues" (p. 5). Five of the association's presentations marketed on their website relate to bringing families together over FMs more often to improve child well-being outcomes. One presentation is directed to "health professionals" whom the association's speakers will teach how to "communicate with moms" so they will "take notice" of the professionals' messages about food and family health and become compelled to "listen and take action" (p. 3) in prescribed ways.

Major corporate brands such as Coca-Cola, J.M. Smucker Company (including Smucker's, Pillsbury, Crisco, and Folgers), Welch's, Del Monte, and General Mills have all been party to the regulating practices of FM discourse. They variously promote the FM research disseminated by CASAColumbia and/or sponsor its national 15-year-long campaign for annual Family Day, and/or sell the critical importance of family dinners through product advertisement and packaging, often tying their claims to CASAColumbia, or secondarily to Weinstein's (2006) widely praised popular press book, *The Surprising Power of Family Meals.*

The Food Marketing Institute (FMI), the trade association for food retailers and food manufacturers, also launched a "Family Meals Movement" in September 2015 aimed at bringing families "back to the table" since "they aren't making it happen often enough" (2016). "Family meals are at a critical intersection in our nation," FMI warned on its Web site, and families "need to know the facts." The Pork Network, Hormel Foods, Campbell's, Meijer, Publix, Harris Teeter, and many others jumped on the bandwagon to back FMI's campaign to declare September "National Family Meals Month." Claiming that greater frequency of FMs "benefits everyone," FMI failed to mention that the food and meal ingredients FMI affiliates sell—and the meal preparation labor those sales then implicate—benefit some of the "everyone" more than others. FMI aimed to pedagogize FM provider activity not only by appointing food retailers and manufacturers as the authoritative sources who can "lead the way" and who are fully equipped to affect FM frequency by virtue of "the facts" they graciously (if calculatedly) share, but also through employing the rhetorical strategy of linking identity to FM frequency (FMI, 2016). Specifically, meal providers were encouraged to "post oven mitt selfies with hashtag #raiseyourmitt" to demonstrate that the campaign "Raise Your Mitt to Commit" (to providing one additional meal each week at home) speaks to the kind of FM providers they are.

The sheer weight and volume of these involvements work rhetorically to reify and venerate the quest for more frequent FMs, thus normalizing the expectation that those who do the FM labor will "simply" do more of it, or risk threats to identity through charges of questionable parenting. How FMs might impact meal providers or what might impact provider interest in or capacity toward taking on more food-related labor seem inconsequential to that expectation. Hence, whether or not a mother adopts that expectation toward herself, she likely is no less encouraged to view her own identity as a mother in terms of whether or not she is "good" enough at mothering to provide routinely shared FMs. The breadth of FM discourse participants also illuminates how perniciously it functions, indicting meal provider/maternal activity while never getting caught explicitly naming it as such.

The implication in this store of messages is that one need only add the single ingredient of frequently shared FMs to the current family dynamic—no matter how pleasant, manageable, uncertain, or even destructive that dynamic may be—to create a recipe for children's success. Or, it follows, one may "choose" to omit or substitute that ingredient, fail to manage risk, and fail to raise healthy and happy children. Family meals are portrayed, borrowing from Seiler's (2012) study of obesity rhetoric, as working "in isolation from the rest of society" (p. 163), disconnected from "the myriad of other factors that influence how, why, and what we eat" (pp. 163, 165). Race and class disparities, cultural practices, varying physiologies and psychologies, and the impact of these on family life in general and foodways in particular are rendered invisible, as meal providers/mothers in general are held morally accountable for child well-being outcomes without regard for family positionality, mental and other health care disparity, corporate investment, or genetic predisposition. The expanse of FM discourse sources and the gross oversimplification of how family foodwork functions is even more troubling when one considers how FM labor is minimized and depoliticized in media representations. This angle on FM labor is further sharpened as it rubs against insistent claims of FM decline and the threat it poses.

Representations of family meals: Pure and simple

The most recent 2012 findings from the frequently cited CASAColumbia projects are identical to those from more than a decade ago: 57% of teens reported meals with their families five to seven days per week, with the recent report admitting that these numbers "have remained relatively consistent over the past decade" (p. 1). In addition, the 2011–2012 National Survey of Children's Health reports that over 70% of children ages 12 to 17 eat dinner with their families four to seven days per week (Data Resource Center for Child and Adolescent Health, 2011–2012), and Child Trends DataBank (2013) reports that number at nearly 80%. Even so, FM discourse crafts a rhetoric of FMs in peril. In sharp relief and with moralizing flair, it sets this rhetoric up against a beatific image of the work that could reverse that peril, thus casting childhood risk as an easy fix and by definition the meal providers/mothers who do not meet the evasive standard as derelict.

Contemporary media and other popular discourse about how the "dying tradition" (Gibbs, 2006, p. 1) and "lost ritual" of the FM results in kids being "short-changed" (Gurian, 2013, para. 2, 4) are fed by insistence on the parallel qualities of pure simplicity and astounding results of FMs, if meal providers/mothers would only serve more of them. Hence this discourse offers suitable context for hyperbolic claims from popular/lay sources about its "magical" qualities (Fishel, 2015; Gibbs, 2006; Weinstein, 2006), "surprising power" (Parrott & Parrott, 2011; Weinstein, 2006), and "big payoff" (Ansel, 2014), which might well "save your life" (Hyman, 2011). Simultaneously, these discourses marvel together at how easily invoked this power and magic is, given that FM labor represents a "small investment" (Ansel, 2014) that takes "little effort" (Kerr, 2010). Even academic discourse is fond of pointing out that the "simple family activity" of mealtime (Hamilton & Hamilton Wilson, 2009, p. 346) is an "uncomplicated affair" (Fiese, cited in Anderson, 2011, para. 16). If we accept that FMs offer up, as Nestlé's Stouffer's foods explained, an environment that is naturally "chockfull of parental engagement, caring conversation, and a healthy dose of light-hearted banter"—all of which are orchestrated "without a whole lot of pressure or anxiety" (Stouffer's, n.d.)—we might be led to the moralistic conclusion that the only variable that could foil such a marvel are the "enemies": parental "laziness and leniency" (Gibbs, 2006, para. 11).

What gets lost in these reductionist accounts are a number of critical concerns. First, meal provision is challenging, mindful, continuous work, and as a body of work it is neither effortless nor simple. Second, FM labor is gendered and the burden that increasing FM frequency puts on mothers is ignored. Third, FMs are not monolithically salutary; like all aspects of family life, they are multidimensional and include a complicated, sometimes troublesome, even darker, side. In what follows, I examine each of these three concerns and work to nuance FM experience, practicality, and struggle drawing from my conversations with mothers about meal habits within their families.

Thinking and talking differently about family meals

In his foreword to Frye and Bruner's (2012) *Rhetoric of Food*, McKerrow (2012) argued that "it is one thing to note the power of language to frame food in positive or negative ways; it is another to suggest ways in which the language might be re-made, that terms might increase or decrease their salience in particular ways in order to create a new matrix of power relations" (p. xiii). I talked with mothers in focus groups to begin grounding alternative forms of FM discourse in the perspectives of the women who do the food labor. My goal was to identify how FM discourse fails to represent FM work (and the mothers who do it) and to lay the groundwork for later discourse that could shift away from a neoliberal view of family culpability and its impact on blame of mothers. I hope to help facilitate a move toward familial foodwork as complex and often difficult, grounded in social structure and not simply in family microcosms, and in need of facilitating social supports that at least match the degree of importance that the discourse assigns to FMs.

Encapsulating the first concern about the limits of FM discourse nearly a decade before it gained traction, DeVault (1991) argued that, as a "complex social event," a meal requires an enormous amount of effort, energy, resources, and negotiation (p. 3). Planning, shopping, scheduling, preparing, serving, navigating table interaction, cleaning, packing away, planning for the next meal, stocking supplemental ingredients, as well as knowing and accommodating family member diets, preferences, and allergies (as more than one-third of the mothers I spoke with did), and adjusting for multiple schedules emerging from divergent and demanding school, work, community, family, and extracurricular activities (as all but one of the study participants did), constitute major, time-consuming, and exhausting involvements. Eva, a mother of three children (16 months, 4 years, and 11 years), manages several of the noted variables as well as family member behavior when her family gathers to eat. Her comments illustrate some of the ways in which FMs are, for her, far from simple:

> I need to shut some of the OCD [obsessive-compulsive disorder] off and shut some of the micromanaging of the "he just spit his food out and it's sitting in his lap, and that's disgusting, and then it's going to go to the floor, and I'm going pick it up' cause we don't have a dog anymore" [laughs]. And the four-year-old, why is he not sitting on his bottom? Or "um, no, you can't have any more to drink because, you know, you'll have an accident." In my head, I am thinking of all the millions of things that are going on at dinner, that are getting ready to have to happen in order for everybody to go to bed, and it—it's this nonstop checklist that's going on. So while I'm looking at my family going "I would really love to enjoy you all," and I would love to enjoy and make the whole process very fun ... in my mind I haven't shut—shut the checklist off.

The provision of meals is an activity that is pursued in interaction with, or competition with, not only a vast expanse of other parenting tasks but also the providers' own schedules, interests, needs, and emotional and psychological states.

Feeding work is all the more complex for poor families and working-class families who may be confronting food insecurity, transportation issues, poor urban planning, and/or work schedules that make routine FMs with the whole of their families barely possible. All of the mothers in my study discussed this interaction/competition with other variables in some way, whether they worked full time in paid employment (17 participants), went to school full time (1 participant), went to school full time and worked part time

(3 participants), worked part time (5 participants), or were neither employed nor enrolled in school (5 participants). Tammy, a mother of a three-year-old, spoke to the issue of workforce impact on family scheduling:

> We always, I mean we always try to do *together*. And it's not always at the table. We sometimes just sit around in the living room, or my son's sitting at his little table and, you know, that sort of thing. It is stressful, though, the nights that [my husband] works, oh my goodness! 'Cause I have to go get my son [from child care], come straight home, have to start cooking like immediately, and you know, just to get it done in time before he has to leave for work.

The commonplace occurrence of a child not eating what is served is profoundly problematic for a mother who struggles to afford the food to start with and who now may be throwing it away or providing a different, additional food option—a drain on time, energy, and money. Some mothers, like Louisa, mother of a toddler, found their own diet disrupted by this dimension of family foodwork:

> I hate wasting food.... I even eat much more junk because I don't wanna throw away all the food on his plate. Like, I would even, at the restaurant, I am like, "Well, I will eat that," because I am a member of that clean-plate club; even if I am full, I keep eating [the child's food]. I don't want to waste it.

Samantha, who has a four-year-old, also wrestled with the impact of food waste. She felt pulled between buying food that is healthier and food that will keep. She talked about preferring to buy fresh produce at Fresh Market but choosing instead to buy canned or frozen produce elsewhere: "It's a cost thing, and it's also a—God, if I saw that [produce] go to waste, if we didn't use it for something, in a certain amount of time, it eats me alive because we don't have three dollars."

The FM campaign model seems content to rely on unrealistic, almost "Stepford moms" images. Such a model not only assumes a heterosexual, White, middle-class life, with all the conceivable privilege that could be associated with it, but also fails to account for the everyday struggles associated with social location and the barriers to family time and meal provision confronting mothers in general. Carla, mother of a three-year-old, illustrated some of the difficulty of juggling family member activities:

> [My daughter]'s involved in two things, but then, you know, my husband plays soccer every Sunday. And I'm on a hundred committees, and ... you know what I mean. It's just, there's always something going on.... So it's hard to—it's hard for me to even make a meal plan and get to the grocery store so we can eat for that week. So then, it's like, last-minute shuffling: *What are we going to eat?*

Frequent FM images also assume a particular kind of commitment to a particular set of familial orchestrations and a certain level of personal satisfaction and family member "payoff" from them.

Further, the discourse fails to acknowledge how exceptionally difficult it is for meal providers to effectively compete with the enormity of demand for children's time and interest. Lydia, who identifies as "one hundred percent the planner of the meals, and the insister that it happens," is raising two teens and two toddlers with her same-sex partner. Aside from the difficulty of finding ways to appeal to such a broad range of ages and tastes among her children, Lydia struggles to get her teens to eat at home because of their busy schedules and their preferences for restaurant industry foods. While she clearly exercises agency in her feeding work, she does so amid deep struggle:

> I have like big issues with the quality of food [when eating] out. I think it's full of sugar, fat, salt, and so from my health perspective I would rather make it at home. So I *fight* for it; it's a fight [to have meals with my kids at home]. So I do it for the health of it, and for the, like, *status* of it. Like our family eats together, so we are a family. That's why I wanted to come [to this focus group]. I feel like strong—I feel like it's really, really important, and it's really a fight in society today to get it done.

The demand for time and energy with which mothers must contend goes beyond that of children or partners; mothers themselves may be pulled in a number of directions simultaneously. For those who are extended-family caretakers among other obligations, for example, and who internalize messages about maternal blame regarding family foodwork, this can weigh heavily. Victoria, mother of two children, two and five years old, explained:

> When I'm with kids at dinner, I'm thinking about: I've got these papers to grade for the class I'm teaching. I've got these papers to write for my classes I'm taking. Um, I'd like to spend some time with my husband ... I've got to fix lunch for in the morning [and think about] what's going on, planning, other family concerns. I'm kind of a caretaker for my mother. She's in assisted living right now, [where] they don't do everything [for her]. And I still have to check on her and things like that, so I definitely have the mommy guilt of everything I'm doing, I should be doing something else at the same time.

Victoria is not alone in this; Gilbert's (2008) autoethnographic analysis revealed a similar finding: "Since my daughter's birth ... I have felt intensely guilty most of the time, no matter what I'm doing and with whom" (p. 204). And several other mothers who spoke with me referenced in some fashion a frequent feeling that they should be doing something other than, or in addition to, whatever they were doing—a nagging sense that even their best time and energy expenditures were not good enough.

The second concern about FM discourse is that messages ostensibly targeted to "families" and "parents" are actually messages that mothers are most likely to be responding to and accounting for, given that research continues to show that women still do the majority of family foodwork. When I asked the women with whom I spoke to identify the percentage of responsibility they held in their home for 11 different tasks related to meal provision (three knowledge and planning tasks, three meal delivery tasks, and five communication tasks),[2] they reported doing 70% of the meal provision labor. Their heaviest burden was in knowledge and planning tasks, where they carried an average of 78% to 86%. This "thought work" (DeVault, 1991, p. 56)—the ways it is shaped, facilitated, and constrained by discourses outside the family, and the ways in which the work is gendered, and in most families unevenly distributed—is rendered invisible. Hence, consideration of how FM discourses might be reemployed to build support for mothers rather than simply assign more responsibility to them remains unexamined. Research has shown that while *parents* were reported to experience feelings of guilt and low efficacy regarding their ability to meet their own ideals about the family eating well, especially when work constraints resulted in what they considered to be less than optimal food choices (Devine, Connors, Sobal, & Bisogni, 2003), *mothers* were found to be more concerned about the nutritional value of what they fed their children than fathers were (Devine et al., 2006, pp. 2596–2597; Owen, Metcalfe, Dryden, & Shipton,

2010). Because the gendering of feeding labor is out of view, FM messages directed at "parents" are not crafted in ways that enlist the participation of fathers or others, or that address the barriers that may uniquely confront mothers.

My conversations with mothers suggested that, regardless of whether their families' feeding practices leaned toward resisting or reproducing meal patterns from their own or their partners' youth experiences, the mothers themselves initiated or struggled with that leaning. Krista, mother of two, ages two and five, explains her effort to resist her own childhood patterns:

> My parents fall into that very traditional gender role, so my mom did the cooking, and in fact my mom makes my father's plates. He goes and sits down, he eats, she comes and cleans up, and everything was put on her.... [In my family now] we're always around the table. My husband makes his own plate, because he has legs and arms [laughs]. But I'm not going there. So he makes his own plates. My five-year-old and my husband are expected to clean up ... I am not. My father, now that I have left the house, he will not cook. He will starve if my mom is not there. He waits on her to get there to make his food and then complains that he's hungry. And mom is like, "There's a kitchen, with a refrigerator. You didn't make—?" She makes his lunches. I don't—I don't go there [with my partner].

Alunda, mother of a four-year-old, worked to have dinners that reproduced family patterns, but her efforts were impeded by the overscheduling of contemporary life:

> I have what I consider a very, like, stereotypical childhood, like, as far as meals and stuff go. My mom, we had breakfast together every morning before school. She would get up, fix it; it was typically hot. Um, she would pack my lunch, take my lunch to school. We would have dinner together every night. She would cook that. It was very stereotypical, Southern, stay-at-home mom situation .... I think for what we actually do [in my own family now], it's very schedule driven. What I would ideally like to be doing, it's my [childhood] family's experience that I would like to be able to replicate more.

Identifying as a latchkey kid who experienced family dinners only intermittently, Eva stood firm on her commitment to shared FMs six nights per week because she wanted her children to have a different experience growing up. Despite the difficulty of orchestrating multiple schedules, behaviors, and tastes, Eva assumed the work of meal provision, though she did speak with some envy about how her husband seemed to coast though dinnertimes without the worry and attention she gave them.

To the extent that well over half of U.S. families share meals regularly, this is due in large part to the efforts of mothers. More specifically, as McIntosh and colleagues (2010) argued, FMs, any priority that family members assign them, and any benefits that derive from them tend to be direct results of mothers' efforts in meal *planning*. The mothers who participated in my study held an average of 81% of the planning responsibility in their homes. Sometimes, partner attempts to take on some of the responsibility failed to save the mothers from labor, as was the case with Krista:

> The only time my husband does the shopping is if I'm sick; something's going on and he has to do the shopping. When I had my second child, he tried to make a habit of going and doing the shopping for like, oh, two weeks, maybe that lasted? Again, his whole thing was, "It's stressful." Because I would have on [the list I gave him], "four cans of Italian diced tomatoes," and I'll get a telephone call: "Krista, there's a half of a freaking aisle of tomato cans. Where is these Italian diced tomatoes?!" So what would take me thirty minutes takes him an hour and a half.

Claudia, mother of a 14-year-old and a three-year-old, carries the planning burden in her family and indicated the heavy weight of it due to its impact on the family when the planning works and on her when it does not:

> So we sit around the table, and it's pleasant conversation and, um, it's—it's a pretty good mealtime. But the real challenge is, I have to make that meal plan. If I don't make it on the weekend and do the shopping, then the whole week is off, because then I'll have to grocery shop on the way home, and then I'll get home later, and then it just doesn't work. So, it's a lot of work for me, I think. And it's challenging.

Planning for meals is a major component of family foodwork that is eclipsed by FM discourse. But planning takes time and energy, both of which can prove elusive for contemporary mothers. DeVault (1991) argued that planning is like putting together a puzzle "in relatively novel ways each day" more than it is "a simple matter of decision-making as conventionally understood" (p. 48). In the meal provider's process of completing the puzzle on a given day, she is "creating one part of the reality of household life" (p. 48).

Despite the work of critical FM scholars who point out that feeding the family begins outside the home—in institutional structures and corporate interests, for example (Fiese & Schwartz, 2008)—and who question "why the frontline in reforming the food system has to be inside someone's kitchen" (Bowen et al., 2014, p. 25), many mothers internalize food risk culpability messages. Paula, mother of two sons, 16 and 20 years old, reflected on the personal burden she felt in feeding her children, highlighting maternal investment in feeding discourse and the understanding that children are at risk if not fed in very particular ways, no matter the impact on eating for adults:

> My youngest son, he has issues with textures. So a lot of times foods, he wouldn't eat because of the way they felt in his mouth [sounds of agreement from other participants]. There was no creativity; we couldn't be creative with the food, and it was more my expectation and the ideal of "this is not what a mother allows." If I were a really good mother, I could get him to eat this other stuff. [You get pressure] from the mother-in-law and from the television and from the, you know, school, and from all these outside sources who are saying, "Well, they need to have this, and they need to have that." Well, I'm not sure how you get it in them, unless you force it down them, right?

The third critical concern regarding reductionist FM discourse is that these meals implicate family relationships and communications that are complex and multilayered, but innumerable accounts of how mealtimes work—well beyond those stemming from the discourse on FMs—fail to acknowledge this relational complexity.

Across disciplines and decades, food and feeding have been appreciated, even lauded, for their role in cultural transmission, identity building, values instruction, language acquisition, and tradition maintenance. Comparatively, the literature rarely notes that FM practices can be, and often are, ideological in terms of normative expectations, including those relating to gendered labor, heteronormativity, class distinction, and motherhood standards, reifying power differences such that "some people serve and obey while others make choices and arbitrary decisions" (Wilk, 2010, p. 429). Further, few scholars have focused on the wider range of human experience with feeding work, including troublesome dynamics and what some might consider a darker side of communication and relating. Indeed, mealtime interpersonal relations disperse across a spectrum of emotional and psychological states, including frustration, unhappiness, hostility, dislike, anger, resentment, boredom, guilt, frustration, defeat, and "everyday unpleasantness" (Lupton, 1996, p. 55; Wilk, 2010, pp. 433–434).

None of my focus-group participants spoke positively about FM provision. Samantha largely found the matter of FMs to be repetitious and uninteresting: "I mean, my thing is just, I get so bored with all of it. It's—it's such a task to me. It's so boring. It's such a boring task.... So the grocery shopping, hence, is boring. The planning, hence, is boring." Samantha said that in fact she "hates" planning, that "it irritates [her] to death." But planning was only part of what she found so frustrating about FMs:

> I hate the idea too of coming home and having to spend, right when you come home, you spend an hour [on dinner]. When I'm working all day and I'm away from my child—when we get home, I mean, we have about a three- or four-hour window to spend together before she goes to bed. I don't want to spend my time doing that.

Other women discussed "hate" regarding aspects of FMs as well: Gail hated mediating arguments; Tammy hated cooking in her "tiny kitchen"; Ruth hated "being the food police." Louisa and Lydia talked about the burden of preparing food they knew the children would hate. For about half of the mothers, matters could take on other aggressive tones, requiring focused attention to the "struggle," the "battle," the "fight" to get children to eat well or at all, the "butting heads" and "fighting" among family members, and the issues of "power" and "control."

Some mothers contended with their partners' psychological or behavioral idiosyncrasies. Ruth talked about a "passive-aggressive tension" between her and her husband at times over dinner, which he expected would routinely be ready between 5:00 and 6:00 p.m., though he provided none of the labor. She said that during times of mealtime conflict, which didn't seem to be particularly rare, he refused to look at her even when speaking. Gail, mother of four children, ages 3, 12, 15, and 16, described dinnertime at her house differently depending on which familial structure she was referencing. In her first marriage, dinnertimes were pleasant and collaborative. However, in her second marriage, FMs shifted due to her husband's eating patterns and psychological struggles:

> I married an individual that only eats meat, never eats a vegetable, and was, just kind of a … uh, he's bipolar and very moody, and I didn't really want the kids around the moodiness. And I personally couldn't deal with it either, so I would try to be away too. So we would all kind of go in our different directions [at dinner] during that time.

Later, Gail divorced her second husband; "the last straw," she said, "was over food." Jasmine, mother of a three-year-old, experienced FMs as less than positive, given that they required additional labor from her if they were to unfold in ways that did not unnerve her:

> I plan it. I set the table. I dish it up. You [laughs]—I bet all of you all are going to smack me when I tell you this: I cut my husband's meat. And my daughter's … Because he's like this person who absolutely hates bones, so I have to like debone everything. And then, I'm talking, if there is like just the tiniest little speck of fat, I mean he's pulling his food apart with his fingers, you know. [I] didn't get those little pieces of fat that he wouldn't even taste if he had just taken a whole chunk and put it in his mouth, you know.... It makes me crazy. It makes me feel like my food's not good if he's picking it apart like that.

While Ruth, Jasmine, and Gail's experiences were more extreme than the ones shared by other participants, the "burden of pleasing others," to borrow a phrase from Bowen et al.'s (2014) research, was a recurrent theme among my focus-group participants and a source of much frustration and concern. Bowen and colleagues noted that they saw few instances across the 12 working-class and poor families they observed during their dinnertimes "in which at least one family member didn't complain about the food they were served" (p. 24).

The narratives of the mothers I spoke with supported DeVault's (1991) argument that the effort to be responsive to family member preferences is not a self-determined "personal favor" but rather "a requirement of the work" (p. 40). In her attempts to meet this requirement, Louisa, like Claudia, felt pulled between her child eating well and him eating at all:

> I think that is my biggest struggle, having to do two meals, like, for our son, and trying to get him to eat things that are different. I don't want to default and cook him something he wants, so I constantly go back and forth between making sure he is eating something and trying to make him eat good things.

The power that Jasmine's and Gail's male partners held to direct energy around the table and negatively impact the meal-sharing experiences of family members is clear, as is the power that young children, like Claudia's son, can similarly wield over the meal.

In some families, power was more equitably negotiated but nevertheless proved relationally taxing. Hazel and her partner's food intake management styles tended to come into conflict over their daughter:

> [My husband's] mother and he and I all have weight issues, and so our mealtime is sort of stressful for me, and I think maybe for our daughter also, who doesn't have a weight problem. Because he really monitors what our daughter eats. And most of it is—she wants a cookie or she wants dessert, but he is saying, "No, you need to eat two more bites of your hot dog, and then you can have a French fry...." It's this closely monitoring and watching. And that's really— that's not my approach... it makes me uncomfortable.... I've pointed out to him before, you know, "You're sort of repeating the same pattern that your mother did with you." ... That's his way of trying to get her to eat a balanced meal and not just eat junk food. And part of my way of doing that would be not to bring so much junk food into the house.

Family food provision, as several scholars have noted, is "fraught" (Anving & Sellerberg, 2010, p. 205; Bowen et al., 2013, p. 21; Paugh & Izquierdo, 2009, p. 189). When FM discourse depicts foodwork devoid of its relational layers, but families are still expected to deliver more frequent FMs, most families can't measure up. They can be interpreted (by themselves or others) as lacking, deviant, or uncaring with regard to feeding-risk management. This interpretation is further facilitated by FM discourse's images of feeding risk juxtaposed with meal labor simplicity. It is a challenge to understand why so much effort and funding has been funneled into the frequent FM campaigns for more than a decade when it has not spoken to meal providers in ways that have resulted in more frequent FMs.

Conclusion

Family meal discourse is a formidable force in mothering rhetorics that functions as a regulatory and reproducing mechanism, emanating from innumerable points and directed at FM providers who are, in most cases, mothers. Such women are compelled to participate in their own monitoring and regulation, although it is unlikely that they experience their meal provision in this way. FM discourse is aimed in part at resuscitating a supposedly moribund social and familial activity that, if revived successfully and in particular ways, holds the promise of freeing adolescents from most of the struggles they variously face. But FMs are neither dead nor dying, and the grandiose claims about their curative effects obscure the ways in which social policy has failed to adequately address the social world in which adolescent children struggle.

Exploring how FM discourse works rhetorically illuminates the ways in which the correlational evidence is distorted as causal, the FM is crafted as a moral responsibility that is directed and monitored by corporate brands and food retailers/manufacturers as much as it is by public health sources, and mothers are simultaneously targeted and silenced while their labor is eclipsed. Frequent FM discourse is a hegemonic rhetorical strategy that reproduces mothers as primarily responsible for producing healthy, happy, fit, and optimally functioning children and blames them if children are perceived as falling short, even as it diverts attention away from state accountability in such outcomes. The widely disseminated and stalwart claims about the efficacy of FMs in mitigating risk to children are employed by public, academic, policy, corporate, and health discourses. And families are prompted to pursue a route to their children's health that actually is directed by myriad social forces and therefore is beyond the simple control of "families," or mothers, as meal providers.

Examining maternal perspectives on the FM can redirect focus from familial/maternal blame and toward a collaborative language of *facilitation* of FMs that speaks and responds to the actual lives that families are living and to some of the real struggles that mothers and other meal providers confront. If FMs have any potential to produce the numerous, significant, and critical adolescent health and well-being outcomes that so many seem readily convinced by simplistic taglines that they do, despite evidence to the contrary (Musick & Meier, 2012), then FM discourse needs to be differently informed. To repeatedly direct education and awareness campaigns almost exclusively at "parents," while neither collecting mothering data nor interrogating the macrosystems situating family feeding work, is irresponsible and ineffectual. The result is likely to be not only regression in gender equity but also a failure to help families help their children.

Acknowledgments

The author recognizes the fine work of her student assistants, Allison Smith and Aimee Trawick, in preparing her to write this manuscript. The author also thanks Lynn O'Brien Hallstein for her careful review of several drafts of this manuscript, and the manuscript reviewers for their crucial insights and direction, each of whose contributions have significantly shaped the final essay.

Funding

The Motherhood and Family Meals project was funded by East Tennessee State University's Research Development Committee.

Notes

1. These demographics may have implications for the findings largely in terms of social class representation because the university is a midsized, public, relatively inexpensive university situated in a rural South Appalachian region with many first-generation college students.
2. Knowledge and planning tasks included planning family meals and menus; knowing the food preferences or diet restrictions of family members; and shopping for groceries and recipe ingredients. Meal delivery tasks included cooking or preparing meals for family members; serving meals for family members; and cleaning up after meals. Communication tasks included encouraging or

managing conversation at the table or during meals; mediating conflicts at the table or during meals; managing family member eating behaviors during meals; delegating tasks to other family members for meal preparation, serving, and/or cleanup; and supervising tasks of other family members for meal preparation, serving, and/or cleanup.

References

Anderson, J. (2011, October 29). Can breakfast replace family dinner? [Web log post]. Retrieved from http://parenting.blogs.nytimes.com/2011/10/29/can-breakfast-replace-family-dinner/?_r=0

Ansel, K. (2014, January 21). Family meals: Small investment, big payoff. Retrieved from http://www.eatright.org/resource/food/nutrition/eating-as-a-family/family-meals-small-investment-big-payoff

Anving, T., & Sellerberg, A. (2010). Family meals and parents' challenges. *Food, Culture, and Society: An International Journal of Multidisciplinary Research, 13*(2), 201–214. doi:10.2752/175174410X12633934463114

Arnold, L. B. (2008). Empowered self. In A. E. Kinser (Ed.), *Mothering in the third wave* (pp. 136–139). Toronto, ON, Canada: Demeter Press.

Bowen, S., Elliott, S., & Brenton, J. (2014). The joy of cooking? *Contexts, 13*(3), 20–25. doi:10.1177/1536504214545755

Burrows, L. (2009). Pedagogizing families through obesity discourse. In J. Wright & V. Harwood (Eds.), *Biopolitics and the "obesity epidemic"* (pp. 127–140). New York, NY: Taylor & Francis.

Cairns, K., Johnston, J., & MacKendrick, N. (2013). Feeding the "organic child": Mothering through ethical consumption. *Journal of Consumer Culture, 13*, 97–118. doi:10.1177/1469540513480162

Charmaz, K. (2006). *Constructing grounded theory: A practical guide through qualitative analysis.* London, United Kingdom: Sage.

Child Trends DataBank. (2013, May). *Family meals: Indicators on children and youth.* Retrieved from http://www.childtrends.org/wp-content/uploads/2012/09/96_Family_Meals.pdf

Columbia University National Center on Addiction and Substance Abuse. (2003, September). *The importance of family dinners.* Retrieved from http://www.casacolumbia.org/templates/publications_reports.aspx?keywords=dinners

Columbia University National Center on Addiction and Substance Abuse. (2005, September). *The importance of family dinners II.* Retrieved from http://www.casacolumbia.org/templates/publications_reports.aspx?keywords=dinners

Columbia University National Center on Addiction and Substance Abuse. (2006, September). *The importance of family dinners III.* Retrieved from http://www.casacolumbia.org/templates/publications_reports.aspx?keywords=dinners

Columbia University National Center on Addiction and Substance Abuse. (2007, September). *The importance of family dinners IV.* Retrieved from http://www.casacolumbia.org/templates/publications_reports.aspx?keywords=dinners

Columbia University National Center on Addiction and Substance Abuse. (2009, September). *The importance of family dinners V.* Retrieved from http://www.casacolumbia.org/templates/publications_reports.aspx?keywords=dinners

Columbia University National Center on Addiction and Substance Abuse. (2010, September). *The importance of family dinners VI.* Retrieved from http://www.casacolumbia.org/templates/publications_reports.aspx?keywords=dinners

Columbia University National Center on Addiction and Substance Abuse. (2011, September). *The importance of family dinners VII.* Retrieved from http://www.casacolumbia.org/templates/publications_reports.aspx?keywords=dinners

Columbia University National Center on Addiction and Substance Abuse. (2012, September). *The importance of family dinners VIII.* Retrieved from http://www.casacolumbia.org/templates/publications_reports.aspx?keywords=dinners

Coontz, S. (1992). *The way we never were: American families and the nostalgia trap.* New York, NY: Basic.

Cossman, B. (2002). Family feuds: Neo-liberal and neo-conservative visions of the reprivatization project. In B. Cossman (Ed.), *Privatization, law, and the challenge to feminism* (pp. 169–217). Toronto, ON, Canada: University of Toronto Press.

Coveney, J. (2002). What does research on families and food tell us? Implications for nutrition and dietetic practice. *Australian Journal of Nutrition and Dietetics, 59*(2), 113–119.

Data Resource Center for Child and Adolescent Health. (2011–2012). National survey of children's health. Retrieved from http://www.childhealthdata.org/browse/survey/results?q=2290&r=1&g=448

DeVault, M. L. (1991). *Feeding the family: The social organization of caring as gendered work.* Chicago, IL: University of Chicago Press.

Devine, C., Connors, M., Sobal, J., & Bisogni, C. (2003). Sandwiching it in: Spillover of work onto food choices and family roles in low- and moderate-income urban households. *Social Science and Medicine, 56*(3), 617–630. doi:10.1016/S0277-9536(02)00058-8

Devine, C., Jastran, M., Jabs, J., Wethington, E., Farrell, T., & Bisogni, C. (2006). "A lot of sacrifices": Work–family spillover and the food-choice coping strategies of low-wage employed parents. *Social Science and Medicine, 63*(10), 2591–2603. doi:10.1016/j.socscimed.2006.06.029

Eisenberg, M. E., Olson, R. E., Neumark-Sztainer, D., Story, M., & Bearinger, L. H. (2004). Correlations between family meals and psychosocial well-being among adolescents. *Archives of Pediatrics and Adolescent Medicine, 158,* 792–796. doi:10.1001/archpedi.158.8.792

Elgar, F. J., Napoletano, A., Saul, G., Dirks, M. A., Craig, W., Poteat, V. P., & Koenig, B. W. (2014). Cyberbullying victimization and mental health in adolescents and the moderating role of family dinners. *Journal of the American Medical Association Pediatrics, 168*(11), 1015–1022. doi:10.1001/jamapediatrics.2014.1223

Fiese, B. H., & Schwartz, M. (2008). *Reclaiming the family table: Mealtimes and child health and wellbeing* (Social Policy Report, Vol. 22, No. 4). Ann Arbor, MI: Society for Research in Child Development.

Fishel, A. (2015, January 12). The most important thing you can do with your kids? Eat dinner with them. *Washington Post.* Retrieved from http://www.washingtonpost.com

Food Marketing Institute. (2016). Let's help family meals happen at home! Retrieved from http://www.fmifamilymeals.com/

Frye, J. J., & Bruner, M. S. (Eds.). (2012). *The rhetoric of food: Discourse, materiality, and power.* New York, NY: Routledge.

Fudge, J., & Cossman, B. (2002). Introduction: Privatization, law, and the challenge to feminism. In B. Cossman (Ed.), *Privatization, law, and the challenge to feminism* (pp. 3–38). Toronto, ON, Canada: University of Toronto Press.

Fulkerson, J. A., Story, M., Mellin, A., Leffert, N., Neumark-Sztainer, D., & French, S. A. (2006). Family dinner meal frequency and adolescent development: Relationships with developmental assets and high-risk behaviors. *Journal of Adolescent Health, 39,* 337–345. doi:10.1016/j.jadohealth.2005.12.026

Gibbs, N. (2006, June 4). The magic of the family meal. *Time.* Retrieved from http://content.time.com/time/magazine/article/0,9171,1200760,00.html

Gilbert, J. (2008). Why I feel guilty all the time: Performing academic motherhood. *Women's Studies in Communication, 31*(2), 203–208. doi:10.1080/07491409.2008.10162533

Giles, M. V. (2012). From "need" to "risk": The neoliberal construction of the "bad" mother. *Journal of the Motherhood Initiative, 3*(1), 112–133.

Gurian, A. (2013, September 16). Family meals matter—Staying connected. Retrieved from http://mikemoses.typepad.com/purple_pastor/2013/09/the-lost-art-of-the-family-meal.html

Hamilton, S. K., & Hamilton Wilson, J. (2009). Family mealtimes: Worth the effort? *Infant, Child, and Adolescent Nutrition, 1*(6), 346–350. doi:10.1177/1941406409353188

Hammons, A. J., & Fiese, B. H. (2011). Is frequency of shared family meals related to the nutritional health of children and adolescents? *Pediatrics, 126*(6), e1–e10. doi:101542/peds.2010-1440

Harvey, D. (2007). *A brief history of neoliberalism.* New York, NY: Oxford University Press.

Hyman, M. (2011, January 9). How eating at home can save your life. *Huffington Post.* Retrieved from http://www.huffingtonpost.com/dr-mark-hyman/family-dinner-how_b_806114.html

Kamberelis, G., & Dimitriadis, G. (2011). Focus groups: Contingent articulations of pedagogy, politics, and inquiry. In N. K. Denzin & Y. S. Lincoln (Eds.). *The Sage handbook of qualitative research* (4th ed., pp. 545–561). Los Angeles, CA: Sage.

Kerr, J. (2010). Bright, strong, healthy, happy children start at your dining table (FitFuture: Strategies for Better Living Series, No. 0403). Retrieved from http://kern.org/mo/wp-content/uploads/sites/40/2013/08/Vol4_Issue3_Happy_Children.pdf

Kinser, A. E., & Denker, K. J. (2016). Feeding without apology: Maternal navigations of distal discourses in family meal labor. In F. Pasche Guignard and T. M. Cassidy (Eds.), *Mothers and food: Negotiating foodways from maternal perspectives* (pp. 1–27). Bradford, ON, Canada: Demeter Press.

Larson, R. W., Branscomb, K. R., & Wiley, A. R. (2006). Forms and functions of family mealtimes: Multidisciplinary perspectives. *New Directions for Child and Adolescent Development, 2006*(111), 1–15. doi:10.1002/cd.152

Levenstein, H. (2012). *Fear of food: A history of why we worry about what we eat.* Chicago, IL: University of Chicago Press.

Lupton, D. (1996). *Food, the body, and the self.* London, United Kingdom: Sage.

MacKendrick, N. (2014). More work for mother: Chemical body burdens as maternal responsibility. *Gender and Society, 28*(5), 705–728. doi:10.1177/0891243214529842

McIntosh, W. A., Kubena, K. S., Tolle, G., Dean, W. R., Jan, J., & Anding, J. (2010). Mothers and meals: The effects of mothers' meal planning and shopping motivations on children's participation in family meals. *Appetite, 55*, 623–628. doi:10.1016/j.appet.2010.09.016

McKerrow, R. M. (2012). Foreword. In J. J. Frye & M. S. Bruner (Eds.), *The rhetoric of food: Discourse, materiality, and power* (pp. xi–xiv). New York, NY: Routledge.

Meyers, M. (2013). An untold story: Mothers' and daughters' connections through food. In A. H. Deakins, R. B. Lockridge, and H. M. Sterk (Eds.), *Mothers and daughters: Complicated connections across cultures* (pp. 211–229). Lanham, MD: University Press of America.

Mudry, J. J. (2009). *Measured meals: Nutrition in America.* Albany: State University of New York Press.

Musick, K., & Meier, A. (2012). Assessing causality and persistence in associations between family dinners and adolescent well-being. *Journal of Marriage and Family, 74*(3), 476–493. doi:10.1111/j.1741-3737.2012.00973.x

National Cattlemen's Beef Association. (2015). Family-focused and school nutrition. Retrieved from http://www.beefnutrition.org/CMDocs/BeefNutrition/Nutrition%20Seminar%20Program/2015%20Topics/FAMILY-FOCUSED%20AND%20SCHOOL%20NUTRITION.pdf

Neumark-Sztainer, D., Larson, N., Fulkerson, J. A., Eisenberg, M. E., & Story, M. (2010). Family meals and adolescents: What have we learned from Project EAT (Eating Among Teens). *Public Health Nutrition, 13*(7), 1113–1121. doi:10.1017/S1368980010000169

Owen, J., Metcalfe, A., Dryden, C., & Shipton, G. (2010). "If they don't eat it, it's not a proper meal": Images of risk and choice in fathers' accounts of family food practices. *Health, Risk, and Society, 12*(4), 395–406. doi:10.1080/13698571003793213

Parrott, L., & Parrott, L. (2011). *The hour that matters most: The surprising power of the family meal.* Carol Stream, IL: Tyndale House.

Paugh, A., & Izquierdo, C. (2009). Why is this a battle every night? Negotiating food and eating in American dinnertime interaction. *Journal of Linguistic Anthropology, 19*(2), 185–204. doi:10.1111/j.1548-1395.2009.01030.x

Rockett, H. R. (2007). Family dinner: More than just a meal. *Journal of the American Dietetic Association, 107*(9), 1498–1501. doi:10.1016/j.jada.2007.07.004

Seiler, A. (2012). Let's move: The ideological constraints of liberalism on Michelle Obama's obesity rhetoric. In J. J. Frye and M. S. Bruner (Eds.), *The rhetoric of food: Discourse, materiality, and power* (pp. 155–170). New York, NY: Routledge.

Sen, B. (2010). The relationship between frequency of family dinner and adolescent problem behaviors after adjusting for other family characteristics. *Journal of Adolescence, 33*, 187–196. doi:10.1016/j.adolescence.2009.03.011

Story, M., & Neumark-Sztainer, D. (2005). A perspective on family meals: Do they matter? *Nutrition Today, 40*(6), 261–266.

Stouffer's. (n.d.). *What dinner at home means for your family: The surprising power of dinner.* Wilkes-Barre, PA: Nestlé USA

Strauss, A., & Corbin, J. (1998). *Basics of qualitative research: Techniques and procedures for developing grounded theory* (2nd ed.). Thousand Oaks, CA: Sage.

University of Minnesota Epidemiology and Community Health Research. (2016). Project EAT publications: How important are family meals for adolescents and young adults? Retrieved from http://www.sphresearch.umn.edu/epi/project-eat/project-eat-publications/

University of Minnesota School of Public Health. (2016). Project EAT. Retrieved from http://www.sphresearch.umn.edu/epi/project-eat/

Weinstein, M. (2006). *The surprising power of family meals: How eating together makes us smarter, stronger, healthier, and happier.* Hanover, NH: Steerforth.

Wilk, R. (2010). Power at the table: Foods fights and happy meals. *Cultural Studies <=>Critical Methodologies, 10*(6), 428–436. doi:10.1177/1532708610372764

#SpoiledMilk: Blacktavists, Visibility, and the Exploitation of the Black Breast

Megan Elizabeth Morrissey and Karen Y. Kimball

ABSTRACT

On September 22, 2014, Medolac Laboratories, a company in Oregon that processes human milk, announced an initiative to purchase pumped breast milk from African-American mothers in Detroit, Michigan. Angry about Medolac's predatory initiative to target this population, a community of Black female breastfeeding activists, or Blacktavists, swiftly took to blogs, Twitter, and Facebook to express their concerns. We argue that Blacktavists—working on, against, and through the Black breastfeeding body—constructed a persuasive narrative about Medolac's campaign that made visible (a) the historical legacy of Black labor for White interests, (b) the economic value of that labor, and (c) whiteness as a racial category. Overall, our study explores the valuable, problematic, and complex characteristics of Blacktavists' advocacy. Future successful advocacy must continue to challenge normative mothering rhetorics to bring about impactful social change.

On September 22, 2014, Medolac Laboratories, a company in Oregon that processes human milk into a shelf-stable product, announced an initiative to purchase pumped breast milk from Black mothers in Detroit, Michigan. Working with the Mother's Milk Cooperative (a milk bank) and partnering with the Clinton Global Initiative (CGI), Medolac planned to recruit 2,000 "urban milk donors" for the cooperative (Medolac, 2014). To rationalize this action, Medolac explained how their efforts to recruit low-income Black women in Detroit would ultimately benefit a population that, according to the Centers for Disease Control and Prevention (CDC, 2013), has the lowest breastfeeding initiation rates of any racial or ethnic group in the United States. The aims were articulated in a press release announcing the program:

> The company seeks to increase breastfeeding rates among urban African American Women by forming a local partnership campaign to support the growth of the Mothers Milk Cooperative's donor base, promoting healthy behavior and prolonged breastfeeding within their communities. (Medolac, 2014, para. 1)

As Medolac is a for-profit company, the plan to purchase these new donors' pumped milk for $1.00 and sell it to hospitals drew criticism from lactation activists. As one prominent blogger, Kimberly Seals Allers (2014), charged, the company "processes the milk into a commercially sterile, shelf-stable product and sells it to hospitals for about $7 an ounce—a 600 percent markup" (para. 2). Noting the demographic makeup of the Detroit area and Medolac's exploitation of this community, Allers (2014) further explained, "It's one thing to commodify mother's milk, but to try to commodify a group of women—specifically black women, who already have a difficult history with breast-feeding—seems, a bit, well, sour" (para. 4).

Angry about Medolac's predatory initiative to target and exploit low-income Black women in Detroit, a community of Black female breastfeeding activists, or Blacktavists,[1] swiftly took to blogs, Twitter, and Facebook to express their concerns. Collaborating to stop Medolac's campaign, Blacktavists produced and shared image macros, blog posts, open letters, Facebook status updates, and Twitter hashtags to voice their complaints. The swell of concern resulted in Blacktavist Kiddada Green penning an open letter to Medolac, wherein she described the company's initiative and listed the questions she and other Blacktavists had about the campaign. The letter was posted to the Black Mothers' Breastfeeding Association's (BMBFA) website—a Detroit-based nonprofit of which Green is founder and executive director—and allowed individuals to sign in solidarity with Blacktavists who sought answers from Medolac. In 10 days, the letter gathered more than 600 signatures (Green, 2015a) and was successful in that it prompted Medolac to retire its campaign on January 21, 2015.

Blacktavists working *on, against,* and *through* the Black breastfeeding body constructed a persuasive narrative about Medolac's campaign that made visible (a) the historical legacy of Black labor for White interests, (b) the economic value of that labor, and (c) whiteness as a racial category—all in ways illustrating the beneficial, problematic, and complex characteristics of Blacktavists' advocacy. Through this analysis, we discuss what these strategies suggest about the rhetorics of reproduction (specifically about discourses that reproduce ideological understandings of Black motherhood), ultimately noting that Blacktavists' use of visibility strategies may have halted Medolac's campaign but failed to shift normative national discourses about Black motherhood.

Focusing particular attention on Blacktavists' "Stop Medolac" campaign, we use refracting lenses of race, class, and sexuality to reveal how contemporary notions of Black motherhood are (re)constructed in discourse.[2] To scaffold this analysis, we begin by contextualizing Black motherhood, discussing how U.S. racial histories contribute to contemporary understandings of Black mothering as a form of labor. Exploring this with particular attention to intersectionality, we explain how discourses of Black motherhood (generally) and the act of breastfeeding (specifically) marginalize Black women's infant-feeding decisions and discuss the implications of this for Blacktavists' rhetoric. Finally, we address the ways that these activists use visibility as a strategy to (re)shape Black mothering rhetorics and how these efforts manage the intersectional positionality of Black breastfeeding women.

Theorizing the visibility of Black motherhood

Medolac sought to profit from Black women's labor, redirecting Black mothers' breast milk *away from* Black infants and *toward* some wealthy White mothers who could afford to purchase it as a commodity. These efforts, while benefiting White mothers and White corporate interests such as Medolac's, marginalize Black mothers along multiple axes of identity (including race, gender, sexuality, and social class) and contribute to contemporary mothering rhetorics that reinforce hierarchical distinctions among and between mothers. Public discourses about Black women breastfeeding draw upon complex histories of race/racism, sexism, and U.S. governmentality[3] and work as cultural forces that elicit advice, support, insult, and disdain. The practice of breastfeeding and its public negotiation, even when supportive, is about surveilling and disciplining women's bodies (Bartlett, 2003) and contributes to the ways that Black motherhood has historically come to be seen as suspect. Blum (1993), recognizing breastfeeding as concurrently cultural, natural, biological, and socially constructed, points to the highly scrutinized position of the lactating breast within U.S. culture. This position is further complicated by discourses of race, class, gender, and sexuality, as well as the visibility politics that manage the public conversation about these intersections. As this section theorizes, the cultural narratives about Black motherhood that have circulated throughout the U.S. cultural imaginary have constructed Black women as bad mothers who, among other failings, do not breastfeed their children as they are supposed to. Tracing the historical relationship between Black women and White women, we discuss how Blacktavists' efforts to increase breastfeeding initiation rates negotiate the historical legacy of Black women laboring outside of the home—often for White women and/or White interests—and the attendant impact of this for Black women's families and for the positioning of Black mothers within the U.S. social hierarchy.

In the past 25 years, public health efforts to raise breastfeeding initiation rates have become more familiar in the United States, with recent statistics indicating that 79% of women now initiate breastfeeding (CDC, 2014). Despite this "high" number, the CDC (2013) also reported that "Black infants still had the lowest prevalence of breastfeeding initiation and duration" (para. 1); despite increasing in the first decade of the 21st century, these numbers remain lower than those of White or Hispanic infants. Attempting to mitigate low initiation rates in the Black community, Blacktavists have established a significant presence online, using blogs, Facebook, and Twitter to make (and keep) Black breastfeeding visible within the public sphere. Adopting a critical rhetorical orientation, we are interested in the constitutive nature of these texts, the ways that Blacktavists' discourses reproduce and challenge the ideological understandings and material conditions of Black motherhood, and the visibility politics that organize these discourses. Medolac's proposal benefits from—and indeed depends upon—increased breastfeeding rates in the Black community. The impact, however, is that White mothers and White-run corporations like Medolac[4] capitalize on the fruits of this lactation labor, reinforcing the historical legacy of exploiting Black labor for White interests.

Occupying a devalued social position (Roberts, 1997) and framed as undeserving of the status of "mother as caregiver" (Triece, 2012, p. 3), Black women have regularly been cast as inadequate mothers (Carpenter, 2012). This deficit is constructed through prevalent cultural narratives that frame Black women as jezebels, matriarchs, welfare queens, and crack mothers, (see, e.g., Carpenter, 2012; Roberts, 1997) and constitute a mythology of Black identity and experience that serves as a backdrop for contemporary U.S. race relations. Specifically, Black women's relationship to labor and their long history in the workforce as slaves, wet nurses, domestics, and agricultural laborers have marked them as employable (Bell, 1965; Mink, 1995; Triece, 2012). This history contextualizes Medolac's efforts to recruit poor Black mothers in Detroit into an economy that is designed to service the breastfeeding needs of privileged White mothers[5] and that benefits such corporations as Medolac, who reap the profits from these arrangements.

Against a racist and exploitative historical backdrop, Black mothers are in an impossible position to reconcile. Cultural narratives suggesting they are overdependent on public assistance call on them to labor to demonstrate their self-sufficiency (and subsequent worth/value); however, when they do enter the workforce, they are framed as inadequate mothers. Ironically, Black mothers have often needed to labor outside the home to manage the systemic and institutional racism that has made it exponentially more difficult for Black women and Black families to attain financial solvency. Thus, when Black mothers go to work to support their families, they face critiques that they are too independent and that their absence from the domestic realm of the home is hurting Black families. Triece (2012), paraphrasing Fraser (1989), explained: "The competing demands of capital and care placed poor Black women in a double bind—if they chose to stay home to care for their children, they were labeled lazy or 'welfare queens;' if they assumed jobs in the labor force they were labeled 'failed mothers'" (p. 2). Indeed, scholarship about mothering suggests that "the Good White Mother in the U.S. social imagination stands as an idealized standard for femininity that constrains all women across various intersections" (Reid-Brinkley, 2011, p. 46). In this way, Black women are positioned within the U.S. cultural imaginary as inadequate and/or bad mothers whose ambition, independence, and sexuality are suspect.

Feminist scholars, conceptualizing the impact of multiplicity in relation to privilege and subordination, have demonstrated the impacts of intersecting cultural discourses.[6] The vulnerability of the women in Detroit that Medolac's campaign sought to exploit cannot be understood without simultaneous attention to the historical contexts and discourses of race, class, gender, and sexuality that denigrate Black women as more employable, sexually irresponsible, and generally bad mothers. For this reason an intersectional approach affords scholars a way to engage the complex, overlapping, and nuanced manner in which power circulates to place Black mothers within the U.S. social hierarchy. Further, using an intersectional lens to examine Blacktavists' discourse reveals how these Black women assert agency within the complex power relations in which they are positioned. Roberts (1997) explained: "For centuries a popular mythology has degraded Black women and portrayed them as less deserving of motherhood. Slave owners forced slave women to perform strenuous labor that contradicted the Victorian female roles prevalent in society" (p. 950). Black motherhood, then, has been articulated as a conflicted category whereby Black women are visible in the public sphere as domestic/slave labor rather than as successful heteronormative mothers. Thus, the history of slavery casts Black women's breasts and their public exposure differently (Blum, 1999).

Blacktavists use visibility to manage the publicity of the Black female body within a heteronormative national landscape that foregrounds whiteness, middle-/upper-class status, and heterosexuality. Rand (2013), explaining some of the complexities of visibility, noted:

> If the radical gesture of visibility politics is the insertion of the vulnerable physical body into public discourse and the relinquishment of the privilege of bodily abstraction, then the effects of visibility politics for those marked by gender, sexuality, race, and class, who are always already hyperembodied and visible, are much less predictable. (p. 123)

Thus, when those who have the benefit of passing as heterosexual, as White, or as middle or upper class decide to "out" themselves, they have some ability to control the impressions they make on others; however, those individuals who are unable to manage concealing or revealing their differences cannot predictably anticipate the ways they will be treated. The concurrent visibility and invisibility of Black women in the public sphere have relied on the normalcy of whiteness and heteronormativity as a standard against which to measure their performance of motherhood (Carpenter, 2012). Thus, Black women courted by Medolac's campaign are at once *hypervisible* in their deviation from whiteness and heteronormativity and *invisible* in the ways multiple axes of oppression have marginalized them from public representation. In this way, Blacktavists must manage visibility to reorient Black women's relationship to motherhood through the practice of breastfeeding. For the non-White female body, visibility is fraught with complications that have profound implications for the publicly breastfeeding body whose practice may at once be a necessity as well as a political action. Indeed, to be subject to interlocking dominant discourses of power and the complementary frameworks of visibility they employ positions Black mothers such that they must embrace (hyper)visibility to assert themselves within the public sphere.

Conducting a rhetorical analysis of online activism

Within a four-month window—between September 22, 2014, when Medolac announced their campaign, and January 21, 2015, when they officially retired their efforts—Blacktavists, lactation consultants, and activists rallied to challenge Medolac's predatory Detroit campaign. Relying on Twitter, Facebook, blogs, and organizational websites to inspire support for their cause, these Blacktavists created texts that are a compelling example of the ways Internet technologies and social media can be used for activism and, as such, are productive sites for rhetorical inquiry. Even though Medolac announced its campaign in September 2014, it was not until December 3, 2014, when Blacktavist Kimberly Seals Allers, a consultant for BMBFA and a blogger, wrote and published a post on *New York Times* parenting blog *Motherlode* that many Blacktavists became invested. Allers's post drew forth a multitude of social media responses from across the nation, including Internet image macros,[7] Twitter comments, Facebook posts, and eventually Kiddada Green's open letter to Medolac, which was widely circulated and shared across the Blacktavist community. Indeed, one of the primary characteristics of this discourse is Blacktavists' synthesis of complex cultural statements and arguments about Black motherhood into highly condensed images, phrases, and hashtags. Employing this strategy, Blacktavists were able to spread their message quickly and widely.

Tracing social media as a text for analysis is challenging and requires attention to not only what is being said and by whom but who is sharing, "liking," and reposting these cultural messages. In particular, for online messages to have resonance they must be portable, accessible, and clear—characteristics that Blacktavists' social media exhibited. Collaborating to repeatedly use certain hashtags (such as #StopMedolac),[8] circulate particular image macros, and link to one another's online content allowed Blacktavists to maintain control over their message and to center the voices of a generally marginalized community of Black women and mothers. Leaving no doubt as to Blacktavists' intention to use social media strategically, BMBFA tweeted to one of the individuals commenting about the campaign to stop Medolac: "@blacktavist plz include the hashtag in your posts: it'll help followers find your tweets #StopMedolac" (BMBFA, 2015a).

Although Blacktavists appear organized and deliberate in their efforts to stop Medolac, their discourses are fragmented, overlapping, and complex. Thus, to assemble a comprehensive set of texts for analysis, we gathered all of the available online material circulating to halt Medolac's campaign that we could find. In total, we collected content from 12 individuals or groups who wrote for the campaign across a variety of forums. This network of activists, in less than five months, generated thoughtful commentary responding to Medolac's initiative, shared one another's posts on their own social media pages, and collaborated to solicit more than 600 signatures petitioning Medolac to stop its campaign in Detroit.[9]

Tracing their contributions, it is clear that four significant moments, punctuated by particular texts, contour the discursive terrain that we analyzed. These four moments include (a) Medolac's (2014) official announcement starting its campaign in Detroit; (b) Allers's (2014) post about Medolac's campaign in *New York Times* parenting blog *Motherlode*; (c) Green's (2015a) open letter to Medolac, soliciting signatures and asking the company to stop the campaign; and (d) Medolac's (2015) official announcement resigning the initiative. These discursive touchstones structure Blacktavists' social media conversation and provide the prompts to which the primary contributors we explore respond. Although there were many other bloggers, Twitter and Facebook users, and online activists to share or link to this content, "like it" on social media, or voice support, we focus our discussion on only those contributors who generated unique content for the Medolac campaign.[10]

Exploring Blacktavists' strategies of visibility

In their efforts to stop Medolac's exploitation of Black mothers in Detroit, Blacktavists used the Black breastfeeding body intersectionally, collaboratively, and resistively, employing specific rhetorical strategies to manage the mainstream visibility of this population. Highlighting the multiple and interlocking subject locations of Black mothers, sharing and commenting on other Blacktavists' online content, and rejecting normative culture's efforts to organize Black motherhood into a rigid social hierarchy that continues to disadvantage minorities, Blacktavists' efforts successfully halted Medolac's campaign. In particular, we have identified three rhetorical strategies of visibility used by Blacktavists that demonstrate how these women momentarily managed the normative civic discourses about Black motherhood. These three visibility strategies include (a) demonstrating the historicity of Black labor for White interests, (b) establishing the economic value of that Black labor, and (c) naming whiteness as a racial category. Using examples from the content created and circulated by Blacktavists, we demonstrate how these women used visibility to manage the marginality of the Black breastfeeding body in public discourse and evaluate their ultimate success in stopping Medolac's campaign.

The historical legacy of Black labor for White interests

In the contemporary United States, many citizens engage in discourses of colorblindness and multiculturalism that obscure the ongoing racial inequalities that originated with U.S. systems of slavery. Omi and Winant (2014) explained:

> From the very inception of the republic to the present moment, race has been a profound determinant of one's political rights, one's location in the labor market, and indeed one's sense of identity. The hallmark of this history has been racism. (p. 8)

Purportedly, postracism marks the end of racial discrimination and separates interpersonal experiences with racism from the historical, institutional, and structural legacies of racial oppression in the United States (see, e.g., Goldberg, 2002; Joseph, 2012; Squires et al., 2010). Blacktavists, as we demonstrate, resist these imposed silences about race and the subsequent discursive invisibility it creates not only by calling specific attention to their raced bodies but by contextualizing Medolac's efforts within a historical and ongoing context of racism. Responding to the inception of the company's campaign, Blacktavists discursively linked Medolac's efforts to the institution of slavery, making U.S. racism and the exploitation of Black female bodies visible within the "postracial" landscape of the United States.

Within popularly circulating discourses of postracism, Medolac's efforts to recruit urban African-American women can be read as colorblind and unmotivated by racism; however, Blacktavists' rhetoric reveals a pattern of Black labor being exploited for White interests and frames Medolac as part of this exploitative pattern. Afrykayn Moon (2015a), in her blog titled *View From a Rack*, noted:

> *How does offering to purchase breast milk from African American mothers compare to slavery? Slavery* is a legal or economic system under which people are treated as property. Knowing that, the essence of slavery is using people as property, exploiting a group because of their race, economic status or religion for financial gain. Does that ring a bell for you? Medolac is proposing to collect African American women's milk from low-income areas of Detroit, and sell it to hospitals for seven dollars. That's a six hundred percent profit made off the backs (or breast in this case) of African American mothers! (para. 5)

Moon's blog post clearly situates Medolac's efforts within a much larger historical context of discrimination and oppression, drawing parallels between the company's use of Black breastfeeding women and slave owners' use of Black labor. Calling attention to Black bodies, Moon remarks that Medolac is profiting "off the backs (or breast in this case) of African American mothers." Race scholars have indicated the tension between discursive and material constructions of race, suggesting that embodiment is essential for understanding marginalization (see, e.g., Moraga, 1983). Using this lens we see how Moon, focusing on the materiality of Black mothers' bodies, moves between the discursive constructions and the material conditions of race to make racism visible *on* and *through* the bodies of Black breastfeeding women.

Rendering U.S. histories of racism visible within civic discourses that circulate the myths of postracism and colorblindness, Blacktavists resist and reject being categorized and labeled through White narratives and instead manage how they are seen by providing an intersectional account of the ways their raced, gendered, sexed, and classed bodies have been abused. As executive director of BMBFA and Internet blogger Kiddada Green (2015a) noted, "African American women have been impacted traumatically by historical commodification of our bodies" (para. 3). Similarly, Allers (2015), a consultant for BMBFA and independent blogger, addressing Medolac, articulated, "You disrespected the historical relationship between Black women and white women and our breast milk by not respecting the community enough to reach out to any Black breastfeeding advocates, advisors or organizations in devising your scheme" (para. 2). In both accounts, Green and Allers resist Medolac's efforts to discursively construct their bodies as commodifiable by calling on the unique intersection of history, race, and gender. Specifically, by rooting their critique within these intersections, Green and Allers frame Black mothers as members of a supported and sustaining community and make an alternate narrative of Black motherhood visible within public discourse.

Blacktavists' strategy to link Medolac's campaign to histories of Black exploitation is articulated discursively as well as represented through powerful visual images, image macros that can shape public discourse and manage the visibility of Black breastfeeding women. Image macros were one Facebook group's primary contribution to the #StopMedolac campaign. The anonymous organizer(s) of the page "Breastfeeding Mothers Unite" posted a number of image macros during the campaign that were circulated and shared by other Blacktavists across various platforms. Both Figure 1 and Figure 2 were posted as profile pictures to the Breastfeeding Mothers Unite Facebook page and contextualize mothering rhetorics within a complex web of history, race, class, gender, and sexuality. In Figure 1, a drawing of a Black woman nursing a White infant appears in the foreground, while a White woman, presumably the infant's mother, lies in a comfortable bed in the background of the image in a well-furnished bedroom. Visually representing the legacy of Black women working as wet nurses for their slave-owning mistresses, the image states, "Those who forget the past are doomed to repeat it" and includes the following: "#StopMedolac from targeting Black mothers in Detroit for breast milk." This comment directs the viewer to connect slavery-era racial exploitation, a narrative that is banished from contemporary discourses of the postrace era in the United States, to Medolac's campaign in Detroit.

The relationship between the mistress, the slave, and the nursing child at once relies on embodiment to reinforce the heteronormativity of whiteness, while propagating the marginal sexuality of blackness. This occurs insofar as the White mother, having satisfied reproductive expectations (Carter, 2007), reclines to rest, while the wet nurse bares her Black breast for a White infant. Drawing together cultural expectations of race, gender, sexuality, and social class, this image macro reinforces generalizations of White motherhood as leisurely, privileged, and separated from the physical care of the infant, while Black

Figure 1. Drawing of Black woman nursing a White baby in White woman's bedroom (Breastfeeding Mothers Unite, 2015a).

Figure 2. Photograph of Black woman nursing White baby (Breastfeeding Mothers Unite, 2014a).

motherhood is exploited, laborious, and inextricable from satisfying the physical needs of White women and infants. Highlighting the ways that Black female sexuality has been milked for White interests, Blacktavists position Black mothers as hypervisible within a postrace discursive landscape—requiring viewers to not only see race and racist relationships but also the complicit ways that gender, sexuality, and social class inform contemporary racial relationships in the United States.

Image macros based on photographs are also powerful discursive tools used by Breastfeeding Mothers Unite to demonstrate the sexuality of Black motherhood. In Figure 2, a photograph lends credence to Blacktavists' critiques of exploitation. Using the photograph (a historical document) and Medolac's logo to censor the Black mother's bare breasts, the image macro ironically claims "Coming to Detroit! 2015"—a discursive framing that marks the Black breastfeeding woman as a spectacle. Resembling a movie poster advertising an upcoming attraction, Figure 2 relies on irony as a strategy of visibility, whereby Medolac's logo—apparently controlling the degree to which the Black nursing body will be visible—is also that which renders Black femininity simultaneously hypervisible. By featuring the laboring Black woman satisfying the physical needs of a White infant in the foreground of the image, Blacktavists critique the narrative of excessive Black female sexuality. Specifically, the text that frames the image identifies Medolac as the reason for Black women baring their breasts in public and also as the ironic authority that must then manage this unrestrained display of sexuality—a move reversing the cultural myth that Black femininity is unchecked and dangerous and instead implying that White interests are what have been responsible for framing Black femininity in this way.

As Blacktavists demonstrate, not only is rendering visible the longevity of racist relations important but so too is featuring the Black female body alongside constructions of whiteness and heteronormativity. As Flores (2014) argued:

> Race, in all of its messiness, ambiguity, and contestation, lies in/between discursivity and materiality in ways that are (almost) always embodied and lived. That is, despite the fall of

popularity of scientific and biological theories of race in the early twentieth century, the visible body retains definitional power in cultural ascriptions of race. (p. 94)

Thus, the circulation of image macros intervenes in contemporary mothering rhetorics, foregrounding the historical labor of the Black body for White interests, and the comparative embodiment of Black motherhood and disembodiment of White motherhood. Taken together Blacktavists' texts make visible "the material existence of 'colored' bodies" (Johnson, 2001, p. 10) and demonstrate the marginality of Black motherhood—a move that allows Blacktavists to organize public conversations about Black motherhood.

The economic value of Black labor for White interests

During slavery, White families who owned slaves relied on the manual labor of Black men and women to cultivate their fields, manage their livestock, maintain their property, and care for their family's needs—all of which produced a sizable income and a generally comfortable lifestyle for some White individuals and families. As Blacktavists communicate, Medolac's predatory campaign to recruit low-income Black mothers to donate their breast milk is deeply connected to this historical legacy of White people using Black people for profit. Anayah Sangodele-Ayoka (2015a), who runs the website called *Free to Breastfeed* and writes for the blog *Moms Rising*, explained:

What is the value of breastfeeding? The answer to this question usually includes a rundown of the myriad health benefits for mothers and children, reduced healthcare costs or the intangible emotional connection nurtured in the mother–infant dyad. Now, a new program by a company called Medolac has given it a dollar amount: $1/ounce. (para. 1)

Sangodele-Ayoka and other bloggers go on to problematize the inflated rate at which Medolac will sell this same product to hospitals desiring a supply of human breast milk for their patients, at a 600% profit.

Although some White families used the Black breastfeeding body to profit, Blacktavists, constructing and circulating persuasive appeals to stop Medolac's campaign, work *through* the Black breastfeeding body to assert Black mothers' agency and to suggest their ability to control their worth in the marketplace. Figure 3 encapsulates these complaints with a drawn image of a Black woman exposing her breast to nurse a White infant. This image, appearing as a profile picture on the Facebook page for Breastfeeding Mothers Unite, is framed by text that reads:

Why are women always being sold … told that they are doing something of "value" … but consistently devalued in the process? Once again we are being exploited for a 600% profit. When you learn how much you're worth, you'll stop giving people discounts.

With a deliberate slippage between Black women being "sold" and "told," this image macro highlights the profit that Medolac stands to earn from Black breastfeeding women. To imply Black breastfeeding women do not know their worth or they would not give discounts resists dominant narratives that Whites control the marketplace, and instead recenters Black mothers as both capable and responsible for valuing their own labor.

A primary way that Black breastfeeding women are rendered valuable within Blacktavists' discourse is through their relationship to heterosexuality. Specifically, within U.S. contexts, heterosexuality (like whiteness) has social value because its normativity can translate to varying degrees of influence for those who embody or can approximate this

Figure 3. Sketch of Black woman nursing White baby (Breastfeeding Mothers Unite, 2014b).

kind of relationality. As Rand (2013) explained, a framework called the heteroeconomy of desire structures social relationships, noting, "Heterosexual desire manages resources by motivating and shaping the consumption of popular culture products, and humans and identities acquire value directly in relation to the standards of the economy" (p. 131). In this way, Blacktavists construct a discourse that renders Black breastfeeding women visible in the consumer marketplace—not as objects/property but as participants within the heteroeconomy of desire whose worth is calculated based on the complex expectations for their performances of race, class, gender, and sexuality.

Blacktavists' efforts to render Black breastfeeding women visible as agents within the U.S. economy are also captured in a second image circulated on the Black Mothers Unite Facebook page. Figure 4 combines a historical photograph of a Black slave playing "horse" with a White child, framed by this text: "Medolac is making a 600% profit off the BACKS of our African American mothers! Selling your breast milk to Medolac will make you breastfeed longer. If you believe that, I've got a bridge you can buy." The message communicated in this image macro works through several different logics. The expression "If you believe that, I've got a bridge you can buy" references a turn-of-the-century scam whereby con artist George Parker attempted to sell the Brooklyn Bridge to people interested in purchasing land (Cohen, 2005). This historical reference equates Medolac's efforts to those of an infamous scam artist. In this way, Blacktavists reveal Medolac as untrustworthy and irresponsible. In particular, the textual part of the image macro addresses Black mothers as audience members capable of making decisions about how and where to invest their money and implying that they have the ability to make smarter choices than the woman in the image or the immigrants who tried to buy the Brooklyn Bridge.

Image macros like those discussed here demonstrate Blacktavists' efforts to render Black breastfeeding women visible as audience members and agents with the ability to act on their own behalf and can be contrasted with other Blacktavists' image macros that position

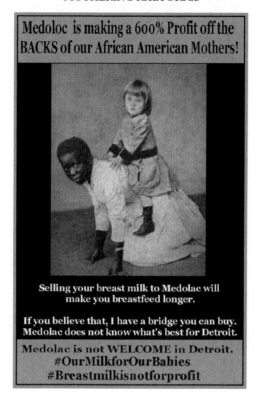

Figure 4. Photograph of Black woman on hands and knees (Breastfeeding Mothers Unite, 2015b).

Black breastfeeding women as subjects within a profit-driven White industrial machine. In Figure 5, an image macro first appearing on Afrykayn Moon's blog *View From a Rack* shows a hand-drawn cartoon portraying incapacitated Black women rolling down an infinite conveyer belt where octopus-like tools reach down from above, attaching to the Black women's breasts to extract milk. The posters hanging on the wall of this illustrated factory show such statements as "We'll pay for your milk $ $ $," "Help NICU babies," and "You can do it." In this image macro, Blacktavists work through the medium of a political cartoon to make visible the profit that White interests reap from Black bodies and Black labor. Further, this image macro illustrates the embodiment of Black mothers' oppression and engages the intersectional ways that race, gender, sexuality, and social class collude to erase Black motherhood—consuming it within a heteroeconomy of desire so that Black femininity can benefit some White, procreative, monogamous couples—and making Black women valuable only insofar as they service White, heteronormative sexuality.

Shortly after Medolac announced its campaign in September 2014, and Blacktavists' discourses began to circulate more widely across social media platforms, Green (2015a) posted an open letter to Medolac in which she solicited signatures of support to stop its campaign. In this letter (one of the four discursive touchstones of this discourse), Green posed a series of questions for Medolac that captured Blacktavists' concerns that White interests regularly profit from Black bodies and Black labor. She asked:

> Why did your company decide to target Detroit, and specifically low-income African-American women within our city? Given the long history in our country of profiting off Black

Figure 5. Cartoon sketch of Black women on a factory conveyor belt (Patrick, 2015).

women's bodies, what steps are you taking to ensure that this process is not exploitative? (Green, 2015a, para. 4)

Though Green communicated her concerns directly to Medolac and provided the company with a specific set of issues she wanted to see addressed, Medolac never provided a response to her questions—something to which we will turn more critical attention in the conclusion. Importantly, Green's letter, along with other Blacktavists' image macros, challenges the historical narratives that mark Black bodies as valuable to the U.S. economy only insofar as they benefit White slave owners and White corporate interests. By creating and circulating a variety of texts to center Black mothers as participants within the U.S. economy, Blacktavists resist narratives implying the invisibility of Black motherhood within the U.S. heteroeconomy and manage national mothering rhetorics through strategic uses of visibility. As we will now explore, a final way that Blacktavists managed the visibility of Black motherhood in the public sphere was to make the whiteness against which it has always been measured a visible category within the postrace United States.

Marking whiteness as a racial category

Against discourses of U.S. racial formation that have marked and marginalized bodies of color, whiteness has been recognized by scholars as occupying a normative, racial center that is privileged, largely unmarked, and uncritically examined (see, e.g., Garner, 2007; Nakayama & Krizek, 1995). Because whiteness is the taken-for-granted normative subject location within U.S. discourses, those who benefit from this identity label experience a number of advantages (see, e.g., Lipsitz, 2006; McIntosh, 1990). Working against the normative discourses of individuals and institutions invested in maintaining the social position and capital of whiteness, Blacktavists' efforts to stop Medolac use rhetorical strategies that make whiteness visible. To do this, they critique the narrative of the "White savior," as well as deploy a vocabulary of "privilege" to call attention to the unearned advantages of whiteness.

In making whiteness visible as a privileged social location, Blacktavists highlight the complexities of (hyper)visibility and invisibility that marginalize Black motherhood. Kimberly Seals Allers (2015), writing her own open letter to Medolac after Kidadda Green's correspondence began to circulate, addresses Medolac chief executive officer (CEO) Elena Medo (specifically) and Medolac (generally) as "White saviors." She remarked:

> Please be clear. If you want to help us—then you should talk to us first. It's a very simple concept. And you seem to be the only one who doesn't get it. Your arrogance and white saviorism is showing, Ms. Medo. And it isn't attractive. (Allers, 2015, para. 11)

Allers's comments charge readers to contextualize Medolac's efforts within familiar U.S. narratives of magnanimous White people saving disenfranchised people of color who cannot help themselves. Making Elena Medo and Medolac's whiteness visible, Allers disrupts normative racial discourses by bringing whiteness to the fore to balance the hypervisibility of the Black body, and the invisibility of Black motherhood.

Blogger Afrykayn Moon (2015a) also described Medolac as offering problematic and unwanted aid to Black mothers in Detroit, noting in her blog post, "It's time for Elena Medo to know she cannot play Savior here without communicating with the people in this community" (para. 27). On a blog radio show several days later, Moon (2015b) reinforced this point, noting, "You can't save me if you can't talk to me." Both Allers's and Moon's primary critique of Medolac is that, within and throughout its campaign, Black mothers remained invisible insofar as they had no voice (and no agency) in constructing their futures. Allers's and Moon's efforts to frame Elena Medo and Medolac as White saviors, however, disrupt this discursive absence, requiring that Black mothers be visible within this narrative, for the trope of the White savior cannot work without a non-White subject who stands to "benefit" from their efforts.

Blacktavists' rhetorical efforts to make race visible work against contemporary color-blind attitudes in the United States and call attention to U.S. racism. Allers's and Moon's references to the "White savior" directly invoke race as an element of contention; however, their critique of the U.S. racial hierarchy persists in language that references privilege as well. On Allers's (2014) *New York Times* parenting blog, *Motherlode*, the blogger wrote:

> Increasing breast-feeding rates among low-income African American women, in Detroit and all over the country, is a goal I support. But there's more to that effort than numbers. So far, Medolac is taking a very privileged "we know what you need" stance. (para. 10)

A month later, and immediately after Medolac decided to pull its campaign, Green (2015b) responded to the news on the BMBFA website using parallel language in her own post. She remarked:

> We have won the battle, but the fight is far from over. We are concerned about Medolac's hubristic condescension. Medolac's press release cited a "toxic atmosphere" as their rationale for giving up the Detroit project. *They never even agreed to sit down with us, but accuse us of creating a toxic atmosphere?* This is the kind of "we know better than you" attitude that started and ended their campaign. (para. 4)

In each of these examples, Blacktavists break out of the pervasive postrace discourses that characterize contemporary U.S. social relations and make race and racism visible in direct and indirect ways. In so doing, Allers, Green, Moon, and others engage in a discursive strategy that depends on rendering the otherwise invisible Black mother and White savior visible within the postracial United States.

As we discuss throughout this analysis, Blacktavists' strategies reveal that rhetorical reproductions and challenges to the ideological understandings of Black motherhood can come from the margins. Nevertheless, we resist a congratulatory reading of these efforts—especially as lingering concerns about some of the Blacktavists' choices, as well as questions over the degree to which their efforts truly intervened in larger discourse of discrimination, remain. It is toward these concerns that we now direct our attention.

Conclusion

Blacktavists' use of visibility as a rhetorical strategy worked to halt Medolac's campaign in Detroit and, for this reason, can be understood as a successful rhetorical effort; however, as we argue, this victory is not without complications. In a press release from Medolac on January 21, 2015, the company explained, "It is with regret that we have taken the unilateral decision to retire this CGI Commitment to Action" (para. 5). Justifying its decision, Medolac directly addressed Blacktavist Kidadda Green, stating:

> Thank you for your letter which we received last week.[11] We welcome the chance to correct the misinformation being circulated regarding our Commitment to Action that we announced last September but never had an opportunity to implement. (Medolac, 2015, para. 1)

Thus, even though Medolac retired its campaign in Detroit, the company nevertheless implied that the good work it could have done was unduly stopped by Blacktavists who never gave Medolac the opportunity to actualize its efforts. In this way, Medolac rhetorically constructed a scenario that cast the company's efforts as "good" and the Blacktavists' efforts as "bad," reproducing Black mothering rhetorics that mark Black women as troublemakers, aggressive, and/or pathological (Carpenter, 2012; Reid-Brinkley, 2011; Roberts, 1997).

Black mothering rhetorics reproduce ideological systems of whiteness and heteronormativity and reinforce an existing social hierarchy that maintains the privilege of these particular intersections. Some scholars have noted the significance of the Moynihan Report (published in 1965) in shaping contemporary Black mothering rhetorics, noting that in this report, Black women were charged with the failure, shortcomings, and poverty of the Black family (Carpenter, 2012; Feldstein, 2000; Roberts, 1997). Taken together, the Moynihan Report from the 1960s, contemporary media content, and other public discourses circulating narratives of Black motherhood have long suggested Black women's shortcomings when measured against the standard of the mythological good White mother (Reid-Brinkley, 2011).

Examining Medolac's language to retire the campaign demonstrates how the authority of whiteness is used to articulate judgments that represent Black women as difficult troublemakers. The company explains: "In light of recent events … this environment has become too toxic for public/private partnership" in ways that prevent Medolac from seeing "a viable pathway forward to advance this campaign, particularly given our desire for continued local partner participation" (para. 2). The "recent events" to which Medolac refers are the bevy of Blacktavists' communication about the company's campaign—a comment that places responsibility for this campaign's failure (and the "toxic" environment that was created) squarely on Black women. Medolac's repeated charges that its campaign in Detroit would help Black mothers and Black children caused a silencing of Black mothers and reinforced their invisibility. When Black mothers and Blacktavists, uninvited, voiced their concerns about the campaign, they were charged with creating a "toxic environment" and labeled difficult community partners who spoiled low-income Black mothers' opportunity to improve their circumstances. In this way Medolac reproduced Black mothering rhetorics that place blame on Black mothers for the failure of their own communities.

Recognizing the troubled ways in which Medolac framed its campaign's retirement, Blacktavist Anayah Sangodele-Ayoka (2015b) noted in her blog post that "the coalition behind the public accountability campaign, led by Black Mothers Breastfeeding Association (BMBFA), counts Medolac's statement as a 'complicated victory'" (para. 4). At once acknowledging the campaign's success as well as the normative discourses about Black femininity that linger to position many Black mothers as aggressive and as troublemakers, Sangodele-Ayoka's statement implies the unfinished work of Blacktavists and the difficulties of producing social change. Indeed, the maternal body is a key site for understanding cultural attitudes about contemporary motherhood (O'Brien Hallstein, 2015); and as Blacktavists' rhetoric demonstrates, the maternal body of the Black breastfeeding woman is the site of intersecting discourses of identity, power, and subversion. The nexus of Medolac's and Blacktavists' discourses reveal the way the body has been used to leverage social control and to advocate for social change. Indeed, managing the visibility of the Black breastfeeding body allowed Blacktavists to challenge Medolac's exploitation of Black mothers, but does not yet appear to have been successful in revising harmful Black mothering rhetorics that continue to inform the positionality of Black women.

Since halting Medolac's campaign, Blacktavists continue their efforts to assert a visible place for Black mothers within the public sphere. Afrykayn Moon produces her weekly blog talk-radio show. Anayah Sangodele-Ayoka's blog posts on *Moms Rising* continue to center the Black breastfeeding body. Kiddada Green and BMBFA (2015b) continue their work to raise awareness and educate Black women about breastfeeding—implementing a webinar series to "illustrate ways to support, protect and promote breastfeeding within the community" (para 4). With a persistent focus on remaining visible, and advocating for low-income mothers on the margins, Blacktavists will continue to challenge the efforts of groups such as Medolac. Passing on the stories of their achievements, demonstrating the value and limitations of their current strategies, Blacktavists will no doubt keep trying to topple—one post at a time—more than just Medolac; however, for meaningful social change to occur, future efforts must address the normative mothering rhetorics that create initiatives like Medolac's in the first place.

Acknowledgments

This article, "#SpoiledMilk: Blacktavists, Visibility, and the Exploitation of the Black Breast," derives from a project initially conceptualized in second author Karen Y. Kimball's master's thesis completed in 2008. Since that time, this essay was developed to further elaborate and theorize the intersections of race, gender, and sexuality inherent in her original project on breastfeeding. The authors thank Jeff Bennett for his generous feedback, Jennifer Aglio for her copyediting assistance, and the staff at Prairie House Restaurant in Cross Roads, Texas, for the wonderful workspace and killer food.

Notes

1. The term *Blacktavist* is a colloquial expression adopted by women advocating for increased breastfeeding initiation rates in the Black community. The expression is a blend of the terms *Black* and *activist* and references the common phrase *lactavist*.
2. We use the term *refracting* to suggest the ways that our analysis shifts and/or bends as it is considered within and/or alongside multiple intersecting subject positions.
3. We use the term *governmentality* to describe the way the state exercises control, established by Michel Foucault in his 1977–1978 lecture series *Security, Territory, Population* (Foucault, Senellart, Ewald, Fontana, & Davidson, 2009).
4. Medolac defines itself as a public benefit corporation.
5. Because of the various positions of marginality that all people may experience, individuals are often simultaneously privileged and disadvantaged (relative to social class, gender performativity, sexuality, race, able-bodiedness, and so on); such is the case for the White mothers and the Black mothers we talk about throughout this article.
6. For a comprehensive accounting of this work, see Chávez and Griffin's (2012) collection, *Standing at the Intersections of Feminism, Intersectionality, and Communication Studies.*
7. Image macros are images which often appear with text and which communicate cultural concepts that are shared publicly by users across Internet platforms.
8. The hashtag #StopMedolac was used 107 times by 44 unique Twitter users over the course of 21 days, often in conjunction with other hashtags—among them #BlackLivesMatter, which was used alongside #StopMedolac in 12 separate instances. Although Blacktavists used multiple hashtags, the title of our article, #SpoiledMilk, was not circulated by Blacktavists in their efforts to stop Medolac's campaign but is rather something with which we took creative license to capture and support Blacktavists' critique.
9. These activists appear to come from diverse backgrounds. Some are mothers who, through their own experiences, have become involved online to share struggles, successes, and tips about breastfeeding. Others are lactation consultants, and still others are directly linked to (or work for) organizations committed to empowering mothers to make their own informed decisions about parenting, breastfeeding, and health.
10. The primary contributors referenced include Blacktavists Kiddada Green, Kimberly Seals Allers, Afrykayn Moon, Anayah Sangodele-Ayoka, Danielle Atkinson, Jodine Chase, and Liz Brooks; Breastfeeding Mothers Unite; Breastfeeding Coalition of Oregon; Rose Incorporated; Health Connect One; and Harambee.
11. Medolac is referencing the letter Kidadda Green wrote on January 12, 2015, that solicited signatures from other individuals concerned that the company was taking advantage of low-income Black women in Detroit.

References

Allers, K. S. (2014, December 3). Inviting African-American mothers to sell their breast milk, and profiting [Web log post]. Retrieved from http://parenting.blogs.nytimes.com/2014/12/03/inviting-african-american-mothers-to-sell-their-breast-milk-and-profiting/

Allers, K. S. (2015, January 13). Dear Elena Medo: You can't claim to support Black breastfeeding and attack Black breastfeeding advocates; now Detroit moms have spoken [Web log post]. Retrieved from http://mochamanual.com/2015/01/13/dear-elena-medo-you-cant-claim-to-support-black-breastfeeding-and-attack-black-breastfeeding-advocates-now-detroit-moms-have-spoken/

Bartlett, A. (2003). Breastfeeding bodies and choice in late capitalism. *Hecate, 29*, 153–165.

Bell, W. (1965). *Aid to dependent children.* New York, NY: Columbia University Press.

Black Mothers Breastfeeding Association. (2015a, January 18). @blactavist plz include the hashtag in each of your posts: It'll help followers find your tweets #StopMedolac [tweet]. Retrieved from https://twitter.com/BMBFA/status/556910028427628545

Black Mothers Breastfeeding Association. (2015b, February 24). Events. Retrieved from http://blackmothersbreastfeeding.org/event/webinar-community-breastfeeding/

Blum, L. M. (1993). Mothers, babies, and breastfeeding in late capitalist America: The shifting contexts of feminist theory. *Feminist Studies, 19,* 290–312.

Blum, L. M. (1999). *At the breast.* Boston, MA: Beacon Press.

Breastfeeding Mothers Unite. (2014a, December 28). Photograph of Black woman nursing White baby. Retrieved from https://www.facebook.com/BFMUnite/photos/pb.240269209350178.-2207520000.1425221595./837821559594937/?type=3&theater

Breastfeeding Mothers Unite. (2014b, December 30). Sketch of Black woman nursing White baby. Retrieved from https://www.facebook.com/BFMUnite/photos/pb.240269209350178.-2207520000.1425243703./839674079409685/?type=3&theater

Breastfeeding Mothers Unite. (2015a, January 14). Drawing of Black woman nursing a White baby in White woman's bedroom. Retrieved from https://www.facebook.com/BFMUnite/photos/pb.240269209350178.-2207520000.1425221595./849255705118189/?type=3&theater

Breastfeeding Mothers Unite. (2015b, January 15). Photograph of Black woman on hands and knees. Retrieved from https://www.facebook.com/BFMUnite/photos/pb.240269209350178.-2207520000.1425243703./843485675695192/?type=3&theater

Carpenter, T. R. (2012). Construction of the crack mother icon. *Western Journal of Black Studies, 36*(4), 264–275.

Carter, J. (2007). *The heart of whiteness: Normal sexuality and race in America, 1880–1940.* Durham, NC: Duke University Press.

Centers for Disease Control & Prevention. (2013). Progress in increasing breastfeeding and reducing racial/ethnic differences—United States, 2000–2008 births. *Morbidity and Mortality Weekly Report (MMWR), 62*(5), 77–80.

Centers for Disease Control & Prevention. (2014). *Breastfeeding report card, United States/2014.* Atlanta, GA: National Center for Chronic Disease Prevention and Health Promotion, Centers for Disease Control and Prevention. Retrieved from http://www.cdc.gov/breastfeeding/pdf/2014breastfeedingreportcard.pdf

Chávez, K. R., & Griffin, C. L. (2012). Standing at the intersections of feminisms, intersectionality, and communication studies. In C. L. Griffin, and K. R. Chavez (Ed.), *Standing in the intersection: Feminist voices, feminist practices in communication studies* (pp. 1–34). Albany: State University of New York Press.

Cohen, G. (2005, November 27). For you, half price. *New York Times.* Retrieved from http://www.nytimes.com/2005/11/27/nyregion/thecity/for-you-half-price.html?_r=0

Feldstein, R. (2000). *Motherhood in Black and White: Race and sex in American liberalism, 1930–1965.* Ithaca, NY: Cornell University Press.

Flores, L. (2014). The rhetorical "realness" of race, or why critical race rhetoricians need performance studies. *Text and Performance Quarterly, 34*(1), 94–96. doi:10.1080/10462937.2013.849356

Foucault, M., Senellart, M., Ewald, F., Fontana, A., & Davidson, A. I. (Eds.). (2009). *Security, territory, population: Lectures at the College de France, 1977–1978.* (G. Burchell, Trans.). New York, NY: Picador/Palgrave Macmillan.

Fraser, N. (1989). *Unruly practices: Power, discourse, and gender in contemporary social theory.* Minneapolis: University of Minnesota Press.

Garner, S. (2007). *Whiteness: An introduction.* London, United Kingdom: Routledge.

Goldberg, D. T. (2002). *The racial state.* Malden, MA: Blackwell.

Green, K. (2015a, January 12). Open letter to Medolac Laboratories from Detroit mothers [Web log post]. Retrieved from http://blackmothersbreastfeeding.org/2015/01/open-letter-to-medolac-laboratories-from-detroit-mothers/

Green, K. (2015b, January 22). Victory!!! Medolac retires campaign!! [Web log post]. http://blackmothersbreastfeeding.org/2015/01/victory-medolac-retires-campaign/

Johnson, E. P. (2001). "Quare" studies, or (almost everything I know about queer studies I learned from my grandmother). *Text and Performance Quarterly, 21*(1), 1–25. doi:10.1080/10462930128119

Joseph, R. L. (2012). *Transcending blackness: From the new millennium mulatta to the exceptional multiracial.* Durham, NC: Duke University Press.

Lipsitz, G. (2006). *The possessive investment in whiteness: How White people profit from identity politics.* Philadelphia, PA: Temple University Press.

McIntosh, P. (1990). White privilege: Unpacking the invisible knapsack. *Independent School, 49*(2), 31.

Medolac Laboratories. (2014). Medolac Laboratories announces Clinton Global Initiative (CGI) Commitment to Action at 2014 CGI annual meeting [Press release]. Retrieved from http://www.ireachcontent.com/news-releases/medolac-laboratories-announces-clinton-global-initiative-cgi-commitment-to-action-at-2014-cgi-annual-meeting-275992691.html

Medolac Laboratories. (2015). Medolac Laboratories retires planned urban donor commitment to action campaign unimplemented [Press release]. Retrieved from http://www.ireachcontent.com/news-releases/medolac-laboratories-retires-planned-urban-donor-commitment-to-action-campaign-unimplemented-289327291.html

Mink, G. (1995). *The wages of motherhood: Inequality in the welfare state, 1917–1942.* Ithaca, NY: Cornell University Press.

Moon, A. (2015a, January 12). Something is starting to smell familiar … Who is Medolac? [Web log post]. Retrieved from https://viewfromarack.wordpress.com

Moon, A. (Presenter). (2015b, January 20). Medolac … The saga continues [Blog radio]. Retrieved from http://www.blogtalkradio.com/viewfromarack/2015/01/21/medolacthe-saga-continues

Moraga, C. (1983). La guera. In C. Moraga, and G. Anzaldúa (Eds.), *This bridge called my back: Writings by radical women of color* (pp. 27–34). New York, NY: Kitchen Table/Women of Color Press.

Nakayama, T. K., & Krizek, R. L. (1995). Whiteness: A strategic rhetoric. *Quarterly Journal of Speech, 81,* 291–309. doi:10.1080/00335639509384117

O'Brien Hallstein, L. (2015). *Bikini-ready moms: Celebrity profiles, motherhood, and the body.* Albany: State University of New York Press.

Omi, M., & Winant, H. (2014). *Racial formation in the United States* (3rd ed.). New York, NY: Routledge.

Patrick, K. (2015). Cartoon sketch of Black women on a factory conveyor belt hooked up to breast pumps. Retrieved from https://viewfromarack.wordpress.com

Rand, E. (2013). An appetite for activism: The Lesbian Avengers and the queer politics of visibility. *Women's Studies in Communication, 36,* 121–141. doi:10.1080/07491409.2013.794754

Reid-Brinkley, S. R. (2011). Mammies and matriarchs: Feminine style and signifyin(g) in Carol Mosely Braun's 2003–2004 campaign for the presidency. In K. R. Chavez, and C. L. Griffin (Eds.), *Standing in the intersection* (pp. 35–58). Albany: State University of New York Press.

Roberts, D. E. (1997). Unshackling Black motherhood. *Michigan Law Review, 94*(4), 938–964.

Sangodele-Ayoka, A. (2015a, January 12). How much is breastmilk worth? [Web log post]. Retrieved from http://www.momsrising.org/blog/how-much-is-breastmilk-worth

Sangodele-Ayoka, A. (2015b, January 23). Open letter, closed in breastmilk bank controversy [Web log post]. Retrieved from http://www.momsrising.org/blog/open-letter-closed-door-in-breastmilk-bank-controversy

Squires, C., Watts, E. K., Vavrus, M. D., Ono, K. A., Feyh, K., Calafell, B. M., & Brouwer, D. C. (2010). Postracism: A theory of the "post-" as political strategy. *Journal of Communication Inquiry, 34*(3), 210–253. doi:10.1177/0196859910371375

Triece, M. E. (2012). Credible workers and deserving mothers: Crafting "mother tongue" in welfare rights activism, 1967–1972. *Communication Studies, 63*(1), 1–17. doi:10.1080/10510974.2011.634477

Standpoints of Maternity Leave: Discourses of Temporality and Ability

Patrice M. Buzzanell, Robyn V. Remke, Rebecca Meisenbach, Meina Liu, Venessa Bowers, and Cindy Conn

ABSTRACT

Our standpoint analysis of 21 women in pink-collar occupations displays how these workers both adhere to and challenge maternity leave discourses by rhetorically positioning their leaves as time off and (dis) ability. They both acknowledge the advantages of and resist discourses of time and (dis)ability by constructing complicated, contradictory, and ironic knowledge that such language both secures their leaves and revokes their images as competent workers. This study illustrates how standpoint analyses can inform changes in organizational policy and workplace practices for mothers employed in pink-collar occupations based on common knowledge and differences in local-specific experiences. Beyond providing such analysis, this study also contributes to greater understandings of the "rhetorical reproduction of ideological systems and logics of contemporary culture" constituting mothering rhetorics.

> "You had your baby. Now it's time to get back to work."
> —Sandy

Although "Sandy," a teletypist in our study, noted that her supervisor and coworkers at a trading company seemed happy and supportive of her pregnancy and maternity leave, she perceived that once she had her baby they were anxious for her to resume her paid work so that things could return to their normal state. In Sandy's and other cases, preferences for and understandings about the meanings of workplace pregnancy, work, jobs, careers, benefits, and work–life balance depend on context. These preferences and understandings shift over time, economic conditions, occupational groups, and differences (e.g., gender, class, race, immigrant status, generational cohorts) nationally and globally (e.g., Buzzanell, 2000; Cheney, Zorn, Planalp, & Lair, 2008; Hanchey & Berkelaar, 2015; Klarsfeld, 2010, 2014; O'Connor & Raile, 2015). For instance, in the United States, pink-collar occupational positions typically have been held by women with job titles such as secretaries, customer service representatives, personnel specialists, and administrative assistants, in which service is essential to the job description (U.S. Department of Labor [DOL], 2001). The U.S.

Bureau of Labor Statistics has indicated that pink-collar work is one of the fastest-growing job sectors, attracting both women and men largely because of greater job security (Francis, 2012), despite low pay and lack of advancement opportunities (Kiesel, 2014). Even so, pink-collar occupations and work, like other instances of occupational segregation by sex, retain gendered organizing processes that pattern sex and gender distinctions in every aspect from tasks to structures, re-creating gender and class distinctions on local and societal levels (Acker, 1990, 2006; Pringle, 1989a; Turk, 2014).

These gendered organizing patterns are most evident when workers' differences become salient as, for example, when leaders are transgender (Muhr & Sullivan, 2013), when different workforce segments question the primacy of work (O'Connor & Raile, 2015), or when women and men participate in occupations socially constructed as appropriate for the other sex (Wingfield, 2009). In trying to understand more about these gendered organizing patterns, we examine how a particular workforce segment—mothers employed in pink-collar positions—perceive their workplace experiences when pregnant and on maternity leaves. Our rationale is that these women occupy positions in which their organizational relationships and work in service/support of others require that they must understand their work vis-à-vis others as well as organizational and societal power structures. During their pregnancies and maternity leaves, women in pink-collar occupations also may struggle to regulate their bodies, conform to others' expectations about ideal workers and priorities regarding paid labor, seek to maintain a professional (nonsexual) demeanor, and negotiate what they need for their well-being and that of their child(ren) (Buzzanell & Ellingson, 2005; Fox & Quinn, 2015; Gatrell, 2013; Liu & Buzzanell, 2004; Turner & Norwood, 2013, 2014). Most organizational research into pregnancy and maternity leave focuses on potential career repercussions for women in relatively privileged positions.[1] By comparison, relatively little has been written about the ways mothers in pink-collar occupations make sense of their experiences. Examining these women's experiences offers counterpoints to published studies by showing how they may have different struggles because they operate in structurally subordinate positions requiring them to see how and where their own and others' perspectives and interests may be similar and dissimilar. These experiences may generate insights useful for organizational and policy change.

In our study, we examine the ways in which mothers working in pink-collar occupations construct maternity leave, that is, how they express awareness of and come to understand the gendered organizing processes involved in their maternity leaves. We use feminist standpoint theories to present women's complicated lived experiences, nuanced knowledge, and individual yet collective voices in ways that can generate change (Buzzanell, 2015; Ashcraft, 2014). Although standpoints reflect political consciousness, Lenz's (2004) point is well taken in that standpoints do not refer to "rigid or permanent stabilization of perspective, but rather to a fluid and dynamic negotiation of experience and point of view that can be temporarily stabilized in order to interrogate dominant ideologies" (p. 98; see also Buzzanell, 2015). Rather than treating women as a monolithic group that holds coherent, shared group understandings, standpoints can be viewed as shifting and socially constructed consciousness, identities, and perceptions of what typically is taken for granted in group members' everyday lives. Because these standpoints emerge and change based on experience, reflection, and evolving political understandings of women's positions vis-à-vis others, they provide opportunities to understand how different groups of mothers couch their pregnancies and maternity leaves in ways that may benefit themselves and/or others. Deconstructing the normative paradigm of White, middle-class experience to enlarge space for diverse women is essential to enrich theory and understand how class and social location play into the marginalization of different women's ordinary lives (see Ashcraft, 2014; Dougherty, 2011; Parker, 2014; Schein, 2002). In short, we explore how mothers who work in pink-collar occupations struggle with gendered organizing structures through the language and values they express about their maternity leaves.

Literature review

Maternity leave

Broadly created and maintained, maternity leave is the period during which mothers recuperate, care for children, and attend to changing relationships after delivering or adopting a child. The leave is provided for the mothers' and children's health and to integrate the children into the family structure. While most countries mandate paid maternity leave for all mothers, the United States, Lesotho, Swaziland, and Papua New Guinea do not (International Labour Office, 2010; see also Klarsfeld, 2010, 2014). These provisions compare with some countries such as the United Kingdom, Sweden, and Canada, where parents are afforded paid leave for up to 480 days. For instance, based on business needs and size, mothers may not qualify as "eligible employees of covered employers," meaning that they technically are not eligible for leave time and for payment through the Family Medical Leave Act (FMLA, 1993; U.S. Department of Labor, n.d.).

Approximately half of U.S. first-time mothers are able to take paid leave (Finnegan, 2011). Mothers who are employed in the United States are not guaranteed paid maternity leave even if they engage in paid labor for a qualifying company (see Guendelman, Goodman, Kharrazi, & Lahiff, 2014; Jorgensen & Applebaum, 2014; Ybarra & Hill, 2014); the federal FMLA grants them 12 weeks of unpaid leave. Individual companies may offer additional maternity leave benefits, including payment or salary continuation, job sharing, telecommuting, and flex time. Payment for mothers while on leave comes from the individual companies' budgets. In countries where leave is mandated, payment for leaves comes from a variety of sources, such as employers, social welfare systems, or a combination of both (Women's International Network, 1998).

Some U.S. organizations recognize the advantage of offering paid maternity leave. The "business case" for maternity leave is persuasive: Paid leave is beneficial not only to mothers and children but to families in general and workplaces (Milkman & Appelbaum, 2013). Organizations and media outlets such as Working Mother (http://www.workingmother. com) offer yearly rankings of the best organizations for women's employment, and maternity leave provisions weigh heavily in the evaluations. Some organizations see these rankings as useful in attracting the very best talent. However, this recruitment (and retention) tactic is usually used by and most effective for highly skilled professionals, not women in pink-collar occupations, whose salaries and working conditions are not considered to be as desirable as those for women professionals.

Classing maternity leave

Past feminist scholarship that dealt with the right to paid work and "the problem that has no name" (Friedan, 1963) was imbued with classist and political gender identifications that both encouraged change for particular groups of women and ignored the issues of working-class, pink-collar, and poor women (Heywood & Drake, 1997; hooks, 2000). As hooks (2000) explained, "many of these working women who put in long hours for low wages while still doing all the work in the domestic household, would have seen the right to stay home as 'freedom'" (p. 102). This difference in vantage points means that, when analyzing class issues, researchers need to focus not only on economics but also on the complex values, behaviors, and belief systems at play. As Weedon (1999) noted:

> [C]lass is a contested term and its precise meaning depends on the discursive context in which it occurs. Moreover, it is a term which has multiple dimensions and levels ... [and can] characterize the lifestyle, values, and attitudes of particular groups within society. (p. 134; see also Dougherty, 2011)

In the case of employees in pink-collar occupations, class also can mean "the combination of limited education and few job skills ... her education and training place her in low-level jobs that do not provide sufficient income" (Schein, 2002, p. 36; see also Women's International Network, 2003). The May 2013 National Occupational Employment and Wage Estimates for secretaries (except legal, medical, and executive secretaries) listed a mean hourly wage of $18.39, making the mean annual wage $38,250 prior to taxes (U.S. DOL, 2013). Importantly, researchers found that women using the FMLA provision for unpaid maternity leave were typically White, married, and with stable income, which suggests differences related to class, race and ethnicity, sexual-social orientation, and occupation in mothers' abilities to take leaves (Gerstel & McGonagle, 1999; Guendelman et al., 2014).

Thus, while discussions of maternity leaves for White, middle-class women center on how and whether these leaves affect careers and leadership (e.g., Ashcraft, 1999; Hewlett, 2007), the issues for other employed mothers may be very different. These issues are not simply economic.[2] They also relate to gendered organizing processes whereby paid work is imbued with hidden rules for which they are not privileged (Payne, 2001). Payne (2001) describes hidden rules as "unspoken cues and habits of a group. Distinct cueing systems exist between and among groups and economic classes" (p. 52). In the United States, these hidden rules relate both to the logic of capitalism, in which managers create and/or use strategies to subordinate labor, and patriarchy, in which discourse articulates relations among social systems, such as organizations and family (see Holmer-Nadesan, 1996; Weedon, 1999). As managerial, class, and gender discourses conspire to "call" pink-collar workers to accept subordinate relations and identities, these employees may find it difficult to find a space for resistance to these meanings of themselves, their paid work, and their relationships with others (Holmer-Nadesan, 1996). However, they also may draw upon alternative ways of knowing and being, as well as performing their identities, given that their standpoints incorporate understandings of others as well as of themselves. Indeed, research on women in pink-collar occupations indicates that they operate creatively within the tensions and contradictions of their situations by "bitching," designing and distributing subversive documents (i.e., office folklore, poetry), engaging in irreverent humor, constructing positive images of themselves and their paid work, and valuing relationships with other women (Bell & Forbes, 1994; Holmer-Nadesan, 1996; Kovicak, 2001; Pringle, 1989b; Sotirin, 2000; Sotirin & Gottfried, 1999). These findings suggest that women in pink-collar positions may have wide ranges of experiences, understandings, and possible actions useful for developing different perspectives not only on the power structures that constrain and enable them and other employees in general but also on maternity leave. Such findings display how they navigate "discursively and materially toward various ends … [and] engag[ing] practical tensions and improvis[ing] tactics that enable both empowerment and productivity" within organizing processes (Ashcraft, 2000, p. 352).

Standing in the margin: Feminist standpoint perspectives

Using feminist standpoints allows us to examine in detail what happens in diverse women's lives, how these women comprehend different lived experiences, and how they construct their identities, voices, and actions in light of these understandings. Bullis and Stout (2000) state that standpoint theories assume "that by starting with the experiences and knowledges of the subordinated, we can better understand how dominations occur" (p. 48). Standpoint approaches position women as central in the study of particular organizing processes, such as maternity leaves. Using women's abilities to penetrate the discourses and practices of oppression creates space for researchers to generate theory about and by women, instead of overlaying theory to "fit" women's experiences. Through the production of studies using standpoints, researchers gain partial situated knowledge, or knowledge developed from different positions in society and the ways these locations and attendant agencies are structured by multiple power relations (Allen, 2000, 2011; Collins, 2000; Hallstein, 2000; Harding, 1987, 1991, 2004). Partial knowledge means not only that knowledge is "not-total" but also that knowledge is "not-impartial," so that standpoint researchers do not claim that "knowledge is generally true, or true for 'women'" (Ramazanoğlu & Holland, 2002, p. 66). As a result, feminist standpoint researchers struggle with the relationships among power, gender, and knowledge. These struggles help develop knowledge that can benefit women through analyses of commonalities and ways to resist collectively domination in varied forms, including trivialization of women's concerns (Ashcraft, 2014; Buzzanell, 2015; Wood, 1992). Thus, while feminist standpoints accommodate difference, they retain commonality "to preserve the analytic and political force of feminist theory" (Hallstein, 2000, p. 4).

In short, our analysis seeks to illuminate experiences of mothers employed in pink-collar occupations and add to understandings of maternity leave and mothering rhetorics. Although we examine a particular group's experiences for patterns, we contend that feminist standpoints integrate both privilege and marginalization, looking for unifying commonalities while admitting differences, and operating with incomplete understandings and awareness of societal positionings for, as Buzzanell (2015) notes:

> Whereas standpoints focus on group members' understandings of their societal positions, these group members' ways of knowing are not and cannot be uniform because of the different circumstances in which individuals live and work. How to build knowledge about the lived conditions of particular collectivities while also admitting the diverse variations and intersectionalities of identity groupings is highly controversial. (pp. 771–772)

With some exceptions, the voices and experiences of women in pink-collar occupations have not been analyzed sufficiently in organizational and communication research. Their struggles for meaning constitute women in pink-collar occupations as knowledgeable agents who actively construct their worlds and are simultaneously complicit with and in opposition to dominant meanings and practices. Their standpoints reveal these discursive struggles as well as their understandings of their situatedness in gendered organizing structures. Achieving standpoints *is* a struggle requiring "conscious reflection on and political understandings of their experiences of oppressions" (Hallstein, 2000, p. 12; see also Buzzanell, 2015; Harding, 2004). Thus, we examine how they make sense of their maternity leaves and policies to develop theory and practices that are richer and more inclusive of different women's lives, particularly mothers employed in pink-collar occupations.

Method

Robinson (2014) argues that feminist standpoint epistemologies regarding motherhood can provide women with a voice that is not absolute or complete but lets women envision a different world, one which values caring and which enables different and more empowering discursive framings. In designing our study to provide space for the voices of mothers working in pink-collar positions, we discuss our participants and procedures, with particular attention to our own positionalities vis-à-vis pink-collar work and maternity leaves.

Participants

The 21 accounts of women in pink-collar occupations used in this study come from a database of 102 interviews with women who discussed their maternity leaves. These 21 women labeled themselves primarily as secretaries, teletypists, and office workers or clerks (67% of our participants in pink-collar occupations), customer service representatives, assistants, financial counselors in institutions of higher education, and receptionists in animal clinics. All 21 participants had at least one maternity leave and up to three leaves, with the majority of participants having just one (67%, or 14 out of 21). The average age of the participants for their first and/or only leave was 27 years, but all leaves were taken when the participants were between the ages of 20 and 44 years old.

Situated within the Midwestern region of the United States, 17 of the participants self-identified as White, three identified as Black, and one identified as Latina. Regarding education, 43% of our participants had at least an associate's degree; all reported having taken some college courses. All but one participant were married, and the one exception reported that she was separated.

The participants were employed at their workplace for a range of years when they took their first or only maternity leave (between three months and 14 years); the average was 4.7 years. Most participants reported being satisfied with their jobs before (90%) and after (81%) their leaves, but two participants did report that they were dissatisfied with at least one of their leaves. The remaining participants reported being neither satisfied nor dissatisfied with their leave experience. Relatedly, most of the participants reported feeling secure in their jobs. Only one woman said that she did not perceive herself as having job security before or after her maternity leave (i.e., she said that she felt neither secure nor insecure at these times).

Procedures

The results draw from survey and interview data to obtain background details (e.g., educational levels, occupations, race, ethnicity, and information pertaining to maternity leaves) and to uncover women's understandings of their experiences. The interview protocol included both open and closed questions and was organized into four key parts: (a) respondents' understandings of maternity leave policies; (b) their descriptions of their pregnancies/adoptions and maternity leave experiences; (c) their (and others') ways of talking about maternity leaves; and (d) their descriptions of their returns to paid work. The goal of the interview and survey was to gain access to the participants' overall experience of maternity leave, particularly the commonalities that could indicate group-level knowledge constructions and awareness of their sociopolitical-economic positions and their consequences for participants' lives understandings. Upon institutional review board (IRB) approval, participants were contacted, and interviews averaged 36 minutes (range of 18 to 90 minutes) and produced 389 pages of single-spaced transcription. All names and locations were changed to preserve confidentiality.

To engage in data analysis, the authors first considered their own positions regarding pink-collar employment and personal relationships. They did so because Ramazanoğlu and Holland (2002) note that feminist standpoint researchers need to be made visible in projects for, like research participants, the researcher:

> "knows" from a specific and partial social location, and so is socially constituted as a "knowing self" in particular ways of thinking and authorizing knowledge …. Making the researcher visible makes power relations between women a critical feature of understanding the complexity and variety of gendered power relations. (p. 65)

All authors were women and from both middle-class and working-class backgrounds. All, save one, had experience as pink-collar workers (e.g., secretary, receptionist, clerk, administrative assistant, executive assistant, and temp worker) prior to graduate school. All, save one, reported having mothers with, and fathers without, pink-collar work experience. The one exception was the author whose mother did not have pink-collar work experience but was a high school teacher and computer programmer.

Two of the authors had paid maternity leaves when they gave birth to their children. Recognizing that maternity leaves were not simply about giving birth but about changing relationships to self, others, and spatiotemporal contexts, we noted that all authors have participated in the joys and constraints associated with family leaves as aunts, daughters, siblings, and friends. The authors used their personal experiences of perceived vulnerability and of being within others' control (e.g., for schedules, breaks, types of work being done) recalled from their past pink-collar positions to work through the transcripts individually and then collectively. They also delved into their own (and observations of others') feelings when frustrated with maternity leave policies, practices, and language. For instance, one author was required to "make up the time" she was granted through FMLA by serving on committees during her leave and taking on an extra class the semester following her "return" to paid work. Feeling frustrated and confused by her inability to accomplish her course preparation, the first author studied herself using time-motion techniques to figure out how much time was being spent caring for her newborn and adjusting to the changing relationships with her partner, coworkers, parents, and others. Other authors, as well as these two researchers who had maternity leaves, commented about how conversations, schedules, and time with their friends and relatives changed dramatically, with new mothers often not being able to shower until midafternoon and expressing amazement at how much they enjoyed just watching their newborns (see also Buzzanell & D'Enbeau, 2009). All the researchers brought these pink-collar work and relational sensibilities to their examination of the interview transcripts. As Charmaz (2000) notes, findings bring in authors' positionalities vis-à-vis their data such that emergent knowledge resides neither in data nor researchers but in the space between.

We also discussed the discursive lens we employed that enabled us to engage with our participants' language choices and sense making (see Alvesson & Kärreman, 2011; Fairhurst, 2007; Fairhurst & Putnam, 2014). Approaching our interview data in this way meant that we examined participants' everyday talk and reported interactions ("discourse") as well as the enduring systems of thought that are rooted in systems of power and knowledge bounded culturally and historically ("Discourses"). Thus, our interpretations of mothers employed in pink-collar positions took into consideration the U.S. context, including general expectations about maternity leaves and governmental and organizational policies, and the women's own expressions about their leave experiences. In working through the data, researchers looked for themes or general semantic patterns identifiable by repeated, similar, or forceful phrasing (see Owen, 1984) but also for particular forms of discourse. We used a constructivist constant comparison technique that involved memoing and generating themes throughout the systematic iterative, inductive, and deductive processes; this procedure was flexible enough to incorporate researchers' own experiences and interpretations (Charmaz, 2000). Collectively, the authors determined how themes constructing and describing maternity leave repeatedly surfaced within each interview and across the interviews. Recalling Smith and Turner (1995), they found that these themes were expressed metaphorically, noting that analysis of these discursive forms and their implications added rich nuance, depth, and possibilities for understanding our participants as mothers employed in pink-collar occupations taking maternity leaves. The authors wrote, revised, and/or commented on different versions by returning to the data and to interdisciplinary sources on gender, class, organizing, and power to develop a more complex account of maternity leave (Janesick, 1994; Ramazanoğlu & Holland, 2002). The authors found their discussions and results both challenged and replicated the ideological systems and logics that constitute mothering rhetorics as they surfaced the power dynamics in their participants' lives and became more aware of their own standpoints in these complex intersections of work and personal life.

Results

This research study was driven by our desire to understand how mothers employed in pink-collar occupations make sense of their maternity leave experiences. Two recurring semantic patterns, or themes, emerged repeatedly within and across the interviews: (a) maternity leave as time off [paid labor] and (b) maternity leave as (dis)ability.

These two themes operated as tensions with which the mothers struggled as their personal experiences, language, and needs seemed to compete with managerialist and organizational temporal values, logics, and procedures. For both, the women's language prioritized their paid worker role as primary. Anything that did not contribute to their time and ability to perform their worker function was perceived as deviant. Their time off paid labor was unusual in their organizational and personal experience. Although our participants enjoyed the time with their babies and felt the time was special, they also subscribed to paid labor and their worker role as primary, with temporal and economic discourses overriding those of caregiving. Moreover, they resisted but also acknowledged that the language of time and disability was needed to reassure others of their returns to work and to secure their leaves within their organizations' human resources policies and practices. Thus, they presented nuanced understandings of maternity leave that exhibited commonalities in awareness but differences based on the particularities of their lives.

We focused on two themes because these were the most consistent throughout the women's interviews and because they indicated how mothers were caught up in corporate language and seemed uneasy in their awareness that organizational and societal language disconnected from their experiences. They struggled with this awareness. As one example, Carla kept returning to her wish that she could have spent more time with her child and not go back to paid work. Yet she understood and expressed that her income was necessary.

Maternity leave as time off

All 21 participants used the phrase *time off* to define maternity leave, meaning "time off" of paid work, phrasing that connoted a deviation from a regular pattern, a disruption of the routine, a devaluation of time for caregiving, and an entrée into a different phase of these mothers' lives that was only momentary as they anticipated the return to paid work.

All participants used the phrasing *time off* alone or with embellishment about the functions of this time. Annie, a medical secretary in an insurance company, defined maternity leave as "time off from work prior to or right when you have your child." Sandy, a teletypist at a trading firm, said, "My definition would be three months off of work." Tanya, a receptionist at an animal clinic, said, "Maternity leave is when a pregnant employee stays out of work until they are recuperated." Lucinda, a customer service representative in a manufacturing firm, emphasized time but also echoed Tanya's emphasis on physical recovery: "Eight weeks to recoup from having—from having a baby." Like the others, Erin, a financial counselor in an institution of higher education, elaborated on the "time off" theme by providing functions served by this period of time:

> My definition is, uh, leave that you can take to recuperate from—to obviously have a baby or an adoption situation. Just that time that is needed for every person who is having a child, or having—or having a child in their life, you know, to be away from work and concentrate on that, and to form a bond with that.

Our participants, then, perceived this time off paid work primarily as a break in their usual paid labor routines. In this main meaning, the women indicated they understood their roles in society. They may now be mothers, but their time primarily has been and will be spent in the labor force. The disruptive "off" in time off paid work meant that they were off the clock (on break in chronological time), off the temporal and linear rhythm of career and labor patterns (Buzzanell & Goldzwig, 1991; Buzzanell & Lucas, 2006; see also Gilbert & von Wallmenich, 2014), and off of the most important aspect of their lives—the aspect that regulates their time throughout their life course, namely, paid work. Their language and conceptualization of time implied devaluation of time for caregiving and for activities not associated with money.

That paid work was prioritized as most important to these women was embedded in the language of "time off" but also in our participants' reported experiences. Some participants' wording foregrounded tensions in time off, highlighting societal prioritization of workers' time as engagement in paid labor and the organizing function of work in everyday life. Without employment, some women expressed difficulty in knowing what to do with themselves. For instance, Jessica said she was confused about what to do when she first took her leave: "[T]he first day I was off on my leave, like, I didn't know what to do with myself." Although not all expressed confusion, other participants did describe how they maintained their employment connections during their maternity leaves by, for example, returning to their offices to introduce their newborns to their coworkers and bosses, thus linking their personal and work lives and their familial and employment relationships. Their office visits also may have served to reassure themselves and others that their workplace relationships were important to them and that they intended to maintain that continuity in their lives despite time off paid work.

Furthermore, participants' definitions evoked discourses of commodification that may have fed into (legal and organizational) justifications for maintaining leaves in the United States as unpaid. There were two reasons for this justification: value is linked to exchange; and the deeply embedded metaphor of "time is money." First, participants perceived that others thought maternity leave was a waste insofar as they were not engaged in useful work, that is, work that has exchange value if viewed from a Marxist perspective (see Weedon, 1999). For example, Sandy reported that while her supervisors and coworkers were "very nice" and supportive throughout her pregnancy, leave, and return to paid work, she perceived their attitude about her return as being "you had your baby, now it's time to get back to work." Now that their leaves were over, they should refocus on work (see Gilbert & von Wallmenich, 2014). Now that they had their babies—apparently considered a singular event with temporary workplace repercussions rather than a whole life change and new set of role obligations and long-term consequences—they should reorient or "get back" to their work, where time is a proxy for performance and their presence or face time signaled their commitment to their work role (Bailyn, 1993; Buzzanell, 2014). Moreover, as they get back to work, their only valued identity as worker is reinscribed into their time and relationships, failing to admit the plurality of identities that operates over the life course and in particular moments (Bidart, 2014).

Second, the "time is money" conceptual metaphor is predominant in Western thinking and guides or justifies much of human behavior in this context (Lakoff & Johnson, 1980). *All* of our participants said that they had to return to paid work for financial reasons, even when *all* said that they would have liked to stay home longer with their newborns. Rita said that she returned to the workplace "because we were putting an addition on to our house to accommodate the family [laughs] and we needed the money." Janice also laughed when she was asked why she returned to paid employment: "We needed the money at the time [laughs]. And it was probably the only reason." Rose laughed when she was asked to respond to her reason for returning to her place of employment after her maternity leave:

> Interviewer: Why did you return to work?
>   Rose: Why? Ah, I ask myself that question. [Laughs]
> Interviewer: [Laughs]
>   Rose: Basically because I—I really enjoyed my job, and for the money.
>   Also for the insurance benefits.

Rose's laughter as well as the laughter of other mothers in our study highlighted women's awareness of the incongruity that they all prioritized work over caregiving, and they all said that they needed to return to work because of financial reasons and material comforts. They struggled to express what they valued in terms or language that would make sense to others.

April said that she knew "all along" that she would return to paid work: "We needed the money ... I thought that the majority of women that had children went back to work, so it was just a natural thing to think that I would go back to work." Susan returned to work "because we needed the money ... we had gotten a new house, so we needed to make the mortgage payments." Thus, for economic reasons, commodification, and the normal or natural thing for a woman to do, these mothers returned to paid employment.

However, other mothers noted their ambivalence, guilt, and regret—not as much about returning to paid work but about not spending the time with their children. When asked why she returned to paid work, Carla replied simply, "I returned for financial reasons." But at other times during her interview, she noted, "There's always these remote guilt feelings where you wish you didn't have to do it, but it's necessary," and talked about the first weeks being "very hard." Kelly replied that she "had to," thus giving her job agency in the sense that she did not question her return to paid work or its timing: "because my job required me to come back in six weeks" and she needed the job. As Chris said, "I really didn't want to [return], because I wanted to stay with my baby. But, you know, I had to financially." Claire had "a very difficult time going back to work, even though it was only part time. Because I had in my mind that I would be home full time with the—with the baby." Jessica expressed guilt about leaving her baby but justified her choice because her job provided tuition reimbursement that would later lead to a college degree and a better job: "I felt guilty thinking, am I gonna make a choice between [my son] and school?"

In short, for all of our participants, the primacy of paid labor in life and the economic decision premise phrased as commonsensical (e.g., at being asked why she returned to paid work, Grace laughed and remarked, "I needed the money"), necessary (e.g., Chris noted, "I had to"), and "natural" with the employer and workplace policy being the force orienting the women's tacit agreement (e.g., Kelly's phrase was, "my job required") encouraged mothers' return to paid labor after their maternity leaves. Their agency to do otherwise was constrained by financial realities (e.g., pink-collar workers' lower pay in comparison to white- and blue-collar workers; see Women's International Network, 2003) but also seemed to have been linked to U.S. societal beliefs that paid (i.e., linear or clock) time has more value than other kinds of time, particularly time for caring activities (i.e., time for physical healing, relational work, and so on, that indicate life-cycle and life-event time orientations; see Ancona, 2001; Gallos, 1989; Gilbert & von Wallmenich, 2014; Wood, 1994) in contrast to other countries that have extensive leaves. Indeed, all participants said that they would like to have had maternity leave extensions. All shared feelings of being "excited" and "happy" about their new mother status which also made our participants so "sad," "upset," "depressed," and "not ready" to return to paid work. As Lora said, and Janice echoed during her own interview, "It [returning to paid work] was horrible. It was one of the worst times of my entire life."

Extending the "time is money" metaphorical line of thinking sustains the unpaid nature of maternity leaves in the United States. Because pregnancy has no immediate exchange value, maternity leaves could justifiably be unpaid (and leaves continue to be unpaid even under 2012 FMLA guidelines). Almost two-thirds of our participants reported being unpaid or only partially paid during their maternity leaves. For those who received additional time off, this extra time was usually unpaid. That caregiving times—individual bodily rhythms, reproductive rhythms, relational development and continuity rhythms—all have their own value at particular moments and throughout the life course (see Bidart, 2014) is evident in the tensions within mothers' unfulfilled desires for more time with their infants that coexist with the temporal and economic discourses prioritizing paid labor. Moreover, the mothers' language echoed Gilbert and von Wallmenich's (2014) nuanced discussion extending Hall's monochronic or M-time into language invoking linear, task-oriented, scheduled, focused, and efficient time; and polychromic or P-time invoking temporal fluidity, relational attention, and changing demands associated with motherhood. As Gilbert and von Wallmenich noted (2014), their participants often had difficulty expressing not only the value of relational time but also what they did when not engaged in paid work activities. They reverted to prioritization of employment time while expressing their longings for extended leaves and more prolonged bonding with their infants.

For instance, similar to Gilbert and von Wallmenich's (2014) participants, Carla tried throughout her interview to let her interviewer know how much she both appreciated her time off of paid work but also the brief time in which she could focus on her baby. Carla noted that maternity leave is first and foremost "a time period when you are out of your [paid] work area" and yet it also is relational and caregiving time:

> It is a time period when, when you are out of your work area [pause] to whether it be before or after to have to have some time to yourself and take care of your health during the—those— uh, last critical moments due to the uncomfort or the receiving of a child when you're home with a child, to dedicate that time to that child, welcoming to the world and giving that child the affection, and getting to know you, giving them the proper care and attention they need during those critical days which are when they're born.

Carla's ambivalence ran throughout her interview and remained bound up linguistically and practically with time. She wished that she could have some flexibility in her employment hours so that she could be with her child at critical times, and yet she realized that this was not possible, namely, that her employment hours were "mandatory" (whereas her implication was that her caregiving hours were not perceived by others as mandatory). Specifically, she remarked at another point in her interview:

> You are missing out on all those things that, you know—it's something that you want to be there, yet you can't be there. And, ah, at that time we didn't have flexible hours, so I couldn't say "I'll start early" or "I'll start later." It was that, you know, these were mandatory hours— were not flexible.

When asked during the final minutes of her interview if there was anything else that might be important to know for interpreting her remarks, Carla paused then added:

> When they [your children] are sick, and you take the next day with them, or you wish you had more time to spend with them, because it's something that is hard—to leave a sick child behind, because your—your concentration even throughout the day is on that child. It just doesn't seem fair that your mind is on both places, on your job and thinking about that child, thinking constantly that you wish you were there for them.

Janice noted that things change after a baby is born:

> Before the baby was born, I really was not concerned that I was returning to work. I thought that I wouldn't mind a bit. [laughter] ... That changed after the baby was born .... I didn't realize how it would affect me to have to leave the little baby.

Thus, mothers perceived that maternity leave and returns to paid labor were filled with ambivalences and contradictions, prompting them to question their priorities and note changes in their relationships and time.

Maternity leave as (dis)ability

Almost three-quarters (71%) of our participants described their maternity leaves as sick leave, medical leave, or disability. *Disability* was not a term they preferred to use for their experiences but language that they appropriated to explain how they assumed their companies were able to position maternity within benefits packages and sometimes provide pay. They perceived a contradiction between maternity as a normal process for women and the company's requirement that maternity be abnormal from a legal and business or managerialist perspective. Moreover, in contrast to our participants' expressed feelings that maternity leave was a special point in their lives to be able to spend time with their infants, the vast majority of our participants said that they and/or others either referred to maternity leave as "a sick leave" or "medical leave" and pregnancy as "a disability," or treated them as though they were sick and different from their normal selves. Our participants perceived this labeling as detrimental to their self-images as capable workers. Moreover, they recognized that their organizations did not grant them their "time off" because it was a nice thing to do or a joyous occasion. Rather, as Polly stated, maternity leave is a requirement: "a leave that's required because of pregnancy." Carla noted that "it was like medical leave, and they paid like eighty, eighty-five percent of my check."

Furthermore, another two women remarked about the nonroutine nature of maternity leave and their understanding that pregnancy and maternity leaves just did not fit into the corporate world. Donna noted that she told everyone at her place of employment about her pregnancy but, in the course of this retelling, she specified the conditions under which she would hide her pregnancy:

> And the environment I was in was—it was nothing that I would want to hide, that I had a promotion coming up or I was interviewing for a job or anything. I guess if that were the case, I would have thought—but I was in the same job, and I was coming back to the same job, and I knew it wasn't going to influence anything, ah, I—you know. So I didn't have any reason not to tell all.

Lora seemed to indicate there was no room to negotiate maternity leave because mothers' pregnancies and leaves did not add value to organizing processes and outcomes: "It was something that didn't benefit the company, and we all knew that, uh, but you knew what the rules were at the time and had to accept them if you became pregnant."

Although Donna and Lora did not explicitly label their leaves as disability, medical, or sick leaves, they did comment on the abnormal or deviant nature of pregnancy in the workplace and of maternity leave. However, those whose disability/medical/sick leave policies or practices paid for their time off work were "grateful" for the benefits while also uncomfortable and struggling with the benefits that accompanied the less than ideal (worker) image that such phrasing connoted.

As an instance of how the mothers struggled against anything that diverted attention from their good or ideal worker status, Chris insisted that she was well, meaning that she "could have still worked" even after she went into early labor and her doctor "was concerned because I was toxemic, [during] which you swell up and everything, and I was just borderline. It wasn't that I couldn't walk or touch my back. I could still get up and everything." When asked about her major concerns during maternity leave, Juliet commented that she did not want her pregnancy to be an issue, that is, to "interfere with my job duties and the performance of my job." She said, "I didn't want people saying behind my back … 'if she wasn't pregnant she'd be doing it right now.'" These comments not only speak to mothers' hard-earned desires to be perceived as competent workers but also to the status of maternity leaves in the United States. Although the FMLA offers 12 weeks of unpaid leave under certain employer conditions (for concise current overview, see Guendelman et al., 2014; Jorgensen & Appelbaum, 2014), state temporary benefits, such as California's State Disability Insurance (SDI), provide paid leaves but not job protection. Thus, our participants' interests in retaining their good worker images throughout their pregnancies were needed not only to retain the status and merit of their work but also to protect their jobs. Their fears are not unfounded, as Fox and Quinn (2015) found that pregnant workers often are stigmatized in the workplace.

Like others, Jessica aligned the maternity–disability connection with corporate logics to make sense of the term: "I guess from, like, the personnel department standpoint and maybe even benefits department,… um, I found it kind of funny that, um, maternity was considered a disability." Much like Gilbert and von Wallmenich's (2014) research participants, who found conventional language describing the different employment–relational rhythms of their lives to be inadequate, our participants found the corporate language of disability to be out of sync with their lived experience of mothering and even perplexing because they did not perceive themselves as disabled. Simultaneously, however, they appreciated how the language could be used for their benefit. Thus, they operated within the space of knowing that the language and procedures of disability were required for necessary outcomes (linear, cause-effect thinking and instrumental rationalities; see Buzzanell & Goldzwig, 1991) and of struggling to grasp how something so natural and normal for many women could become so convoluted. Our participants, like Grace and Janice, even noted that there were somewhat different circumstances whereby some mothers received "extended" rather than "standard" time off depending on their medical conditions: "Some people had taken an extended time off; that was granted without pay other than just the standard time off."

For instance, our participants remarked that they had to bring in proof of pregnancies and sign documents about being pregnant; other participants described elaborate procedures for maternity leave. Recalling the leave procedures she underwent, Claire remarked, "They gave me the form; you had to sign it and state why you were leaving, if it was a medical leave. It was the same kind of form for a maternity as it was for a medical leave." She noted that signing these papers "terminate[d] my position" (meaning that she would not be engaged in paid work even temporarily after childbirth), and that she needed to state why she was leaving and undergo an exit interview. Claire appreciated the irony: "There was an initial form to fill out for your maternity leave stating why you were leaving even though you were not going to not come back."

Whereas some participants described others' discourse of maternity leave as disability to be odd, they expressed full awareness of its necessary discursive positioning in benefits packages. Our participants perceived discourses of disease and disability as constituting attempts by their companies to locate ways using "legitimate" language to create leaves. In this respect, they perceived their organizations as agents struggling to uphold the logics and policies of justice or equality for all members and those of care and difference for members requiring accommodations for particular times in their lives (see Liu & Buzzanell, 2004) without considering the interdependencies of justice/equality and care/difference (Scott, 1998).

Our participants were grateful that organizations provided maternity leaves. April observed, "I got disability pay, for part of the time." As she explains, "I had a tailbone injury during birth [for her first child], so it was hard to sit at my computer. So they gave me an extra two weeks" with pay, whereas her other four- to six-week leave periods after the births of this child and her other children were unpaid. April remarked that a friend of hers was "lucky" because the friend's company labeled maternity leave as disability, meaning that her friend had six weeks of paid leave. In general, then, participants accepted—and some even wished for—language of disability so that they could have at least partially paid maternity leaves (i.e., they wanted a "real policy," as Juliet put it) although as Sandy noted, her first maternity leave experience was more flexible than her policy-based second leave.

The fact that they considered the language to be somewhat odd meant that they were aware to some extent that maternity was marginalized in or different from regular organizational policies (see Peterson & Albrecht, 1999) and that maternity as disability metaphorically positioned them as sick, not normal, and unable to work (see Coopman, 2003). They made sense of the language by calling on the logic of personnel or corporate benefits, but even there the fit was uneasy because maternity (leave) as disability (leave) failed to displace the current incompatibility of pregnancy and the (male) workplace (see Martin, 1990), failed to bridge sameness–difference arguments (see Tavris, 1992; see also Ashcraft, 2014), and even failed to correspond with "disability" as defined in disability laws (see the Americans with Disabilities Act [ADA], Equal Employment Opportunity Commission [EEOC], 2000: http://www.dol.gov/dol/topic/disability/ada.htm).

Varied groups have attempted to resolve this uneasy fit. While liberal feminists stress pregnant women's capabilities for work, emphasizing that these women are like everyone else (i.e., male workers), these equality or sameness arguments position pregnant women as men with temporarily disabled bodies: "According to equal-rights advocates, pregnancy should be treated like any disability that might cause workers of either sex to lose a few days' or a few months' work" (Tavris, 1992, p. 117). The argument, while effective in passing legislation (e.g., the Pregnancy Discrimination Act [PDA]; see EEOC, 2016), causes discontent because other feminists focus on difference and find it "ridiculous, demeaning, and antiwoman to ignore the special condition of pregnancy" when forming laws and policies (Tavris, 1992, p. 118). Furthermore, the ADA has denied disability status for pregnancy (see EEOC, 2000). Pregnancy is one of a number of "serious health conditions" but not an ADA disability, because "the condition is not an impairment" (EEOC, 2000). It is no wonder that our participants found the wording of maternity as disability both detrimental and helpful. With President Barack Obama's call to revisit and revise family leave to assist U.S. families in managing work and family needs (see Council on Women and Girls, 2014; Eilperin & Zezima, 2014), perhaps language can be crafted to lessen the (dis)ability tensions and to achieve understandings that disability and ability as well as work and family are necessary contrasts that enrich each other rather than act as antithetical terms, that they intersect differently based on context and perpetuate gendered workplaces (Scott, 1998). Even so, as Gilbert and von Wallmenich (2014) note, the problems are rooted deeply in language itself and the value judgments about women's relational experiences. Even in the language of disability the temporal order of contemporary life emerged: time spent in the activities of caregiving and mothering is valued so little in comparison to employment that one would need to be "disabled" to even consider not engaging in paid work, thus forfeiting ideal worker status. Williams (2000) suggests "nongendered rhetorics of community," such as selflessness decoupled from motherhood and promoted in pursuit of common good, can lessen tendencies to dichotomize particular language and associated values. Similarly, language that promotes maternity leaves—particularly paid leaves—as benefiting all by prioritizing caregiving and well-being in families and at places of employment as part of "sustainable lifestyles" might offer a different vision (see Buzzanell, 2012; Gilbert & von Wallmenich, 2014).

Discussion

Our analyses display how mothers employed in pink-collar occupations struggle with the primacy of paid life along with the ideal worker body as indicated by their awareness of, ambivalence about, and contestation of maternity leave as time off paid work processed through organizational procedures that classified their leaves as disability/medical/sick, thus affording the women with pay. As such, our analyses explore maternity leaves within tensional discursive space that allows researchers and caregivers to understand better how the lives of mothers employed in pink-collar occupations are both constrained and enabled by organizations. How mothers assert their constrained agency provides insight into how motherhood, gender, and communication are being shaped rhetorically.

These findings hint at a response to Ashcraft's (1999) question: "What would organizing —specifically, maternity leave—crafted around women's experiences and meanings look like?" (p. 276). In this discussion we sort through what maternity leave might look like if considered through the standpoints of mothers employed in pink-collar occupations. As Tavris (1992) points out, most laws, organizational policies, and practices associated with pregnancy and maternity leave fail to consider the lives of women in low paid and less prestigious occupations. In our study, we wanted to know not only what maternity leave would look like from the standpoints of mothers working in pink-collar occupations but also what kinds of theoretical and pragmatic implications could be drawn from such locally situated knowledge.

We found that time, caregiving, and able-bodiedness (as mothers and as competent workers) were issues fraught with contradiction and entangled with knowledge that corporate language could undermine women while also being used for the workers' benefit. Indeed, our participants expressed gratitude for the time, even if unpaid, that they were able to take after the births of their children, and also recognized that the human resources language of disability, although far from their own embodied experiences and desired ideal worker status, was necessary to secure their maternity leaves. They also realized that having policies on the books was insufficient to provide the kinds of leaves that they wanted. Indeed, one of our participants, Sandy, made explicit reference to the FMLA when describing the differences in her two maternity leaves, noting that, for her first:

> You took into consideration how many years you were there. After ten years it was for every week you were there, you received a week off. Then they changed the policy when the new law went into effect … [restricting her leave to] twelve weeks' maternity family leave with the second pregnancy. [Later in the interview] First pregnancy, [my company was] very flexible. Second pregnancy, um, I had a supervisor who didn't have children. It was a little bit harder but, um [pause], it didn't matter because it was in the rules.

Thus their discourses embedded the constrained agency and perceived tensions, ironies, and contradictions found throughout mothering rhetorics, particularly as reproduced in organizational contexts. They appreciated how rules were implemented to provide leaves within systems that needed loopholes like disability to equalize legally women's and men's experiences. Past research on pink-collar and working-class women documents the structural restrictions, subordinate positioning within gendered occupational relations, and economic factors that dominate their lives (e.g., Holmer-Nadesan, 1996; Pringle, 1989a, 1989b) and ways in which they locate discursive spaces for agency, collegiality, and resistance to others' conceptualizations of them (e.g., Bell & Forbes, 1994; Holmer-Nadesan, 1996; Kovicak, 2001; Sotirin, 2000; Sotirin & Gottfried, 1999). As one of our reviewers put it, our participants gave voice to these struggles "by simultaneously resisting language which frames childbirth and infant care as a disability and time as productivity/earning, and accepting leaves which ultimately undermine their professional competence."

Limitations

First, the group of women interviewed for this study numbered only 21, was primarily White, and lived in the Midwestern region of the United States. Many of these mothers worked for organizations that had developed maternity leave policies mirroring provisions in the FMLA, offering unpaid leaves, but did not need to pursue legal compliance with FMLA because of company size. Indeed, only 20% of new mothers and 50% of all mothers in the United States are covered by the FMLA (Guendelman et al., 2014). As Ybarra and Hill (2014) note, low-income working women in the United States typically are ineligible for maternity leave policies. Even when states such as California offer paid pregnancy and maternity leaves through state disability insurance (SDI), jobs are not protected. Examining maternity as well as other forms of family leave in their analysis of the Department of Labor's 2012 FMLA Survey, Jorgensen and Applebaum (2014) report:

> Surprisingly, fully 21.0 percent of FMLA-eligible employees reported that they thought they might lose their job as the main reason for not taking leave, even though the FMLA gives eligible employees the right to job-protected leave.... This suggests that some eligible employees are not knowledgeable about the protections provided under the FMLA, and/or some covered employers do not comply with the law. (p. 3)

Indeed, only half to three-quarters of private-sector organizations falling within the FMLA actually comply with guidelines (Armenia, Gerstel, & Wing, 2014). In sum, whether paid or unpaid, U.S. Census Bureau reports indicate that most mothers return to paid labor within three months of giving birth (Laughlin, 2011).

Second, the women's accounts were retrospective. While reflecting how they made sense of their experiences over time, the interviews also lacked the moment-by-moment struggles that methods such as participant observation during maternity leaves and multiple interviews over the course of their pregnancies and leaves could have produced. Finally, we had neither others' perceptions and insights into maternity leave processes and practices at the participants' organizations nor copies of company policies or benefits packages. Because we were interested in the ways our mothers made sense of practices in their workplaces, we asked only for their perceptions. As a result, we did not analyze the role our participants perceived that their children's fathers played in their maternity leaves and return to paid work.

Theoretical and pragmatic implications

As Trethewey (1999) pointed out, organizational discourses have very real consequences for women, including women's perceptions of their embodied selves. Calling pregnancy or motherhood "a professional stumbling block," with mothers arguing that it is those without children who perpetuate this thinking, Trethewey highlighted the personal and organizational toll that language incommensurate with women's experiences can have. Furthermore, Trethewey (2000) traced possibilities for resistance amid concertive control (i.e., where women would identify with and embody organizational decision premises) and argued that such possibilities lie in autonomous organizational agents. For professional women, controls are aligned with advancement. For our participants in pink-collar occupations, discourses about time and ability enabled and constrained: Time off work enabled them to take a leave yet these leaves were bound by regulations, with language of disability and medical leave rendering them as imperfect objects subject to disciplinary actions. The first author noted that she was explicitly told not to come to her place of employment while on maternity (disability) leave because the policy meant that she was physically unable to work, which defied her own sense of bodily well-being. Thus women's bodies as sites of struggle deserve further attention in research on the workplace.

Moreover, a full metaphorical analysis might reveal additional ways in which awareness and change could take place for women's benefit. To understand what different women's lives are like as well as how change can be made to enhance their own and others' lives, researchers and practitioners might delve more fully into the metaphorical "ground," underlying assumptions and politicized dynamics, and discursive pathways for transformation that are deeply embedded in language (see Buzzanell, 2004; Gilbert & von Wallmenich, 2014; Meisenbach, Remke, Buzzanell, & Liu, 2008; Scott, 1998; Smith & Turner, 1995). For instance, our analysis indicated that our participants had few illusions about workers' place in organizations. They strategically enacted organizational priorities and logics by expressing their prioritization of paid labor and by adhering to the rules to secure what they needed. However, they also defied others' implications that they were not fully competent while pregnant. They might have worked for financial reasons, but they did not entangle paid labor with self-fulfillment, personal worth, or calling, thus creating avenues of self-empowerment to distance themselves from their employers and the work itself when they were not being paid for their labor, unlike professional women and men. Delving further into figure-ground configurations and the ways attention to multiple readings that can usurp binaries (see Scott, 1998; Smith & Turner, 1995), we use iterative processes to challenge notions of maternity and maternity leave in organizational life and society as a whole. In these ways we illuminate how mothering rhetorics are produced and reproduced through tensions of contestation and complicity in ideologically and materially charged spaces.

Specifically, maternity/maternity leave (figure) is understood in terms of time off paid labor (ground) and disability (ground). In combination, these metaphors affirm the primacy of paid work, ideal worker, and masculine organizing in which members are passive and difference is disruptive, deviant, and acknowledged only when useful for achievement of organizational goals. Yet one possible initial shift in the ground might make maternity/maternity leave (figure) understood in terms of time for caregiving (ground) and in terms of health and well-being (ground), thus prioritizing other life aspects as our participants struggled to do (see Smith & Turner, 1995). In these shifts, we do not simply replace the original ground with its opposites but resist closure and binaries, thus using the mutability of organization and intersections of communication, organizing, and structure, so that time and ability can be enlarged, restructured, and refocused on their (and organizations') constitutive rather than sedimented natures. Thus, maternity and maternity leave can operate as sites for reprioritized personal life, regeneration, and relationships rather than marginalizing individual and relational interests, particularly those of childbearing and adopting women (and men). By examining the fissures in the dominant time and ability metaphors created by our mothers employed in pink-collar occupations, we find space to challenge denial of payment for leaves and of policies supporting difference that can benefit workers and organizations.

Furthermore, in the case of mothers working in pink-collar occupations, standpoint theory requires that researchers advance knowledge grounded in "particular, culturally-specific, women's experiences, lives, or activities (or 'labor')," by uncovering the conceptual practices through which dominant institutions exploit women (Harding, 2004, p. 29; see also Hennessy, 1993). For women in pink-collar occupations, the temporal and embodied language choices and spaces of action function as deeply embedded cultural formations that override desires to pursue caregiving rather than paid employment. They stated that they worked for financial reasons—money and what that money can buy—and were grateful for time off paid work. Their interviews contained no mention of meaningfulness of work, personal fulfillment through employment, desires to return to paid positions as soon as possible, or career aspirations often noted in the studies of managerial and professional women cited earlier. Far from powerless within the bureaucratic control, these mothers employed in pink-collar occupations explored and exploited contradictions within their own and bureaucratic phrasing. For example, they used rules and procedures they deemed helpful, even while they appreciated the incongruity of corporate logics, such as "disability" discourses. As such, their discourse exhibited how productive ways of utilizing and managing contradiction and tensions in everyday life can be enacted (e.g., Ashcraft & Trethewey, 2004). An implication of our feminist standpoint analysis, then, is that discursive analyses centering on contradiction might help explain how social structures of society and organizing work to advocate change (see Buzzanell, 1994). Additional studies on maternity leaves from the standpoints of other groups may display ways that diverse women, particularly those in different occupations and with different perceived employment and career opportunities, construct meanings about leaves and negotiate, or fail to negotiate, their own needs and desires.

Specifically, with current academic and industry emphases on well-being and work-life "balance," findings indicate increasing patterns among U.S. working mothers for early return to work after childbirth, depending on access to and duration of employer-offered maternity leaves (Guendelman et al., 2014). Reasons for early return to work are not only unpaid leave and lack of job protection but also because pregnant workers experience stigmatization in the workplace—experiences that carry over into job satisfaction, psychological well-being, and turnover intentions (Fox & Quinn, 2015). Findings such as these along with the implications of time and (dis)ability discourses could be used to craft persuasive arguments to push agendas around women's well-being further into political adoption. However, as Gilbert and von Wallmenich (2014) note, the language would need to change, as would the inherent value judgments, meaning that a wholesale reprioritization of relational attention and caregiving in general and of mothering rhetorics in particular would need to take place.

Conclusion

In closing, most maternity leave scholarship in communication studies focuses on managerial or professional women. In asking what maternity leave might look like if considered through the standpoints of mothers employed in pink-collar occupations, we orient around organizational members who labor for relatively low pay and in service to or support of clients or other members. By capturing their perceptions of their workplace pregnancies and maternity leaves, our standpoint analysis of 21 women in pink-collar occupations displays how these mothers adhere to and challenge maternity leave discourses by positioning their leaves as time off and (dis)ability. In their (re)production and contestation of contemporary mothering rhetorics, they both acknowledge the advantages of and resist discourses of time and (dis)ability by constructing complicated, contradictory, and ironic knowledge such that language both secures their leaves and revokes their images as competent workers. By using standpoint analyses, changes in organizational policy and workplace practices for mothers working in pink-collar occupations can be made based on common knowledge and differences in local-specific experiences.

Funding

The first author expresses her gratitude to the Velux Foundation and the Copenhagen Business School for her Research Fellow funding during spring–summer 2014 that contributed greatly to her efforts to pursue this work.

Notes

1. Most of this research focuses on women executives' and professionals' career concerns (e.g., Ashcraft, 1999; Buzzanell et al., 2005; Gatrell, 2013; Martin, 1990; Turner & Norwood, 2013, 2014) or on individuals' organizational commitment, job satisfaction, and intent to return to the same employers after maternity leaves (e.g., Fox & Quinn, 2015).
2. To contrast these possible differences, Williams (2000) provides an example of maternity leave consequences for middle-class mothers: "'Since I came back from maternity leave, I get the work of a paralegal,' protested one Boston lawyer. 'I want to say, look, I had a baby, not a lobotomy'" (p. 69). The female attorney being quoted did suffer disadvantages, but she still had a job. A pink-collar worker might aspire to the paralegal work that the attorney is denigrating. A woman with less transferable job skills, formal education, and income to secure representation (if necessary) upon returning to paid work after a maternity leave might incur more severe penalties.

References

Acker, J. (1990). Hierarchies, jobs, bodies: A theory of gendered organizations. *Gender and Society, 4,* 139–158.

Acker, J. (2006). Inequality regimes: Gender, class, and race in organizations. *Gender and Society, 20,* 441–464.

Allen, B. J. (2000). "Learning the ropes": A Black feminist standpoint analysis. In P. M. Buzzanell (Ed.), *Rethinking organizational and managerial communication from feminist perspectives* (pp. 177–208). Thousand Oaks, CA: Sage.

Allen, B. J. (2011). *Difference matters: Communicating social identity* (2nd ed.). Long Grove, IL: Waveland.

Alvesson, M., & Kärreman, D. (2011). Organizational discourse analysis—Well done or too rare? A reply to our critics. *Human Relations, 64,* 1193–1202.

Ancona, D. G. (2001). Taking time to integrate temporal research. *Academy of Management Review, 26*, 512–529.

Armenia, A., Gerstel, N., & Wing, C. (2014). Workplace compliance with the law: The case of the Family and Medical Leave Act. *Work and Occupations, 41*, 277–304.

Ashcraft, K. (1999). Managing maternity leave: A qualitative analysis of temporary executive succession. *Administrative Science Quarterly, 44*, 240–280.

Ashcraft, K. (2000). Empowering "professional" relationships: Organizational communication meets feminist practice. *Management Communication Quarterly, 13*, 347–392.

Ashcraft, K. (2014). Feminist theory. In L. Putnam & D. Mumby (Eds.), *The Sage handbook of organizational communication* (3rd ed., pp. 127–150). London, UK: Sage.

Ashcraft, K., & Trethewey, A. (2004). Developing tension: An agenda for applied research on the organization of irrationality. *Journal of Applied Communication Research, 32*, 171–181.

Bailyn, L. (1993). *Breaking the mold: Women, men, and time in the new corporate world.* New York, NY: The Free Press.

Bell, E. L., & Forbes, L. C. (1994). Office folklore in the academic paperwork empire: The interstitial space of gendered (con)texts. *Text and Performance Quarterly, 14*, 181–196.

Bidart, C. (2014). What does time imply? The contribution of longitudinal methods to the analysis of the life course. *Time and Society, 22*, 254–273.

Bullis, C., & Stout, K. (2000). Organizational socialization: A feminist standpoint approach. In P. M. Buzzanell (Ed.), *Rethinking organizational and managerial communication from feminist perspectives* (pp. 47–75). Thousand Oaks, CA: Sage.

Buzzanell, P. M. (1994). Gaining a voice: Feminist organizational communication theorizing. *Management Communication Quarterly, 7*, 339–383.

Buzzanell, P. M. (2000). The promise and practice of the new career and social contract. In P. M. Buzzanell (Ed.), *Rethinking organizational and managerial communication from feminist perspectives* (pp. 209–235). Thousand Oaks, CA: Sage.

Buzzanell, P. M. (2004). Metaphor in the classroom: Reframing traditional and alternative uses of language for feminist transformation. In P. M. Buzzanell, H. Sterk, & L. H. Turner (Eds.), *Gender in applied communication contexts* (pp. 179–193). Thousand Oaks, CA: Sage.

Buzzanell, P. M. (2012). How can we sustain commitments to the work and personal aspects of our lives? In A. Goodboy & K. Shultz (Eds.), *Introduction to communication studies: Translating communication scholarship into meaningful practice* (pp. 317–323). Dubuque, IA: Kendall-Hunt.

Buzzanell, P. M. (2014). Work and family communication. In L. H. Turner & R. West (Eds.), *The Sage handbook of family communication* (pp. 320–336). Thousand Oaks, CA: Sage.

Buzzanell, P. M. (2015). Standpoint theory. In J. Bennett (Ed.), *The Sage encyclopedia of intercultural competence* (pp. 771–774). Thousand Oaks, CA: Sage.

Buzzanell, P. M., & D'Enbeau, S. (2009). Stories of caregiving: Intersections of academic research and women's everyday experiences. *Qualitative Inquiry, 15*, 1199–1224.

Buzzanell, P. M., & Ellingson, L. (2005). Contesting narratives of workplace maternity. In L. Harter, P. Japp, & C. Beck (Eds.), *Narratives, health, and healing: Communication theory, research, and practice* (pp. 277–294). Hillsdale, NJ: Erlbaum.

Buzzanell, P. M., & Goldzwig, S. (1991). Linear and nonlinear career models: Metaphors, paradigms, and ideologies. *Management Communication Quarterly, 4*, 466–505.

Buzzanell, P. M., & Lucas, K. (2006). Gendered stories of career: Unfolding discourses of time, space, and identity. In B. J. Dow & J. T. Wood (Eds.), *The Sage handbook of gender and communication* (pp. 161–178). Thousand Oaks, CA: Sage.

Buzzanell, P. M., Meisenbach, R., Remke, R., Bowers, V., Liu, M., & Conn, C. (2005). The good *working* mother: Managerial women's sensemaking and feelings about work-family issues. *Communication Studies, 56*, 261–285.

Charmaz, K. (2000). Grounded theory: Objectivist and constructivist methods. In N. K. Denzin & Y. S. Lincoln (Eds.), *Handbook of qualitative research* (2nd ed., pp. 509–535). Thousand Oaks, CA: Sage.

Cheney, G., Zorn, T. E., Planalp, S., & Lair, D. J. (2008). Meaningful work and personal/social well-being: Organizational communication engages the meanings of work. In C. S. Beck (Ed.), *Communication yearbook 32* (pp. 137–186). New York, NY: Routledge.

Collins, P. H. (2000). *Black feminist thought: Knowledge, consciousness, and the politics of empowerment* (2nd ed.). New York, NY: Routledge.

Coopman, S. J. (2003). Communicating disability: Metaphors of oppression, metaphors of empowerment. In P. J. Kalbfleisch (Ed.), *Communication yearbook 27* (pp. 337–394). Mahwah, NJ: LEA.

Council on Women & Girls. (2014). Obama administration initiatives fact sheet. Retrieved from http://www.whitehouse.gov/administration/eop/cwg/work-flex-kit/get-started/factsheet

Dougherty, D. S. (2011). *The reluctant farmer: An exploration of work, social class, and the production of food.* Leicester, UK: Troubador.

Eilperin, J., & Zezima, K. (2014, June 23). Obama uses personal experience to advocate for family leave, workplace flexibility. *Washington Post.* Retrieved from http://www.washingtonpost.com/politics/obama-uses-personal-experience-to-advocate-for-family-leave-workplace-flexibility/2014/06/23/b98b3410-faf0-11e3-b1f4-8e77c632c07b_story.html

Equal Employment Opportunity Commission. (2000). The Family and Medical Leave Act, the Americans with Disabilities Act, and Title VII of the Civil Rights Act of 1964. Retrieved from http://www.eeoc.gov/policy/docs/fmlaada.html

Equal Employment Opportunity Commission. (2016). The Pregnancy Discrimination Act of 1978. Retrieved from http://www.eeoc.gov/eeoc/publications/fs-ada.cfm

Fairhurst, G. (2007). *Discursive leadership: In conversation with leadership psychology.* Thousand Oaks, CA: Sage.

Fairhurst, G., & Putnam, L. (2014). Organizational discourse analysis. In L. Putnam & D. Mumby (Eds.), *The Sage handbook of organizational communication* (3rd ed., pp. 271–295). London, UK: Sage.

Family Medical Leave Act, 5 U.S.C. § 630 (1993).

Finnegan, A. (2011, August 26). Everyone but U.S.: The state of maternity leave. *Working Mother.* Retrieved from http://www.workingmother.com/best-companies/everyone-us-state-maternity-leave

Fox, A., & Quinn, D. (2015). Pregnant women at work: The role of stigma in predicting women's intended exit from the workforce. *Psychology of Women Quarterly, 39,* 226–242.

Francis, D. (2012, September 10). The pink-collar job boom: Traditionally female jobs are booming and attracting men. *U.S. News & World Report.* Retrieved from http://money.usnews.com/money/careers/articles/2012/09/10/the-pink-collar-job-boom

Friedan, B. (1963). *The feminine mystique.* New York, NY: W. W. Norton.

Gallos, J. V. (1989). Exploring women's development: Implications for career theory, practice, and research. In M. B. Arthur, D. T. Hall, & B. S. Lawrence (Eds.), *Handbook of career theory* (pp. 110–132). Cambridge, UK: Cambridge University Press.

Gatrell, C. (2013). Maternal body work: How women managers and professionals negotiate pregnancy and new motherhood at work. *Human Relations, 66,* 621–644.

Gerstel, N., & McGonagle, K. (1999). Job leaves and the limits of the Family and Medical Leave Act: The effects of gender, race, and family. *Work and Occupations, 26,* 510–534.

Gilbert, J., & von Wallmenich, L. (2014). When words fail us: Mother time, relational attention, and the rhetorics of focus and balance. *Women's Studies in Communication, 37,* 66–89.

Guendelman, S., Goodman, J., Kharrazi, M., & Lahiff, M. (2014). Work-family balance after childbirth: The association between employer-offered leave characteristics and maternity leave duration. *Maternal and Child Health Journal, 18,* 200–208.

Hallstein, D. L. (2000). Where standpoint stands now: An introduction and commentary. *Women's Studies in Communication, 23,* 1–15.

Hanchey, J., & Berkelaar, B. (2015). Context matters: Examining discourses of career success in Tanzania. *Management Communication Quarterly, 29,* 411–439.

Harding, S. (1987). The instability of the analytical categories of feminist theory. In S. Harding & J. F. O'Barr (Eds.), *Sex and scientific inquiry* (pp. 283–302). Chicago, IL: University of Chicago Press.

Harding, S. (1991). *Whose science? Whose knowledge? Thinking from women's lives.* Ithaca, NY: Cornell University Press.

Harding, S. (2004). A socially relevant philosophy of science? Resources from standpoint theory's controversiality. *Hypatia, 19,* 25–47.

Hennessy, R. (1993). Women's lives/feminist knowledge: Feminist standpoint as ideology critique. *Hypatia, 6,* 14–34.

Hewlett, S. A. (2007). *Off-ramps and on-ramps: Keeping talented women on the road to success.* Boston, MA: Harvard Business School Publishing.

Heywood, L., & Drake, J. (Eds.). (1997). *Third wave agenda: Being feminist, doing feminism.* Minneapolis: University of Minnesota Press.

Holmer-Nadesan, M. (1996). Organizational identity and space of action. *Organization Studies, 17,* 49–81.

hooks, b. (2000). *Feminist theory: From margin to center.* Cambridge, MA: South End Press.

International Labour Office. (2010). *Maternity at work: A review of national legislation. Findings from the ILO Database of Conditions of Work and Employment Laws* (2nd ed.). Geneva, Switzerland: International Labour Organization.

Janesick, V. J. (1994). The dance of qualitative research design: Metaphor, methodolatry, and meaning. In N. K. Denzin & Y. S. Lincoln (Eds.), *Handbook of qualitative research* (pp. 209–219). Thousand Oaks, CA: Sage.

Jorgensen, H., & Applebaum, E. (2014). *Documenting the need for a national paid family and medical leave program: Evidence from the 2012 FMLA survey.* Washington, DC: Center for Economic and Policy Research.

Kiesel, L. (2014, August 20). Men in pink-collar jobs face a tradeoff: Lower pay, more job security. Retrieved from https://www.mainstreet.com/article/men-pink-collar-jobs-face-tradeoff-lower-pay-more-job-security

Klarsfeld, A. (Ed.). (2010). *International handbook on diversity at work: Country perspectives on diversity and equal treatment.* Cheltenham, UK: Edgar Elgar.

Klarsfeld, A. (Ed.). (2014). *International handbook on diversity at work: Country perspectives on diversity and equal treatment* (2nd ed.). Cheltenham, UK: Edgar Elgar.

Kovicak, K. (2001). Between L=A=N=G=U=A=G=E and lyric: The poetry of pink-collar resistance. *NWSA Journal, 13*(1), 22–39.

Lakoff, G., & Johnson, M. (1980). *Metaphors we live by.* Chicago, IL: University of Chicago Press.

Laughlin, L. (2011). *Maternity leave and employment patterns: 2006–2008.* Washington, DC: U. S. Census Bureau.

Lenz, B. (2004). Postcolonial fiction and the outsider within: Toward a literary practice of feminist standpoint theory. *NWSA Journal, 16*(2), 98–120.

Liu, M., & Buzzanell, P. M. (2004). Negotiating maternity leave expectations: Perceived tensions between ethics of justice and care. *Journal of Business Communication, 41,* 323–349.

Martin, J. (1990). Deconstructing organizational taboos: The suppression of gender conflict in organizations. *Organization Science, 1,* 339–357.

Meisenbach, R., Remke, R., Buzzanell, P. M., & Liu, M. (2008). "They allowed": Pentadic mapping of women's maternity leave discourse as organizational rhetoric. *Communication Monographs, 75,* 1–24.

Milkman, R., & Appelbaum, E. (2013). *Unfinished business: Paid family leave in California and the future of U.S. work-family policy.* Ithaca, NY: ILR Press.

Muhr, S. L., & Sullivan, K. (2013). "None so queer as folk": Gendered expectations and transgressive bodies in leadership. *Leadership, 9,* 416–435.

O'Connor, A., & Raile, A. (2015). Millennials' "get a 'real job'": Exploring generational shifts in the colloquialism's characteristics and meanings. *Management Communication Quarterly, 29,* 276–290.

Owen, W. F. (1984). Interpretive themes in relational commuinication. *Quarterly Journal of Speech, 70,* 274–287.

Parker, P. (2014). Difference and organizing. In L. Putnam & D. Mumby (Eds.), *The Sage handbook of organizational communication* (3rd ed., pp. 619–641). London, UK: Sage.

Payne, R. (2001). *A framework for understanding poverty.* Highlands, TX: Aha! Process.

Peterson, L. W., & Albrecht, T. L. (1999). Where gender/power/politics collide: Deconstructing organizational maternity leave policy. *Journal of Management Inquiry, 8,* 168–181.

Pringle, R. (1989a). Bureaucracy, rationality, and sexuality: The case of secretaries. In J. Hearn, D. Sheppard, P. Tancred-Sheriff, & G. Burrell (Eds.), *The sexuality of organization* (pp. 158–177). Newbury Park, CA: Sage.

Pringle, R. (1989b). *Secretaries talk: Sexuality, power, and work*. London, UK: Verso.

Ramazanoğlu, C., & Holland, J. (2002). *Feminist methodology: Challenges and choices*. London, UK: Sage.

Robinson, F. (2014). Discourses of motherhood and women's health: *Maternal Thinking* as feminist politics. *Journal of International Political Theory, 10*, 94–108.

Schein, V. E. (2002). *Working from the margins: Voices of mothers in poverty*. Ithaca, NY: Cornell University Press.

Scott, J. W. (1998). Deconstructing equality-versus-difference or, the uses of poststructuralist theory for feminism. *Feminist Studies, 14*, 23–50.

Smith, R. C., & Turner, P. (1995). A social constructionist reconfiguration of metaphor analysis: An application of "SCMA" to organizational socialization theorizing. *Communications Monographs, 62*, 152–181.

Sotirin, P. (2000). "All they do is bitch bitch bitch": Political and interactional features of women's officetalk. *Women and Language, 23*(2), 19–26.

Sotirin, P., & Gottfried, H. (1999). The ambivalent dynamics of secretarial "bitching": Control, resistance, and the construction of identity. *Organization, 6*, 57–80.

Tavris, C. (1992). *Mismeasure of woman: Why women are not the better sex, the inferior sex, or the opposite sex*. New York, NY: Touchstone.

Trethewey A. (1999). Disciplined bodies: Women's embodied identities at work. *Organization Studies, 20*, 423–450.

Trethewey, A. (2000). Revisioning control: A feminist critique of disciplined bodies. In P. M. Buzzanell (Ed.), *Rethinking organizational and managerial communication from feminist perspectives* (pp. 107–127). Thousand Oaks CA: Sage.

Turk, K. (2014). Labor's pink-collar aristocracy: The National Secretaries Association's encounters with feminism in the age of automation. *Labor: Studies in Working Class History of the Americas, 11*, 85–109.

Turner, P., & Norwood, K. (2013). Unbounded motherhood: Embodying a good working mother identity. *Management Communication Quarterly, 27*, 396–424.

Turner, P., & Norwood, K. (2014). "I had the luxury…": Organizational breastfeeding support as privatized privilege. *Human Relations, 66*, 385–406.

Wingfield, A. H. (2009). Racializing the glass escalator: Reconsidering men's experiences with women's work. *Gender and Society, 23*, 5–26.

U.S. Department of Labor. (n.d.). Family Medical Leave Act. Retrieved from http://www.dol.gov/whd/fmla/

U.S. Department of Labor. (2001). Bureau of Labor Statistics. Retrieved from http://www.bls.gov

U.S. Department of Labor. (2013). May 2013 National Occupational Employment and Wage Estimates" for Secretaries, Except Legal, Medical, and Executive. Bureau of Labor Statistics. Retrieved from http://www.bls.gov/oes/current/oes_nat.htm#43-0000

Weedon, C. (1999). *Feminism, theory, and the politics of difference*. Malden, MA: Blackwell.

Williams, J. (2000). *Unbending gender: Why family and work conflict and what to do about it*. Cambridge, UK: Oxford University Press.

Women's International Network. (1998). United Nations survey of paid maternity leave for mothers. *Women's International Network News, 24*(3), 8.

Women's International Network. (2003). USA women continue to face discrimination in the workforce. *Women's International Network News, 29*(3), 67.

Wood, J. T. (1992). Gender and moral voice: Moving from woman's nature to standpoint epistemology. *Women's Studies in Communication, 15*, 1–24.

Wood, J. T. (1994). *Who cares? Women, care, and culture*. Carbondale: Southern Illinois University Press.

Ybarra, M., & Hill, H. (2014). The effects of state workforce and safety net policies on maternity-leave job quitting among less-educated workers. W.E. Upjohn Institute for Employment Research. Retrieved from http://research.upjohn.org/grants/89/

Rhetorics of Unwed Motherhood and Shame

Heather Brook Adams

ABSTRACT
Identifying recent historical instances of rhetorical shaming, such as the verbal and nonverbal shaming practices related to unwed motherhood during the mid-twentieth century, contributes to a diachronic study of mothering rhetorics that can queer more recent histories of motherhood. This article analyzes narratives of once-unwed mothers who cite shame as a primary factor that shaped their "decision" to surrender a child for adoption. As rhetorics of reproduction, these stories account for an unspoken raced and classed purity practice of hiding unwed pregnancy and erasing an illicit mother identity due to the threat of communicable shame. As reproducing rhetorics of shame, the narratives demarcate the pure from the impure and serve as a mechanism that figures unwed pregnancy as proof of what I call *ontological failure*.

Between 1945 and 1973, an estimated 1.5 million women in the United States faced unwed pregnancy but—through one manner or another—were *effaced*, disappearing from school, community, and family to secretly have a child and, most typically, relinquish that child for adoption. During these post–World War II years, the notion of romance could sweep a "good girl" off her feet, but planning for (or even knowing about) one's own sexuality was the sure sign of a "bad girl." For White women, especially those in middle-class or upwardly mobile families, "getting *yourself* in trouble" was perhaps the ultimate sin. Consider, for example, author Grace Metalious's 1956 fictionalized version of a real New England town and book by the same name, Peyton Place, where "there were three sources of scandal: suicide, murder, and the impregnation of an unmarried girl" (241).

In the 1960s, ideals of social and sexual purity constrained open discussions about sexuality. From the late 1950s there was an alleged rise in unwed pregnancy, an uptick that underrepresented the actual number of such pregnancies, as many were never officially reported (Solinger 13). This article examines published and unpublished personal narratives of once-unwed and pregnant women of the 1960s and considers such experiences as useful, if partial, representations of these unwritten and unspoken reproductive histories. These histories enhance the study of mothering rhetorics because they populate a partial and secreted portion of the recent history of motherhood in the United States and demonstrate how motherhood was an identity that was paradoxically both rhetorically foreclosed and factually true for these women. In addition, the narratives illustrate how, within the rhetorical ecologies[1] described by once-unwed mothers, rhetorics of shame functioned to maintain an ideal of morally pure motherhood recognized within the context of marriage.

This article considers rhetorics of reproduction vis-à-vis the culturally situated construction of an "unwed mother" identity, taking seriously the claim that "reproductive decision-making and maternity [are] practices and roles that are constituted through and within communication" (Hayden and O'Brien Hallstein xviii). Unlike work that explores such terrain in a post–second wave context, my study questions the rhetorical constructions of mother identities in an earlier, pre–*Roe v. Wade* era.[2] This approach aids in constructing a diachronic understanding of how motherhood has been figured and expressed through various communicative practices and encourages scholars to more fully index the variable constructions of women's sexual(ized) identities and the changes of these constructions over time. As Lindal Buchanan argues, discursive configurations of "mothers, mothering, and motherhood" can grant "authority and credibility" in some cases, but can also position women "disadvantageously within the gendered status quo" (xvii). I extend Buchanan's focus on rhetorical credibility through sanctioned motherhood to ask which women are recognized as mothers, on what basis the identity of mother has been denied to some women, and how this (dis)identification has been communicated to and understood/ accepted by the women discussed here.

White women's depictions of their experiences as unwed mothers in the 1960s suggest that shaming discourses were, by far, the most prevalent way these women and those around them recognized and communicated the state of White unwed pregnancy as a transgression against a gendered, classed, and raced purity ideal located within and performed by the heteronormative, White, middle-class family. Shame rhetorics related to unwed pregnancy during this era, then, function as reproducing rhetorics[3] that (re)produced logics of sexual purity, coded "correct" motherhood as situated within marriage, and staked out the moral and gendered boundaries of heterosexual autonomy. Of course, unwed pregnancy during the 1960s was not exclusive to White and middle-class women, but its construction as a shameful moral problem that necessitated secret keeping and the denial of an unmarried woman's mother identity was concentrated on those particular bodies. In the postwar years, "nice, Waspy unwed girls" (Fessler 239) who became pregnant through consensual sex, quasi-consensual sex,[4] rape, or incest were likely to hide their pregnancies by going to maternity homes where they could keep their "shameful" predicament secret. A woman with fewer financial resources might have gone to a wage home, where she would work as a maid in a private residence for room and board. A story was concocted: *Sally is visiting a sick aunt in Florida; Mary was chosen to be an intern in Washington, DC.* At this time, to be White, unwed, and pregnant was to be stigmatized and bring unspeakable shame to one's class-conscious and upwardly mobile family. These mothers went away to erase their pregnant bodies and, in most cases, were practically forced to surrender their children for adoption to keep those pregnancies secret. In almost every case, they were told by adults who were aware of the pregnancy that they would forget all of this happened.

Although spaces at maternity homes were sometimes available to Black women, fewer unwed mothers from African American communities were ostracized from their families and larger kinship and community networks. Instead, these communities more frequently accepted and accommodated unwed mothers and their children—who often faced other wider, institutional obstacles based on prejudices against their "illegitimate" status.[5] This article, while not offering a comparative analysis of unwed mothers' raced experiences, focuses on acts of shaming, shunning, and expelling unwed mothers and methods of denying motherhood based on heteronormative and hegemonic White, middle-class norms. These activities were enacted through complex rhetorics of shame that figure prominently in mothers' personal narratives.

I draw from scholarship on shame and purity to analyze how and to what ends rhetorics of shame[6] functioned in unwed mothers' experiences. In what follows, I first explain how this focus on shame and purity suggests a queering of histories of motherhood and outline my method. I then argue for recognizing the communicable quality of shame evident in mothers' descriptions of their experiences, which both (a) signals a wider cultural anxiety over an inability to regulate desire and sexuality according to strict moral standards[7] and (b) distinguishes acts of rhetorical shaming from more temporary communicable threats. My analysis of mothers' memories of being shamed demonstrates how amplification colluded with the cultural mandate to erase White, unwed, pregnant bodies. Amplification, in this case a hyperbolic performance of shame, demarcated the figurative boundary between purity and impurity and signaled disidentification with the transgressing unwed mother by those who were threatened. I go on to define the result of rhetorical shaming as *ontological failure,* a state that rendered mothers emotionally isolated and unable to self-advocate. Many mothers continued to keep their secrets and carry a profound sense of shame for many years, thus upholding a standard of purity whereby a woman's moral quality is determined by not only her sexual restraint but also her general passivity (Valenti 24–25). I conclude by speculating how a recent historiographic approach like the one I use here can enable scholars to recognize and attend to other cultural logics, like those of purity, that shape and reshape notions of gender and sexuality over time.

Queering histories of motherhood

Considering the rhetorical construction of motherhood in relationship to shame encourages queering received histories of motherhood and gendered expectations of sexual purity. Here I embrace Jimmie Manning's move to queer heterosexuality by interrogating the "illusions" of it being "monolithic" that are "communicatively constructed in everyday life" (100). Manning's scholarship on the symbolic function of purity rings to "mark" some forms of heterosexuality as distinct from others counters and queers the assumed indivisibility of heterosexuality, providing a model for further investigating how certain types of normative sexuality are surveilled and demarcated. In exploring the intersections among rhetoric, gender, sexuality, and emotion, I also rely on work by Catherine Olive-Marie Fox, who contends that queer theory enables an examination of cultural norms that are meaningful on both individual and collective bases and allows scholars to track "ruptures in normativity that tend to coalesce around questions of propriety and civility" ("Queerly Classed" 340). In particular, Fox's interest in "reprosexuality," which relies on Michael Warner's notion of "the interweaving of heterosexuality, biological reproduction, cultural reproduction, and personal identity" (qtd. in Fox, "Reprosexuality" 245), aligns with my questions about how unwed motherhood functions as a crucible for reproducing rhetorics that have significant material effects—namely mothers' loss of children conceived outside of marriage—as well as implications for understanding how norms of gendered, heterosexual purity are activated and maintained. Such a focus can add to recent work that extends queer theory to analyze heterosexual rhetorical practices and social formations (e.g., Manning; McAlister), while also inviting new explorations of mothering rhetorics.

This article also responds to Alyssa A. Samek and Theresa A. Donofrio's recent call for scholars to take part in "the queer project" by accounting for the "power and centrality of sexuality in general, and heterosexuality in particular, as an ideological discourse that often goes unrecognized and unquestioned" (45). Finally, this article relies on a queer theoretical interest in shame as a collective, or social, emotion (Ahmed, *Cultural, Promise*; Fox "Queerly Classed"; Rand, *Reclaiming*; Sedgwick; Sedgwick and Frank). I conclude by reflecting on how this analysis demonstrates a paradox whereby the collective threat of shame that spurred unwed mothers to take part in a fictive performance of hiding and revirginalization failed to mobilize them toward publicly addressing their experiences and thus forming collective (or even individual) agency.

On method and adaptation

My analysis engages two general types of data. I rely on published memoirs as well as accounts included in Ann Fessler's trade paperback *The Girls Who Went Away: The Hidden History of Women Who Surrendered Children for Adoption in the Decades before* Roe v. Wade (which includes extended segments of interviews with mothers). I also use data from my institutional review board–approved, face-to-face, oral history interviews with once-unwed mothers. I interviewed twenty-five mothers after having recruited self-identifying participants in local newspapers in several Midwestern and East Coast cities and through snowball sampling methods. All participants were women who hid a pregnancy at some point between 1950 and 1971, with most being pregnant during the 1960s.[8] Broadly commensurate with the demographic markers of those who hid an unwed pregnancy, twenty-four of these participants were White (although of varied ethnicities, including Irish and Italian) and one was African American. I used inductive coding and analysis to draw findings from these data.

My decision to find and investigate mothers' stories in both published and unpublished forms relates to my specific inquiry as well as to the challenges of doing feminist rhetorical scholarship that is frequently marked by "struggle, borrowing, invention, and adaptation" (Schell 6). My ongoing work on rhetorics related to unwed pregnancy seeks to shed light on a recent history that is still largely secreted and misunderstood as well as to interrogate sites of productive and unproductive silences (Glenn, *Unspoken*) related to unwed mothers' realities. Although feminist rhetorical historiographers commonly rely on published and archival documents as primary sources for investigating more distant historical figures and times (Glenn and Enoch; Ramsey, Sharer, L'Eplattenier, and Mastrangelo; Royster and Kirsch), I found early in my research that archival holdings of former maternity homes almost never include the voices of women who hid at these institutions. In addition, published accounts of mothers' experiences, such as the two I draw from in this article, address hiding a pregnancy mostly as a precursor to longer and more detailed discussions of the experience of searching for and (sometimes) reuniting with a child surrendered for adoption. In practical terms, these publications do not fully answer the many questions I have had related to the communicative acts that shaped women's experiences during and immediately after a pregnancy as well as mothers' feelings and attitudes about these experiences. Thus, I decided to "exten[d] my methods to include qualitative research" in the same way that Eileen E. Schell did when researching the working conditions of female contingent writing faculty in U.S. institutions (5). Like Schell, I faced a dearth of published sources that I could draw upon and thus have chosen to "partially invent and combine methods and methodologies from across the disciplines" to move forward with my work (5). It is important to note that the interviews excerpted here focus almost exclusively on the experiences of mothers and thus might be viewed as performing a form of silencing in relation to how men as sexual partners/fathers figured into these histories. This focus on women's experiences accurately reflects the reality that men were overwhelmingly not held responsible for the "problem" of an unwed pregnancy; thus, their omission from this article is not a rhetorical choice on my part but a reflection of the historical experiences of mothers.

I refer to my method as "feminist historiography of the recent past" because it incorporates methodological considerations based on Renee C. Romano and Claire Bond Potter's work on recent history as a unique, emerging form of historiographic inquiry. I continue to incorporate published memoirs and interview excerpts from Fessler's project into my scholarship for two reasons: (a) the memoirs reflect carefully crafted and sometimes researched perspectives on authors' personal experiences, thus providing written accounts that allow me to consider mothers' historiographic framing of their own experiences; and (b) each of these sources offers additional perspectives on a relatively silenced history. I value all of these sites of information—from the published and polished narratives to the more improvisational and raw, if no less honest, interview comments to those "memoried"[9] texts in between—that can shed light on this long-secreted practice. This mixed-methods and mixed-data approach is one that I contend adds richness to feminist rhetorical practices that are valued because they remain "in constant motion" (Schell 6–7) and because of the feminist rhetorical historiographic commitment to resist closure (Glenn, *Rhetoric Retold* 174). In addition, historiographic investigations of the recent past can provide useful antecedents for investigations that trace how concepts (e.g., "purity" and "motherhood") shift and move over time.[10]

Communicating shame, communicable shame

Memoirist Margaret Moorman recalls the experience of being sixteen in 1964, learning about her pregnancy, and reluctantly sharing this information with her mother. "My mother's reaction was instantaneous and explosive," Moorman writes. "'How could you DO this to me?' she shrieked" (39). Moorman interpreted the question literally, admitting that she "didn't know how to answer" because she "had never intended to do anything at all to her, certainly not something like this." Surprised at her mother's suggestion of intentionality, Moorman quips that she "had not thought of her [mother] once, in fact, while achieving this remarkable feat of negligence and irresponsibility" (39). This reflection offers bittersweet and instructive humor. Moorman asks her readers to witness an incongruity that other young mothers experienced: She both lacked the experience and perspective of an adult and had to account for her implication in a serious, life-changing, even family-changing (and thus "adult") situation. Memoirist Meredith Hall recounts a similar moment when she prepared to disclose her unwed pregnancy to her mother, who intuited, "'You're pregnant, aren't you?'" Reflecting on these "hard, fierce" words, Hall explains that in that moment she "cannot find [her] mother; she is gone, a million miles away, back in a place where there were no terrible surprises, where good girls don't draw shame on good mothers" (16). At the end of Hall's account of searching for the child she surrendered for adoption, she returns to the emotion that was most central to her experience: shame. "Shame, crushing shame," she writes, "silenced me for those nine months, and for the next twenty-one years" (182).

Recollections of feelings of shame like those shared by Moorman and Hall are especially present in the accounts of mothers' experiences with unwed pregnancy that I collected through oral history interviews. By asking once-unwed mothers to share their stories with me, I have been able to identify shame as the most salient emotion related to these mothers' experiences of being unwed and pregnant as well as a principal feature of their initial—and, in many cases, their ongoing—relationships with the identity of unwed mother. As Lois explained to me when she recounted her story of doing "an unspeakable thing" by becoming pregnant outside of marriage, "they used shame on us." Lois's vague invocation of an agential *they* draws attention to rhetorics of shame that functioned to delimit unwed mothers' options, suggesting that this shame was communicated by specific persons (e.g., parents, religious leaders, social workers) but also that it emanated from an indirect source: the socially held standard for women's sexual purity. Lois's assertion that "[shame] is a powerful weapon, and they used it" indicates that shame functioned rhetorically to designate the severity of unwed pregnancy as a transgression of appropriate and gendered heterosexual expectations—a transgression with severe ramifications.

The responsibility for becoming pregnant outside of wedlock as a young, White woman was often directed singly to mothers; fathers were infrequently expected to acknowledge, much less act upon, their roles in the pregnancies. Shame was funneled to the unwed mother, who was expected to hide her pregnancy to preserve the reputation of her family, herself, and her unborn, "illegitimate" child who would be "given" to a married couple. The intensity of this shame, however, and its connection to the women's disidentification as mothers (which I discuss in greater detail later in this article), has prevented the shame they experienced as young women from disappearing over time. Akin to the ways mothers did not simply "forget" this experience as adults had told them they would, lingering shame remains central to mothers' depictions of their experiences and senses of self. As these memories suggest, the presence of shame invokes the fear that an unwed mother's shame will (or has already) spread to those around her, making it not only communicated but also communicable. A fear of shame's contagious qualities contributed to a number of unwed mothers being expelled from school in the years before and even after Title IX legislation. Some unwed mothers were forced to labor in segregated, even isolated, hospital rooms—an arrangement that separated them from other "legitimate" mothers.

Many mothers who recount their experiences indicate receiving messages about the communicable nature of their shame. For example, when speaking to Fessler, Madeline recalls knowing that by being pregnant and unmarried in 1960 she had "done the worst thing possible," and that, according to her mother, the pregnancy was "killing" her father, compromising his ability to work, and threatening the happiness of her parents' marriage (Fessler 239). Cynthia, a mother I interviewed, also remembers the surprise she felt when she approached her mother about being a pregnant nineteen-year-old in 1962 and was met with fury:

> I had been dating this guy about six months, and it was my first sexual experience. I was really naive. Um, when I got pregnant I went to my parents and my mother was *furious* with me.

I was looking for a hug and, "Oh, honey, it will be all right." And she was furious with me. (Interviewee's emphasis)

Similarly, Lois explained to me that her mother "came at [her]" when she learned of her pregnancy. Remembering the shock of this extreme reaction, Lois continued:

[It was] like I just did something to her. She didn't have any concern for me; it was more punishment. And it was okay to do that back then. It was really okay [because] "you disgraced this family." [As her mother:] "Your father is going to lose his business." [As herself:] He was a businessman. A lot of people knew him.

As with Moorman's and Hall's feelings of dislocation when faced with anger and accusation from their families, other mothers' accounts express how they were encouraged to see themselves: as agents who were responsible for dire effects—both symbolic and material—that would implicate entire families. All three of these examples demonstrate that this particular deployment of shame runs counter to what Sara Ahmed refers to as *"the affective cost of not following the scripts of normative experience"* that functions as "a failure of myself to myself" (*Cultural* 106–107; emphasis in original). Rather than shame solely resting on the unwed mother (a deployment of a sexual double standard), in these instances it rhetorically resituates an individual's failure of the self in ways understood to propagate, disseminate, and thus threaten the social and economic viability and interpersonal wellness of the family.

Even though each of the mothers with whom I spoke—with one exception[11]—felt stigmatized by their unwed pregnancy and thus went into hiding until the birth of their child, not every mother was explicitly shamed by authority figures. For example, Mary remembers Father Arthur visiting her at the maternity home and encouraging her to recognize that through her, God provided the "gift" of a child to a married couple. This message comforted Mary but was premised on her inability to be a socially acceptable mother because she was not married. It also configures an unknown married woman as the legitimate mother for Mary's child.

Faye, another mother with whom I spoke, remembers interacting with her parents after she found out that she was pregnant: "My dad—I don't know what he thought. I mean, they [Faye's parents] never, ever chastised me. Ever. They just never spoke about it at all. It was like it didn't exist." Although Faye's parents did not explicitly direct shame upon her, the family's silence and Faye's hiding and eventual surrender of her child was the result of her implicit position in a broader shame culture that privileged sexual purity among young, White, unmarried women. Faye's reflection suggests that even an ostensibly sympathetic and caring family was constrained by a cultural purity mandate. The family was potentially rendered mute by the disparity between this strict expectation for women's sexual purity and their daughter's violation of it. Faye does not know how to explain this silence, and thus I cannot draw conclusions from it. But Faye's experience does illustrate that shame is not necessarily deployed directly from those with more power onto those with less power. As Fox contends, power is *enacted through shame* that is already present rather than being created by some and then distributed to others ("Queerly Classed" 343). In other words, Faye's family was "performing heterosexuality" (Manning 102) as gendered sexual purity in a way that they did not (and did not have to) reproduce verbally through explicit messages of shame, but that they rhetorically enacted by silently sending her to a home for unwed mothers.

Shame's contagiousness has been considered by scholars including Eve Kosofsky Sedgwick, who notes shame's "uncontrollable relationality" (37), and Ahmed, who theorizes emotions' "sticky" qualities that can be communicated "atmospherical[ly]" (*Promise* 40). Shame is indeed a sticky emotion that threatens to adhere to those who saw or even knew about a woman's unwed pregnancy. A paradox in shame's communicability, though, is that it coalesced people who were complicit with the agenda of hiding but it did not further galvanize mothers toward resistance, even when they were living communally in a maternity home. Many women with whom I spoke remember this as a time of isolation and sadness, and nearly all of these mothers vehemently express having been denied any choice in determining the outcome of the pregnancy, in large part because of their responsibility to family members that dictated hiding as mothers' only viable option. Ahmed argues that such shame "secures the *form* of the family by assigning to those who have failed its form the origin of bad feeling ('You have brought shame on the family')" (*Cultural* 107; emphasis added).

I would argue that this security of familial form is rendered rhetorically through communicated and communicable shame. Such shame denotes—or threatens to denote—that which mars the form, in this case, the optics of the mythic "family" as "happy object," what Ahmed elsewhere notes is an object "on display" that "makes visible a fantasy of a good life" (*Promise* 45). Likewise, the narrative of the shame-threatened family that links so many mothers' stories and the material practices related to hiding in a maternity home can be understood as "figural" iterations that are "fitted to and shap[e]" (McAlister 281) a desire to manage women's sexuality in the name of heterosexual purity through the wedded mother. Whereas Ahmed argues that shame can be restorative if it is witnessed and understood as "temporary, in order to allow us to re-enter the family or community" (*Cultural* 107), shame functioned in a more destructive way for these mothers. Hiding was meant to allow reentry but was contingent upon surrendering their children and indefinitely secreting and forgetting their identities as "illicit mothers" in order to perform a revirginalized purity. This purity would outwardly uphold (and secretly restore) a family's reputation through the unwed mother's "secret" atonement[12] that would then render her eligible to become a wife and proper mother at some future time. As mothers' narratives demonstrate, however, the internalized trauma of such a performance has had psychic and social effects that, in many cases, are only now being reckoned with publicly, as mothers puncture their silences and share their stories more widely.

Demarcation and disidentification

Another way in which shame functions rhetorically in once-unwed mothers' memories is by marking deviance in an exaggerated manner that performs what I would call a ritual[13] of demarcation and disidentification. Shame, as an experienced emotion, "feels like an exposure" and thus typically moves the ashamed to hide (Ahmed, *Cultural* 103). The larger practice of secreting and hiding an unwed mother, then, can be situated as an extreme, if indefensible, manifestation of this shame logic. But rhetorical performances of hyperbolic[14] and pseudoprivate shaming that mothers recount in their narratives suggest that these shame rhetorics marked the magnitude of the alleged deviance. These performances also discursively positioned mothers as outside the acceptable boundaries of heterosexual normativity, a move that accentuated a symbolic border separating the pure from the impure. As narrative excerpts from two mothers demonstrate, the exaggeration in these rhetorical performances simultaneously called mothers' attention to their transgressions and provided a justification for why the transgression needed to be made invisible to others.

This paradox is similar to Michele L. Hammers's recent analysis of Eve Ensler's production, *The Vagina Monologues*. Hammers argues that the sexualized and shamed female body, particularly the vagina, is a "symbolic fulcrum" positioned at the "border of amplification and erasure," the latter occurring as the sexual female body is effaced from public view and discourse (227). This dialectical relationship between amplification, or what Hammers refers to as "heightened, even hyperbolic" attention (227), and the erasure promoted by sexual taboo is present in mothers' experiences of hiding their bodies from view during their (visible) pregnancy.

When in her memoir Moorman recalls her mother's reaction to the news of her pregnancy as "instantaneous and explosive" (39), she highlights the severity of the response. But other mothers' accounts allude to the *performed* quality of hyperbolic shame rhetorics. For example, Susan shared with me that when she found out in 1967 that she was pregnant at age twenty, she was at a loss as to how to handle the situation. Unmarried and living at home with her parents, Susan remembers:

> When I found out I was pregnant, I knew, number one: I could not tell my mother because I probably wouldn't live to see the next day. So, I just—I was a mess, I don't know, for a couple of weeks. Just trying to figure out what to do. I was going to run away. I was—I was just trying to figure out what I was going to do. And I couldn't *share* what was happening to me. There was no one to go to for help.

Feeling silenced, Susan decided to do "the only thing she could think to do," which was to tell her father about her pregnancy. Finding her father supportive, Susan nevertheless had to share this information with her mother. She remembers the day of this disclosure:

> Her gynecologist was the one I was going to. His office called her and said, "Harriet, we've noticed that you haven't been here for a while. Maybe you need to make an appointment." And so she did. So the doctor told Mom, and I was sitting out in the reception area, and I heard her screaming all the way out to the reception area. And I was like, Oh God, do I just get up and leave? What do I do? Well, the nurse came and got me and I went back there. And her reaction was so horrible. She called me a slut. She said, "Where did this happen?" She referred to his thing as a "big, hard," whatever her words were. I mean, it was devastating. It was beyond devastating. I felt like trash.

Susan's recollection centers on her mother's shaming discourse, which began with an eruption of disappointment—a scream that pierced the professional space of the gynecologist's office. The scream inaugurated the shaming, and Susan's mother's revulsion was then amplified in her barrage of humiliating questions. Rhetorically, this performance functioned partially as communication to Susan, but even more significantly as a performance of shaming that could be witnessed by those within earshot: Susan was humiliated not only by her mother's punishing questions but by the fact that others surely overheard them.

When Yvonne became pregnant in 1967, her parents arranged for her to have regular meetings with a social worker, a woman who consistently discouraged Yvonne from imagining the possibility of keeping her child. Yvonne explained to me that presumably the role of the social worker was "to counsel me, I guess," but that she spent more time and energy repeating performances of shame that cemented Yvonne's knowledge of her moral transgression:

> I mean, really, I mean, I think that the role [of a social worker] for the public was to counsel me about how horrible I was for becoming pregnant. I mean, back in those days, people would say, "You went and got yourself pregnant!" Like that's possible. And I mean, it was a very, very common thing to say. Um, to make sure that I understood that there probably was—I really truly felt that there was *nothing* I could have done worse, including killing someone coldheartedly ... that could have possibly been any worse than getting pregnant and not being married. My parents never asked, [the social worker] never asked, the nuns at the maternity home never asked—no one ever asked me anything about the relationship that led up to me being pregnant. It was just assumed that I was a slut and got pregnant. (Interviewee's emphasis)

Yvonne remembers that during one of the sessions, the social worker asked her whether she enjoyed "it," a question that initially caught Yvonne by surprise. "She's asking me if I enjoyed sex!" she remembers. "We're Catholics here, aren't we? We don't talk about this stuff! It was just really, really, really, really creepy that she asked me that. Shockingly creepy."

Yvonne's surprise and repulsion have eclipsed memories of feeling shame. Understanding it within the context of the role of the social worker demonstrates that more than just being "creepy," the question functioned for Yvonne as an experienced, amplified performance of shame. Instead of counseling and deliberating on Yvonne's options as an unwed mother, the meetings repeatedly encouraged Yvonne to feel ashamed about the pregnancy. The exchanges function as a fulcrum on which Yvonne understands how she was distinguished from her allegedly morally pure peers. Yvonne differentiates between the supposed and actual rationale for these "counseling" sessions, and her discussion of the role of the social worker seamlessly shifts to her description of how she understood, through the experience of hiding, her social role as a marked and impure woman regardless of the details of her specific situation.

Yvonne's experiences of rhetorical shaming are also reflected in her discussion of receiving a letter from her fourteen-year-old sister that explained, in her sister's words, how "dreadful" Yvonne was. Yvonne's sister also described how her shame was discussed "around the dinner table and the supper table and the breakfast table" because she was a "slut" and a "whore" who had "ruined the family name." These epithets emphasized Yvonne's deviancy through allegations of hypersexuality. Many mothers explained to me that to be White, unwed, and pregnant elicited accusations of being a "slut" or "whore," even when there was no evidence of a woman having had multiple sexual encounters. Yvonne was devastated by the letter but did not hold her sister accountable; she knew that talk of her sexual impurity came from her parents and that her sister had just absorbed and regurgitated this shaming language. In recollecting the letters, Yvonne seems to recognize the ritualistic quality of her sister's shame, and she finds solace in distinguishing between her sister's rhetorical performance and what she imagines to be her sister's true feelings.

These specific examples of demarcation and disidentification help explain other performed shaming practices that are consistent across most mothers' stories. For instance, more than half of the women with whom I spoke offered their stories of being physically segregated from wedded pregnant women in the hospital, often left in isolation as they labored, and met with messages (by some medical staff) of their shamefulness.[15]

In addition to extending the logic of contamination expressed previously, these practices explicitly call attention to—at least among those present in the hospital—the alleged deviance of the mother and the conditional assistance that the medical facility was willing to give her. I contend that labor represented a potentially unmanageable time for upholding distinctions of purity and impurity, "right" motherhood and "wrong" motherhood, which could have been rendered meaningless through the universalizing act of delivering a baby. The exaggerated performance of shaming served to mitigate this possible disorder, because as purity theorist Mary Douglas asserts, "ideas about separating, purifying, demarcating, and punishing transgressions have as their main function to impose system on an inherently untidy experience" (5).[16] Mid-twentieth-century U.S. suburban culture valued the hypervisibility of purity and class status; young mothers could then function as a visual and embodied representation of goodness and social propriety, but only if they were married. White, unwed mothers, then, functioned figuratively as a touchstone of impropriety and a denial of the so-called maternal qualities of self-sacrifice and moral purity (Buchanan 17). What all of these examples share is a sense of women's sexuality that legitimates oversight and categorization as acceptable or transgressive in ways that are always determined by others rather than by the woman herself. In Valenti's words, "we don't trust young women to be able to control their own bodies" (199).

Shame as ontological failure

An examination of how shame is distinct from guilt can further explain how rhetorics of shame function. Specifically, the self-directed orientation of shame warranted the *practice* of hiding and surrendering (an act) but also depended on a mother accepting that her illicit pregnancy signaled her inability to be a mother to the child that she was carrying (an identity). I refer to the result of this shaming rhetoric as ontological failure, or a deficiency in the very being of a person that is beyond remedy or repair. Whereas problematic actions or breaches of judgment can be recognized and potentially rectified, ontological failure represents a state of perpetual inadequacy as a human being that—in these cases of sexual shaming—becomes manifest in a woman's impure, impregnated body. I contend that mothers' feelings of ontological failure based on shame discouraged them from speaking out for themselves while pregnant; deterred them from feeling solidarity or seeking a collective, counterpublic voice; and arrested their ability to self-identify as mothers despite having birthed children.

When an unwed pregnancy was confirmed, a girl was likely to be reconfigured as a "bad girl," an identity that eclipsed who she was thought to be before the pregnancy and revealed her supposedly true nature. Martha Nussbaum theorizes that projecting shame outward is an act that "normals" use to distinguish themselves from "deviants" in an attempt to achieve a surrogate bliss and avoid having to confront their own weaknesses (218–19). Similarly, Fessler concludes that the "scorn and blame" that other young people directed toward unwed mothers had a strategic function: "by focusing attention on women whose sexual behavior was evident [via a pregnant body], others could deny their own" (36). In both explanations, shame stems from the underlying knowledge of a fundamental shared humanity—in this case between "good" and "bad" girls. It also reflects a need to deny this similarity to reproduce the ideological system of hierarchy that could manage motherhood by upholding a sanctioned type of "good" mother. Significantly, this distinction is one that did not reverse itself, even when women were complicit in a hiding practice that would allow them to reenter their old lives and adopt the yoke of "good" girl again. The secret keeping of illegitimate motherhood, then, signals more than just a maintenance of the fiction of revirginalization. For Cynthia, shaming led to rejection by loved ones and then to her own protective silences. As she disclosed to me:

> I told my boyfriend. He came to the house once. He told my mother that he would stick by me and help me financially—because we knew we weren't going to get married—help me financially and emotionally. And a month later I called him and he had moved to North Carolina or something to be with his parents. So he was gone. I told my one girlfriend and she never called me again. So, that's my feeling. You tell people about this and they run away from you. So I never told my [now] husband.[17]

To be sure, Cynthia's secret keeping is one manifestation of shame's ability to silence those in a position of vulnerability. Told by those in positions of authority that they would forget their experience of surrendering a child, many once-unwed mothers kept their secret as part of their role in the cultural practice of hiding to outwardly perform and surreptitiously "restore" purity. But as Moorman's memoir *Waiting to Forget* titularly suggests, forgetting never came. Silence, then, cannot be understood as proof of having forgotten the experience of illicit motherhood. As Glenn distinguishes in her study of rhetorical silences, silence as self-protection is not the same as being rendered mute (or in this case, forgetting); it is a rhetorical art that allows one in a nondominant position to exert some level of power over an asymmetrical rhetorical situation (*Unspoken* 52–55).

In other words, silence is not only made rhetorical by those imposing it on others who wield less power than they do (through the act of silencing the other, as in the case of unwed mothers being forced to keep a pregnancy secret); it can also be deployed purposefully as a rhetorical act. In the case of unwed mothers, the "choice" to hide pregnancy and continue to keep the secret for years thereafter is a complex one because of the women's extreme sense of disempowerment as allegedly illicit mothers. But the protectiveness of the ongoing silence that Cynthia's comment illustrates should be recognized as a demonstration of mothers' ability to enact some kind of rhetorical choice about where, when, and with whom to break that silence about their still-present past. The mothers that I interviewed helped me understand that, in many cases, identifying oneself as a once-unwed mother does not only entail simply speaking the long unspoken but rather requires a reckoning with one's supposed identity as a "bad" mother.

Shame's distinction from guilt provides another opportunity to interpret the way in which unwed mothers experienced rhetorics of shame. Psychologists June Price Tangney and Ronda L. Dearing argue that shame and guilt are "distinct emotions" that lead to separate feelings and responses (24). Challenging the long-held notion that an experience of guilt or shame is determined by the situation that elicits it, Tangney and Dearing contend that the emphasis is what makes them distinct. I refer to such emphasis as "the socially constructed meaning and embodied feelings" of these emotions. Specifically, guilt is a localized and contextualized emotion that results from the negative evaluation of an action—a "*thing* done or undone" (Tangney and Dearing 18). Guilt is a sense of regret related to an action, and thus it encourages a response of "confession, reparation, and apology" that will address, even amend, the violation (19). Shame is different from guilt in that its focus is not an action but instead the devalued self. Unlike guilt, which might elicit consideration of how one's actions might affect others, feeling ashamed "typically concerns disappointment or despair over what kind of person I am (or have failed to be)" (Manion 37). Ahmed explains that unlike the action orientation of guilt, with shame *"the badness of an action is transferred to me,* such that I feel myself to be bad and to have been 'found' or 'found out' bad by others" (*Cultural* 5; emphasis in original). In short, "shame is experienced less as about what the self has done but what the self is" (Biddle 229).

These definitions suggest how rhetorics of shame connote ontological failure rather than signaling a mistake or misstep. Notably, many more mothers articulate feelings of shame rather than those of guilt related to their experiences of relinquishing a child for adoption. For many of these women, such feelings have been an ongoing part of their lives, long after experiencing pregnancy. Consider Susan's description of her mother's questions in the gynecologist's office as mentioned previously: Susan describes the interaction by indicating that "it was devastating. It was beyond devastating. I felt like trash." Susan does not recount feelings that respond to the actions leading up to the pregnancy or her temporary state of being pregnant. Instead, her expression of feeling ashamed reflects her sense of herself: "I felt like trash." If unwed mothers experienced guilt rhetorics, then they ostensibly could have amended an "error" in propriety or understood their pregnancies as resulting from sexual ignorance, for example. But doing so would have extended the culpability to others—to the man with whom they had sex, to the family or community through which they could have become educated about their reproducing bodies, and so on. Through shame, however, the burden of sexual discretion could coalesce in and on the unwed, pregnant body to salvage "mother" as a purity term reserved for permissible iterations of women's reproduction.

The collateral damage of this ontological failure has had a profound effect on many of the women with whom I have spoken. For Mary Ann, the messages of shame related to being an unwed mother:

> [It] confirmed that I was a worthless person, an odd person. I always felt like I was odd. I still feel odd. Looked fat. Yes, [my unwed pregnancy] made it much worse. I felt like I was an outsider to the life that I lived before. But I was no longer entitled to be the person I thought I was going to be.

Hearing shame rhetorics as an indictment of the self is something that Audrey, another participant in my research, also experienced. Upon returning to her parents' home after residing in a home for unwed mothers and relinquishing her child for adoption, Audrey described herself as:

> a persona non grata. When I went home, I was not allowed to eat at the dinner table. I had to eat up in my room or in the basement. My brothers and sisters were not allowed to talk to me. You know, it was total isolation. Not—I mean—it was bad enough to be shunned at school. And ordinarily you go home because that's—that's where you live and you have reasonable expectations that you are safe there and you are protected and it is a good place for you to be. That's not how my home was—at all.

As these memories suggest, the rhetorical function of shame threatened to influence mothers' senses of themselves beyond the transgression of the pregnancy, thus cementing the distinction between "right" and "wrong" motherhood. As a result, mothers were less likely to renegotiate the boundaries of propriety and reconfigure themselves as mothers in an alternate form. The power of these shaming rhetorics to shape one's sense of self was most apparent to me when I spoke with Elizabeth, a woman from Ohio who hid her pregnancy in 1961. During her interview, Elizabeth repeatedly assured me that she was "not sorry" for the pregnancy and adoption because she had "made a mistake and […] paid for it." Elizabeth refuses to remain conscripted by shame because, according to her logic, she paid penance for a deed. She undercut her own rationale at the end of the interview, though, by looking at me and adding, "I hope you—I hope you don't think I'm a terrible person."

The reason that scholars of communication should care about the distinction between rhetorics of shame and rhetorics of guilt relates to the ways in which researchers have observed emotion's relationship to rhetorical and communicative ecologies and, more specifically, emotion's ability to circulate and function as what Emily Winderman describes as a "collectivizing" rhetorical force in her study of anger (386). Erin Rand also theorizes the rhetorical function of emotion as she compellingly writes about shame's "tremendous affective potential" (*Reclaiming 138*). In her analysis of AIDS activist group ACT UP, Rand argues that "the more powerfully felt the emotion and the more tenacious its roots in the constitution of particular identities and subjects, the greater its promise as a resource for agency" (*Reclaiming* 138). Although this assertion aligns with Rand's project, it fails to represent the experiences of women featured here. The resulting disparity raises an important conceptual question: What makes shame "sticky" in one situation and not in another? In relation to this study, for example, why did the mothers' shame threaten to stick to and shame the people around them but fail to lead to bonding with other unwed mothers, who were also physically ostracized and emotionally spurned by many they loved?[18]

I argue that rhetorical shame as ontological failure is one way to answer these questions. Consider, for example, Mary Ann, who realized how atypical it was for her to be able to see her son in foster care. In many cases unwed mothers of children in foster care were not permitted to touch or even see their child after delivery. Mary Ann concludes that she "still blew it" by not advocating for her own desires or needs as the mother of her so-called "illegitimate" child. She did not speak up because she was "so afraid. I was so afraid that I was crazy, that I would be crazy forever. That I would never be able to take care of the child, or myself, or anything else. So I just went, I went passively along with anything anyone ever told me to do or not do." Similarly, Pam, who became pregnant at fourteen and subsequently surrendered her child, admits to Fessler that she struggled for years with the fear that any children she had later would also be taken from her. As she explains, "It was trapped in my brain … I was not allowed to be a mother" (Fessler 172).

This state of permanent arrest in recognizing the self as a mother—any type of mother—indicates the power of emotionally saturated reproducing rhetorics. In such cases, emotion can be "deployed to determine which arguments and which voices are heard and taken seriously" (Rand, "Bad Feelings" 163) and thus can undergird gendered and patriarchal expectations of reproduction and mothering. Although some of the mothers with whom I spoke are active in adoption reform or otherwise open to publicly sharing their stories, nearly all women described a long period of silence in the years after the pregnancy, speaking minimally or not at all about their experiences of hiding and surrender.[19] Thus, this examination of mothering rhetorics encourages further exploration of the differences between rhetorical ecologies in which shame does remain a sticky, mobilizing emotional force and those in which it does not.

Emphasizing the ontological can be a persuasive and malleable strategy in relation to ideological commitments, as Christine J. Gardner's recent study of rhetorics of abstinence campaigns suggests. Gardner demonstrates that some contemporary purity campaign leaders embrace the move from defining abstinence behaviorally (e.g., losing one's virginity[20] through a sexual act) to thinking of purity as an identity, a matter of "being rather than doing" (30). The collectivizing power of softening the edges of moral purity to connote lifestyle choices, health, and well-being allows young people who have had some sort of sexual encounter to choose a "renewed" or "second virginity" (31–32). This rhetorical construction "manage[s] the liminality of teenagers" in a larger effort at "social control" for "ostensibly religious ends," according to Gardner (40). Teenagers in earlier decades and those today who are implicated in these rhetorical constructions of purity can have surprisingly analogous experiences; they understand their own sexuality—indeed, themselves as sexed and sexual human beings—through particular figurations that render partaking in or averting sex before marriage a metonym for the impure or pure self.

Senses and ruptures: Concluding thoughts on unwed mothering rhetorics

This essay has traced three ways that rhetorics of shame function as mothering rhetorics (rhetorics of reproduction and reproducing rhetorics) in relation to recent unwed motherhood in U.S. culture from the mid-nineteenth century to the early 1970s. First, the communicable threat of shame that unwed mothers could "bring on" their families was one critical basis for the imperative that they visibly hide and later deny their pregnancies. Second, rhetorical performances of demarcating and disidentifying "impure" or "bad" girls from "pure" or "good" girls worked to simultaneously amplify shame and underscore the need to erase the proof of errant motherhood as well as the identity of illicit mothers. Amplification functioned to mark the significance of the transgression of being pregnant (that is, being a mother) outside of marriage and to perform hyperbolically the management of purity and enactment of control over young women's sexual desires and actions. And third, distinguishing between rhetorics that express shame and those that connote guilt is instructive in accounting for why the shame rhetorics did not work as a collectivizing emotion for women hiding a pregnancy and grappling with ontological failure. In these overlapping ways, shame can be thought of as a rhetorically deployed emotion that "mold[s]" the "moral standards" (Winderman 385) of acceptable and unacceptable motherhood. This analysis suggests how rhetorics of shame enact a rhetorical strategy for upholding "Mother" as a god-term that articulates with culturally sanctioned concepts of home, morality, nationhood, and self-sacrifice (Buchanan 8–9). In the process, it queers the history of motherhood by pointing to the paradoxes by which some mothers were compelled to perform a revirginalized identity that they did not truly embrace in order to uphold the optics of heterosexual normalcy.

Attention to rhetorics of shame that function in complex ways within the recent history of unwed pregnancy can serve as a useful index of earlier rhetorical and heteronormative constructions of motherhood. Fox advocates relying on queer theory to investigate the "operation of heteronormativity" through discursive constructions ("Queerly Classed" 345) and, more generally, "how norms affect us individually and collectively" by attending to "ruptures in normativity" ("Queerly Classed" 340). Admitting that norms, like shame itself, are unavoidable, Fox provokes readers to take notice of "ruptures in the normative horizon" and especially experiences of shame, which "often demarcat[e] those ruptures as openings into critical inquiry" ("Queerly Classed" 352). Fox's point, which she applies to the professional field of English studies, can easily pivot to historiographic moments when rhetoric and communication scholars can survey normative landscapes of the past.

Further examination of shame's communicability, rhetorics of demarcation/disidentification, and ontological failure may be fruitful as scholars continue to investigate issues of gender and sexuality as well as motherhood in particular. In general, these areas of inquiry are marked by a merging of embodied experience, performativity, and notions of identity that reside within, through, and on the body and that are implicated by desires of bodies politic. The notion of ontological failure in this analysis has explained secreted scripts of shame from earlier decades. The concept might usefully be applied to other sites, such as contemporary public discussions of sexual assault, consent, and the ongoing gendered silences and blame rhetorics that constrain conversations related to sexual violence.[21]

In addition, a focus on rhetorics of shame and ontological failure prompts us to ask where else we might locate tacit assumptions about who is "allowed" to be a mother. One might consider poet Robin Coste Lewis's recent admission of being unable to see herself as a viable mother because of her limitations from a brain injury (Remnick). Lewis credits seeing another mother with a disability as the reason she finally was able to merge what had been mutually exclusive sites of identity: cognitively impaired person and mother. With her story, Lewis draws attention to the ways in which motherhood might be figured as an ontological status that applies to only some women. How might other women—those with cognitive and/or physical disabilities, those who have had an abortion, or those who otherwise have not delivered a child that would live—frame (or let others frame) their ontological un/fittedness for motherhood?

Cindy L. Griffin and Karma R. Chávez identify the "logic of purity" as a colonial one that seeks to uphold "a proper gender/sexuality for all members of the nation" as well as "clear gender roles for men and for women" (10). Although invoked to note the oppression of heteronormativity and suppression of queer identities, this nationalistic logic also explains the silencing and secreting practices related to White unwed bodies in the United States during the middle of the twentieth century. What other oppressions might become more visible or apparent if rhetorics of shame were used as a discursive tracking device that could point to normative ruptures of the past? With a diachronic record of sexual shaming, scholars might be better able to recognize how, when, and under what conditions norms shift and measure the durability of mothering through time—a capability that can help us account for those secrets still hiding in the not-so-distant past.

Acknowledgments

This article represents a modified portion of my unpublished dissertation, "Secrets and Silences: Rhetorics of Unwed Pregnancy since 1960." I would like to thank study participants who generously shared their experiences with me and who have challenged my thinking about mothering rhetorics. Lynn O'Brien Hallstein generously provided thoughtful and detailed responses to every draft of this article. Thank you to Joan Faber McAlister, Isaac West, and two anonymous reviewers who found this to be a compelling project and guided me through necessary revisions. My thanks also to Lindal Buchanan, Cheryl Glenn, Jessica Enoch, Michael Faris, Bonnie Sierlecki, Sarah Summers, Judy Holiday, Sarah Rude, and Matt Biddle for their thoughtful responses. Thank you to participants of the 2015 Rhetoric Society of America Institute "Rhetoric and Sensation" seminar, seminar leaders

Notes

1. I use Jenny Edbauer's notion of "rhetorical ecologies" rather than rhetorical situation here because Edbauer theorizes "a framework of affective ecologies that recontextualizes rhetorics in their temporal, historical, and lived fluxes" (9). Such a dynamic understanding of rhetoric as a "circulating ecology of effects, enactments, and events" (9) aligns with my own thinking about the multidirectional movements and multifaceted implications of rhetorics of shame.
2. My larger research program is dedicated, in part, to challenging the notion that *Roe v. Wade* marked a watershed moment for women's agency that resulted in a lessening of the shame of unwed pregnancy and women's sexuality, more generally. In this instance, however, the ruling offers a useful index that situates my work alongside other work on reproduction in the field of communication studies.
3. Here I apply the definition of reproducing rhetorics that Lynn O'Brien Hallstein articulates in the introduction to this special issue: "the rhetorical reproduction of ideological systems and logics of contemporary culture."
4. My language here draws attention to the complexities of consent as a historically situated concept. Considered at the contemporary moment, consent functions as a significant and largely discursive aspect of sex and sexual self-advocacy. Yet as contributor Squeamish Kate writes in the online magazine *XOJane*, even today there is "no clear understanding of consent" as a general concept. Investigating rhetorics of consent is outside the scope of this project; however, I choose to highlight the vexed historical notion of consent by using the term "quasi-consensual." By "quasi-consensual," I refer not to partial *agreement* to the sex act, but rather to the partial *awareness* some women had about sex. As an agential matter, this terminology nuances what might otherwise result in a discussion of giving or not giving consent. For example, one mother with whom I spoke explained to me that she did not know what sex was even though she had engaged in sexual intercourse and subsequently became pregnant, representing a different level of awareness than understanding sex as an act but not reproduction as a process. Thus, I am calling attention to the fact that women *may have* indicated some form of consent for a physical act, but even so, they might not have been sexually literate enough to knowingly agree to sexual intercourse. This note is meant to disrupt rhetorics of blame and insufficient notions of consent-as-agreement in order to shed light on how sexual literacy/sexual awareness is a crucial precursor to informed sexual consent.
5. See work by reproductive scholar Rickie Solinger, especially *Wake Up Little Susie: Single Pregnancy and Race before* Roe v. Wade (Solinger 6–7).
6. I think of rhetorics of shame as an amalgam of communicative and communicated words, feelings, and performances, as this article demonstrates.
7. Such anxiety is similar to what Joan Faber McAlister identifies in relation to her analysis of *Habits of the Heart*, a 1985 book reflecting on "a new middle-class familial crisis" (284).
8. Only three mothers I interviewed gave birth outside of the 1960s. Although Fessler's and Solinger's work relies on popular notions that the practice of hiding ended with the passage of *Roe v. Wade* in 1973, I learned of other women who hid a pregnancy during the 1980s. Thus, hiding a pregnancy—while less of a cultural mandate after the *Roe* decision—was still an option for some women who, according to one informant, were bound by a religious mandate to not have an abortion but who were still unwilling (or unable) to show their unmarried and pregnant status publicly. More research is needed on women who went away after 1973, since they do not figure in the historiography of "going away" and continue to be an unrepresented portion of once-unwed mothers.
9. I became aware when conducting interviews that mothers are at various places in terms of sharing their stories. Some shared with me an experience that, at this point, they have shared

with family and even in public venues. Other women's stories are still secreted from even immediate family members. All of the stories are "memoried," a term that I use to denote the fact that memory actively shapes these interview "data," which I consider to add rhetorical richness rather than detract from the validity of these stories that exist in few places other than memory.

10. I am indebted to Rebecca Dingo's methodology of "networking" arguments, so as to shift from analyzing discrete texts to tracing how rhetorics are "picked up" and how rhetorical meaning can subsequently shift and change over time, place, and iteration (2). Although this essay does not follow Dingo's methodology in detail, I hope that my work here supports the larger project of networking that Dingo advocates.

11. The exception is Dorothy, a Black woman who relied on the Salvation Army home's support primarily out of financial rather than moral need.

12. My use of the word *atonement* is meant to suggest the symbolic punishment of hiding the shamed body, which is distinct from but overlaps with the more "practical need" to "deal with" an unwed pregnancy. I also qualify the word *secret* because, although hiding involved complicated scripts and acts meant to make it a clandestine activity, the practice was well known. Also, there is little way to gauge how truly secret or nonsecret hiding was in individual cases.

13. I use the terms *ritual* and *performance* here to emphasize the dramatic quality of these expressions in which the affective quality of the message seems to communicate as much as or more than the sematic meaning of the message.

14. I rely on McAlister's recent definition of hyperbole as "a figure of overstatement, exaggerations, and excess" that primarily functions as "emphatic amplification" (288).

15. Not every mother who shared such a story had the same experience. Some were shamed by nurses, others by doctors, and others by other (wedded) mothers in the facility. Although the details differ, the allowance of shaming rhetorics in the space of the hospital and during the time of laboring was consistent across a number of mothers' stories.

16. The logics of shame present in these performances also uphold Buchanan's explanation of a cultural "code of motherhood" (15) as a construct based on mothers' "sexual disinterest" and reproduction linked to a practice of (social, familial) duty rather than personal sexual desire (17).

17. Cynthia went on to explain that she didn't tell her husband about her unwed pregnancy for four decades of marriage. Her eventual decision to tell her husband about the pregnancy was linked to her later reunion with her son.

18. To clarify, this is a question of how shame functioned rhetorically at the time of a mother's pregnancy. At this point in time, some mothers have joined support groups in order to share their experiences and seek healing together.

19. Just as Fessler heard from mothers she interviewed, many of the women with whom I spoke reported feeling alone until a decade or more later, when they joined a support group or experienced a reunion with their adopted child.

20. See Gardner for a more detailed discussion of how the notion of virginity is, itself, a rhetorical construction that has been defined in varying ways.

21. Actress, director, and writer Lena Dunham's description of being raped during college, which she discloses in her 2014 memoir *Not That Kind of Girl*, was met with sharp criticism and disdain from some. Dunham's discussion of the controversy surrounding her memoir suggests that typical ways of talking about sexual violence could foster feelings of ontological failure among victims. Dunham penned an op-ed posted to the social media site *BuzzFeed*, admitting that she broke her eight-year silence after dealing with feelings of "confusion," "shame," and fear. "I know just how classic these fears are," she writes. "They are the reason that the majority of college women who are assaulted will never report it." Dunham adds that "[s]urvivors are so often re-victimized by a system that demands they prove their purity and innocence," suggesting that, frequently, women's character, not situational decisions, serve as the basis for deliberating about a sexual encounter and, often, for subsequently assigning blame to the woman for what happened. Dunham's framing of how publics talk about sexual violence and assault warrants additional investigation into the communicative functions of shame and blame and the tendency for victims to cast blame on themselves.

Works cited

Ahmed, Sara. *The Cultural Politics of Emotion.* New York: Routledge, 2004. Print.

———. *The Promise of Happiness.* Durham, Duke UP, 2010. Print.

Biddle, Jennifer. "Shame." *Australian Feminist Studies* 12.26 (1997): 227–39. Print.

Buchanan, Lindal. *Rhetorics of Motherhood.* Carbondale: Southern Illinois UP, 2013. Print.

Dingo, Rebecca. *Networking Arguments: Rhetoric, Transnational Feminism, and Public Policy Writing.* Pittsburgh: U of Pittsburgh P, 2012. Print.

Douglas, Mary. *Purity and Danger: An Analysis of Concepts of Pollution and Taboo.* 1966. New York: Routledge, 2002. Print.

Dunham, Lena. "Why I Chose to Speak Out." *BuzzFeed Ideas.* 9 Dec. 2014. Web. 18 Jan. 2016.

Edbauer, Jenny. "Unframing Models of Public Distribution: From Rhetorical Situation to Rhetorical Ecologies." *Rhetoric Society Quarterly* 35.4 (2005): 5–24. Print.

Fessler, Ann. *The Girls Who Went Away: The Hidden History of Women Who Surrendered Children for Adoption in the Decades before* Roe v. Wade. New York: Penguin, 2006. Print.

Fox, Catherine. "Reprosexuality, Queer Desire, and Critical Pedagogy: A Response to Hyoejin Yoon." *JAC* 26.1/2 (2006): 244–53. Print.

———. "Toward a Queerly Classed Analysis of Shame: Attunement to Bodies in English Studies." *College English* 76.4 (2014): 337–56. Print.

Gardner, Christine J. *Making Chastity Sexy: The Rhetoric of Evangelical Abstinence Campaigns.* Berkeley: U of California P, 2011. Print.

Glenn, Cheryl. *Rhetoric Retold: Regendering the Tradition from Antiquity through the Renaissance.* Carbondale: Southern Illinois UP, 1997. Print.

———. *Unspoken: A Rhetoric of Silence.* Carbondale: Southern Illinois UP, 2004. Print.

Glenn, Cheryl, and Jessica Enoch. "Drama in the Archives: Rereading Methods, Rewriting History." *College Composition and Communication* 61.2 (2009): 321–42. Print.

Griffin, Cindy L., and Karma R. Chávez. "Standing at the Intersections of Feminisms, Intersectionality, and Communication Studies." *Standing in the Intersection: Feminist Voices, Feminist Practices in Communication Studies.* Ed. Karma R. Chávez and Cindy L Griffin. Albany: State U of New York P, 2011. 1–31. Print.

Hall, Meredith. *Without a Map: A Memoir.* Boston: Beacon, 2007. Print.

Hammers, Michele L. "Talking about 'Down There': The Politics of Publicizing the Female Body through the *Vagina Monologues.*" *Women's Studies in Communication* 29.2 (2006): 220–43. Web. 1 Dec. 2014.

Hayden, Sara, and Lynn O'Brien Hallstein D. Introduction. *Contemplating Maternity in an Era of Choice: Explorations into Discourses of Reproduction.* Ed. Sara Hayden and D. Lynn O'Brien Hallstein. Lanham: Lexington, 2010. xiii–xxxix. Print.

Manion, Jennifer C. "Girls Blush, Sometimes: Gender, Moral Agency, and the Problem of Shame." *Hypatia* 18.3 (2003): 21–41. *Project Muse.* Web. 3 Feb. 2012.

Manning, Jimmie. "Paradoxes of (Im)Purity: Affirming Heteronormativity and Queering Heterosexuality in Family Discourses of Purity Pledges." *Women's Studies in Communication* 38 (2015): 99–117. Print.

McAlister, Joan Faber. "Figural Materialism: Renovating Marriage through the American Family Home." *Southern Communication Journal* 76.4 (2011): 279–304. Print.

Metalious, Grace. *Peyton Place.* 1956. Boston: Northeastern UP, 1999. Print.

Moorman, Margaret. *Waiting to Forget: A Motherhood Lost and Found.* New York: Norton, 1998. Print.

Nussbaum, Martha C. *Hiding from Humanity: Disgust, Shame, and the Law.* Princeton: Princeton UP, 2004. Print.

Ramsey, Alexis E., Wendy B. Sharer, Barbara L'Eplattenier, and Lisa S. Mastrangelo. *Working in the Archives: Practical Research Methods for Rhetoric and Composition.* Carbondale: Southern Illinois UP, 2010. Print.

Rand, Erin J. "Bad Feelings in Public: Rhetoric, Affect, and Emotion." *Rhetoric and Public Affairs* 18.1 (2015): 161–75. Print.

———. *Reclaiming Queer: Activist and Academic Rhetorics of Resistance.* Tuscaloosa: U of Alabama P, 2014. Print.

Remnick, David. (Host). Sarah Koenig on "Serial," and A Resilient Poet (Episode 12). *New Yorker Radio Hour.* 7 Jan. 2016. Web (Podcast), http://www.wnyc.org/shows/tnyradiohour/.

Romano, Renee C., and Claire Bond Potter. "Just over Our Shoulder: The Pleasures and Perils of Writing the Recent Past." *Doing Recent History: On Privacy, Copyright, Video Games, Institutional Review Boards, Activist Scholarship, and History That Talks Back.* Athens: U of Georgia P, 2012. 1–19. Print.

Royster, Jacqueline Jones, and Gesa E. Kirsch. *Feminist Rhetorical Practices: New Horizons for Rhetoric, Composition, and Literacy Studies.* Carbondale: Southern Illinois UP, 2012. Print.

Samek, Alyssa A., and Theresa A. Donofrio. "'Academic Drag' and the Performance of the Critical Personae: An Exchange on Sexuality, Politics, and Identity in the Academy." *Women's Studies in Communication* 36.1 (2013): 28–55. Print.

Schell, Eileen E. "Introduction: Researching Feminist Rhetorical Methods and Methodologies." *Rhetorica in Motion: Feminist Rhetorical Methods and Methodologies.* Ed. Eileen E. Schell and K. J. Rawson. Pittsburgh: U of Pittsburgh P, 2010. 1–20. Print.

Sedgwick, Eve Kosofsky. *Touching Feeling: Affect, Pedagogy, Performativity.* Durham: Duke UP, 2003. Print.

Sedgwick, Eve Kosofsky, and Adam Frank. *Shame and Its Sisters: A Silvan Tomkins Reader.* Durham: Duke UP, 1995. Print.

Solinger, Rickie. *Wake Up Little Susie: Single Pregnancy and Race before* Roe v. Wade. New York: Routledge, 2000. Print.

Squeamish Kate. "The Other C Word: Why We Need to Talk about Consent More." *XOJane.* 25 Feb. 2013. Web. 13 May 2016.

Tangney, June Price, and Ronda L. Dearing. *Shame and Guilt.* New York: Guilford Press, 2002. Print.

Valenti, Jessica. *The Purity Myth: How America's Obsession with Virginity Is Hurting Young Women.* Berkeley: Seal, 2010. Print.

Winderman, Emily. "S(anger) Goes Postal in *The Woman Rebel*: Angry Rhetoric as a Collectivizing Moral Emotion." *Rhetoric and Public Affairs* 17.3 (2014): 381–420. Print.

Empowering Disgust: Redefining Alternative Postpartum Placenta Practices

Elizabeth Dickinson, Karen Foss, and Charlotte Kroløkke

ABSTRACT

This article examines communication practices surrounding the unconventional yet emerging trend of postpartum placenta use: eating, encapsulating, or burying the human placenta. Through interviews with both supporters and nonsupporters of postpartum placenta practices, we explore conceptualizations of placenta consumption and burial within larger mothering, childbirth, and postpartum rhetorics. We argue that placenta practices function rhetorically within a core frame of disgust, which both supporters and nonsupporters initially use to respond to placenta use. Yet supporters rearticulate the literal meaning of disgust to create an empowering rhetorical frame from which to view placenta practices and mother-hood. In effect, supporters reframe the meaning of disgust toward the mainstream Western medicalization of birth in order to position placenta practices, natural childbirth, and mothering as empowering.

Issues of choice surrounding reproduction, childbirth, and mothering have been central to contemporary feminist discourses and theory (e.g., see Hayden & O'Brien Hallstein, 2010). With the availability of birth control and the legalization of abortion in the 1970s in the United States, access to reproductive choices became a reality for many. This access was followed by myriad choices about pregnancy and mothering as well, including where to receive pre- and postnatal care and where to give birth (in a hospital, a birthing center, or at home). There are birthing intervention and treatment options, such as "mainstream"/"Western" medicalized induced labor, epidurals, or Cesarean sections, as well as what are generally called "alternative," "natural," or "midwifery" decisions, such as home births, hypnosis, and water births.[1] Additional birthing and motherhood choices can include the birthing position (e.g., on the back in bed, squatting, or reclining in water); the practitioners one uses (obstetricians, nurses, midwives, or doulas); breast or formula feeding; crib sleeping or cosleeping; and so on.

One of the more recent options mothers face is what to do with the placenta after childbirth. During pregnancy, the body creates the placenta—a one-pound, dark reddish-blue, disk-shaped organ that connects the fetus to the uterine wall via the umbilical cord. The placenta transfers nutrients, oxygen, and microorganisms to the fetus and disposes of fetal waste; it is delivered after the baby, thus the name "afterbirth." While some cultures consider the placenta valuable or sacred, in many modern hospital births the placenta is considered "waste" and is discarded.[2]

Instead of discarding the placenta, a growing number of mothers consider and negotiate an unconventional yet intriguing option: to consume, bury, or even make art from the placenta. Consumption can take the form of eating it raw, in a smoothie, or in a baked dish (such as a lasagna or casserole). An increasingly popular practice is placenta encapsulation (see Figure 1). Performed by the mother, partner/spouse, family member, friend, or professional placenta-services provider, encapsulation involves stripping the placenta's membrane, dehydrating it (or sometimes leaving it raw), grinding it into a powder, and putting it into pills, which the mother then consumes over several months. While placenta consumption, burial, and art making are still uncommon (Cremers & Low, 2014), the trend continues to grow in popularity and draw media attention (e.g., see Friess, 2007; Independent Placenta Encapsulation Network, 2015). However, laws, regulations, research, hospital policies, and practitioners' decisions, among other issues, make placenta practices complex.[3]

Placenta choices relate to another, larger option that can emerge: What kind of mother to be? How far, for example, will mothers go for their children? Recent examinations of "intensive mothering" (Ennis, 2014) and the "new momism" (Douglas & Michaels, 2005) ask what it means to be a "good mother," when some mothers devote extensive energy to their children and many are expected to do so. Dillard (2015) notes, "Intensive mothering is consistent with a neoliberal regime that places the risks of family life on the shoulders of mothers" (pp. 151–152). In some ways, placenta practices can be considered part of this ideology: Consuming the placenta is thought to help mothers increase their energy, assist in postpartum recovery, and improve lactation. While mothers often are judged negatively for consuming or burying their placentas, they do it anyway, even against the advice of family and hospitals. Placenta practices, then, become constitutive of a particular orientation toward childbirth, postpartum issues, and mothering rhetorics.

Figure 1. Encapsulated human placenta. (Photograph by author).

In this article, we situate placenta practices within mothering rhetorics. Similar to Frye and Bruner's (2012) understanding of food as rhetoric, we note that placenta practices are material as well as rhetorical. The placenta is constitutive of a particular orientation toward childbirth, postpartum issues, and motherhood; it serves as synecdoche, symbolizing a challenge posed both to and by mothers in regard to the reproductive system of which they are a part. We explore conceptualizations surrounding placenta practices to understand this relatively recent mothering rhetoric.

To understand how mothers frame placenta practices, we conducted interviews with supporters and nonsupporters of placenta practices.[4] Through a framing analysis of interviewees' feedback, we identify a process whereby supporters and nonsupporters initially respond similarly, discussing placenta practices as disgusting. Ultimately, however, supporters rearticulate the literal meaning of disgust to create an empowering rhetorical frame within which to view placenta practices, motherhood, and childbirth. Focusing on placenta practices, then, is a fruitful way to explore how a mothering rhetoric and the rhetoric of disgust work both to reproduce and challenge childbirth within medicalized childbirth norms.

Theoretical and methodological approach

In this study, we position our research in literature on framing, wherein symbols function as frames or lenses through which humans see the world (Burke, 1945; Goffman, 1974; Kuypers, 1997). Burke positions frames as terministic screens that dictate how an experience or event is conceptualized. Here, we use *framing* to analyze the perspectives or lenses participants use to make sense of and communicate about what people do with their placentas. The questions guiding our investigation are these: What rhetorical strategies do interviewees use to express and construct the position they come to hold, and to what effect? And what do placenta practices communicate about larger ideologies surrounding reproduction, birth, and motherhood? Essentially, we examine rhetorics of placenta practices while analyzing how a contemporary culture views these practices.

Our data consisted of transcripts from 35 loosely structured interviews (six face-to-face and 29 by telephone) of between 20 and 120 minutes each with supporters and nonsupporters of placenta consumption.[5] To find supporters, one U.S. author placed flyers in public places (including a birthing center and local businesses) and posted announcements on birthing- and placenta-related electronic mailing lists and social media sites. We sought to interview those who engaged in and/or supported placenta practices, including professional placenta preparers, consumers, and special handlers, midwives, and health care professionals.[6] The only criterion for selecting research participants was their support of placenta practices. The Danish author, Charlotte Kroløkke, found interviewees in Copenhagen through a private alternative birthing clinic run by two Danish midwives. Kroløkke interviewed both midwives and, upon gaining consent, the midwives also provided a list of former clients who had consumed their placentas. Kroløkke then contacted these participants.

Many supporters responded immediately; they wanted to be interviewed because they felt passionately about placenta practices. Despite a desire for a diverse interview pool of supporters, only White women of higher socioeconomic status came forward and explicitly responded to our advertisement. Placenta practices can be understood and critiqued as performed mainly by middle- to upper-class, college-educated, heterosexual, White women who are strong proponents of natural childbirth. These supporters have the resources to seek information about birthing alternatives, to engage midwives (and perhaps doulas) as attendants, to pay for encapsulation practices, to vocalize their choices, and to learn about birthing practices in other cultures through reading and travel. Supporting this assessment, Bobel (2002) identified a population that can afford (through financial resources, social capital, and time) alternative birthing, mothering, and lifestyle practices. Our supporters indeed fit Bobel's findings and suggest that the demographic homogeneity among mothers who engage in placenta practices is not accidental. Despite the relatively narrow demographics of people who engage in placenta practices, studying these practices among interviewees in this demographic contributes to understanding how women give meaning to their own childbirth practices.

We similarly advertised for nonsupporters, asking for "anyone who does not believe in, is dubious of, or is deterred by placenta practices." We had a difficult time, however, recruiting nonsupporter participants. After several unsuccessful recruiting efforts, we posted on electronic mailing lists at a local large, public university.[7] We were able to generate a pool of 16 nonsupporters, seven males and nine females. Seven self-identified as White, two as Hispanic, two as African American, two as Asian American, and one as both Hispanic and White. The 16 nonsupporters were generally similar to the supporters in their levels of education and socioeconomic status.

The nonsupporters illustrated another feature of placenta practices: that placenta and placenta practices often are not discussed. Of those nonsupporter interviewees who had previously heard of placenta practices, several first heard about the practice through friends, one from finding a placenta recipe in a cookbook, and several through the media. In addition, several nonsupporters previously had not heard about placenta practices but looked it up online before the interview. Many people who are uncomfortable with placenta practices may not have come forward because it is unknown and rarely discussed.

Using the process of generative rhetorical criticism and a framing analysis of interviewees' feedback, we coded for participants' conceptualizations. With generative criticism, rhetorical critics decide about analysis—and explanations of and theorizing about that analysis—from the artifact(s) rather than applying a previously developed method of rhetorical criticism imposed on the text (Foss, 2009). In our interviews, then, we paid special attention to how supporters answered the questions about their "initial response" and about a "particularly memorable or significant experience" involving placenta use. We examined the words supporters used to define their experiences and then clustered those words to identify major and shared characteristics that constituted how participants then framed those experiences. Several supporters initially described placenta practices positively (e.g., "cool," "beautiful," "logical"), yet they also noted how others think it is strange. Others used terms such as "weird," "disgusting," "gross," and "yucky" to describe either their initial reaction or others' reactions.

With nonsupporters, we also paid special attention to their "initial responses" as well as what they would think or do if a family member planned to use the placenta. As with supporters, we looked for patterns across responses that would help us determine whether a common rhetorical response or frame was evident. Nonsupporters responded with many more words relating to disgust, with nine calling the practice "gross" or "disgusting." Other terms included "bizarre," "unsanitary," "extreme," "not tasty," "not pleasant," "earthy," "unsanitary," "uneducated," "weird," "surprising," and "amusement."

From both supporters' and nonsupporters' interviews, then, we identified the term *disgust* to represent their reactions. The dominance of *disgust*—either as a word participants used to describe their own initial response or society's larger view of placenta use—led to an examination of the rhetoric of disgust as a useful framework. A framework of disgust helps us understand how people conceptualize, respond to, and communicate about placenta practices, and, in turn, about pregnancy, mothering, and motherhood. The rhetoric of disgust provided a way to identify larger understandings about mothering rhetorics within the contemporary medical system.

Rhetoric of disgust

Numerous scholars have examined disgust and its various synonyms—such as the grotesque (Burke, 1984; Mandziuk, 2014; Prior, 1997) and the abject (Kristeva, 1982)—as rhetorical concepts. In essence, disgust is revulsion at the prospect of dealing with offensive objects, prompting a strong, urgent, visceral reaction. In addition, as Burke (1984) notes, juxtaposed contradictory elements are the essence of the grotesque, where two unusual objects or processes are jammed together unexpectedly. Disgust is a mental construct as much as it refers to an object's properties. In other words, disgust depends on an audience's and a culture's reception and definition, as seen in Harpham's (1982) assertion that "[n]o definition of the grotesque can depend solely upon formal properties, for the elements of understanding and perception, and the factors of prejudice, assumptions, and expectations play such a crucial role in creating the sense of the grotesque" (p. 14). The grotesque, then, is not simply a collection of objects strangely combined but "the end result of a train of experiences and developments" (Prior, 1997, p. 50). For example, in some human groups, insects such as ants, cockroaches, beetles, and worms are commonly eaten. Other groups consider even the thought of eating insects to be gross. Disgust, then, is based on agreed-upon patterns of meaning among people.

Related to our study, disgust and grotesqueness often concern the body's borders. Something can become particularly disgusting when it leaves the body. While humans generally are comfortable with body parts and fluids where they belong, when they exit the body (e.g., feces, phlegm, menstrual blood, and, of course, placenta) one cultural response is disgust, as if humans want borders between themselves and their animality (Nussbaum, 2004). Kristeva (1982) suggests that part of the power of what she labels "the abject" exists because such bodily fluids show us what we "permanently thrust aside in order to live" (p. 3).

The pregnant body can be conceptualized within the context of the grotesque, as out of control and disgusting, wherein the "fat" of pregnancy is unappealing, unhealthy, and even repulsive (Dworkin & Wachs, 2009; Earle, 2003; Nash, 2012; Ussher, 2006). Ussher uses *grotesque* to discuss how Western cultures negotiate, regulate, and medically manage perceptions of pregnant bodies. At the very moment that pregnant women are performing femininity (by creating life), pregnant women are likely to be viewed as aesthetically unappealing and even disgusting as women (Dworkin & Wachs, 2009). Dworkin and Wachs (2009) show how fitness magazines encourage women to stay "fit" during pregnancy—allegedly to decrease risk during birth, to help "bounce back" faster postpartum, and to have a healthy baby. In fact, the real reason may be that thin and fit pregnant bodies do not look quite so disgusting. Thus, while modern Western women often are pressured to adhere to a particularly lean, mostly White physical feminized form, pregnancy disrupts that form. As the body grows larger, the distortions of the pregnancy become a contradiction of ideal femininity, making them in effect "disgusting."

Analysis: Framing placenta practices through disgust

Here, we are interested in how supporters and nonsupporters express and frame placenta use. While both groups initially identify "disgust" as central to their understandings of placenta use, each group notably frames disgust differently, demonstrating the instability of its meaning. In this analysis section, we trace and then explain a three-step process by which both groups express and rhetorically frame placenta practices.

In the first step of the disgust cycle, both groups predominantly use disgust to articulate their reactions to and conceptualizations of placenta practices. Both respond similarly to the juxtaposition of two incongruous concepts: eating and human organs. Within the second step, this juxtaposition exposes a particular kind of order, notably the mainstream Western, obstetric-based paradigm of pregnancy and birth. However, supporters and non-supporters then diverge in their framing of disgust, with supporters reframing the meaning of placenta practices so they are no longer disgusting. Last, in the disgust cycle's third step—a step that nonsupporters do not take—supporters make a different move: They challenge medicine's taken-for-granted order and transfer their sense of disgust from placenta practices to Western medicine itself.

Step one: Juxtaposing incompatible elements

In our interviews, both supporters and nonsupporters either expressed or acknowledged surprise at two typically incompatible things: eating and human organs. As one supporter summarized, "The idea of eating any organ is repulsive." In this first step of the disgust cycle, two unlikely things are slammed together, a point both groups acknowledge, often alongside nervous laughter. Of the supporters, one-third personally found this juxtaposition initially disgusting; several described it positively; and others were neutral, open, or unsure. Of those supporters who initially expressed disgust but came to support the practice, the following is a typical response: "No way, it sounded disgusting. It's gross to think of smoothies or drying [a placenta]. I thought, this is the most absurd thing I'd ever heard of." A comment by one eventual supporter summarizes the typical disgust reaction: "That's gross, that's disgusting, isn't that cannibalism?" One supporter described the practice as "off-putting," and her husband's remark aptly summarizes this perspective: "What if your own toe fell off? Would you eat it?"

Even when supporters view placenta practices positively, they still acknowledge that many others do not. "That's gross" is the typical response when the issue is raised. One supporter said, "I think it's sad when we think of it as gross." Thus, regardless of their initial responses, all supporters came to support placenta practices while simultaneously recognizing that the practice is "shocking" and "gross" for many to contemplate.

All nonsupporters we interviewed consider eating the human placenta to be somehow strange, gross, or disgusting. Nonsupporters said they were initially "freaked out," "thrown off guard," and "grossed out" when confronted with placenta use. They noted that "[e]ating something that came out of my body is unappealing"; it is not a "natural thing to do"; it is "very disturbing"; and "it's gross, disgusting, leftovers." Others compared placenta practices to "drinking one's own urine," "eating a lung," "eating a kidney," "eating your own vomit," and "eating skin or body waste." Another nonsupporter compared it to blood-drinking rituals of earlier cultures: "I think of this as going back to the Incans and the Mayans when they thought drinking people's blood [laughter] was good for you, or a sacrifice to the gods or whatever [laughter], a kind of nature religion."

In addition to finding the concept of eating a human organ jarring, the appearance and smell of the placenta is another "gross" aspect for supporters and nonsupporters alike. Interviewees described the blood-smeared, odd-shaped placenta, with the umbilical cord still attached and veins protruding, as not easy to look it. Phrases such as "very bloody and squishy" and "brings to mind a cat or dog eating afterbirth" were typical comments. In addition, to consume it, the placenta must be stripped of its membrane and cut into pieces. It gets chopped into bits in a blender for a smoothie, diced into small pieces for a casserole, or dehydrated in strips and ground into pills. Processing the organ exposes the preparer to all of its visceral features. One supporter, a vegetarian, barbecued her placenta, fed it to her chickens, and then ate the chickens' eggs (see Figure 2), which was how she made the task palatable. She could still reap some benefits from its consumption but not have to think about eating "meat." Another supporter said the placenta had a "meaty aftertaste" that was not pleasant. When one supporter was steaming her placenta in the kitchen, her husband came downstairs "sniffing" and joking that it "smells like newborn cooking." Ultimately, thinking about handling and consuming the placenta in any form often gives one—as an interviewee noted—"the skeevies."

All nonsupporters similarly reacted to the juxtaposition of consuming human organs, even though most had never seen a placenta, in person or in a picture. Two nonsupporters looked up placenta pictures online before their interviews. One described it as "this thing with veins. It looked very disturbing. It looked like something from a David Cronenberg movie." No other nonsupporters talked about the appearance or smell, perhaps because they never had access to either. Even those who had been pregnant (or had partners

Figure 2. One interviewee's placenta, barbecued before being fed to her chickens. (Photograph by interviewee).

who had been) were generally unfamiliar with the placenta, not to mention placenta practices. In our interviews, then, nonsupporters' understandings of the placenta were generally theoretical and often included misunderstandings about the placenta and its function. Typically, they fell back on assumptions about the placenta and the unusual pairing of *eating* with *human organ*.

Last, most interviewees in both groups laughed in response to these shocking, incompatible elements as a nod to the tension of the grotesque. When we asked about nonsupporters' initial reactions to placenta use, five nonsupporters laughed in surprise, two others described surprise in an amusing tone, and several others noted how it was gross but intriguing. Among the supporters, some did not laugh initially; however, many laughed when they described how others responded or might have responded had they known that someone they knew was consuming a placenta. As one participant said, while chuckling, "I certainly didn't tell anyone where it was when I stuck it in the freezer." Another added, "[We] joked about the placenta in the freezer [laughter]." This laughter may point to an acknowledgment of the oddity of placenta use—one that interviewees describe as extreme and nonmainstream, as "so outside the realm of reality." In effect, laughter either diffuses the tension that arises when people mention placenta use or points to those practices as being unusual.

Clearly, these reactions acknowledge Western rhetorics that frame placenta practices in terms of disgust because of the distortion of what most people expect. Disgust and the grotesque essentially rely on contradiction—the connection of two incompatible elements that are jarringly forced together (Burke, 1984). Kayser (1963) describes disgust as the "distortion of all ingredients, the fusion of different realms, the coexistence of beautiful, bizarre, ghastly, and repulsive elements, the merger of the parts into a turbulent whole" (p. 79). The grotesque is a fusion of surprise and horror, the unknown and abnormal, the profound and the degenerate. The elements create a disharmony because they are fragmented, absurd, and ludicrous in their juxtaposition (Harpham, 1982).

In the case of placenta practices, *human organ* and *consumption/burial* constitute the jarring juxtaposition. The disorientation jolts the audience out of their "accustomed ways of perceiving the world" and confronts them "with a radically different, disturbing perspective" (Thomson, 1972, p. 58). A stunning and sudden fusion, then, is responsible for the audience's uncomfortable response and nervous laughter that accompany disgust, an amusement that Kristeva (1982) calls a "horrified laughter" (p. 204) that indicates shock and fascination. The outcome simultaneously is satisfying and horrifying: An audience appreciates and is amused by the incongruity, and they laugh as they shudder (Danow, 1995). The grotesque and laughter are, in this manner, brought together.

Step two: Exposing and challenging categories, systems, and order

Within the second step of the disgust cycle, juxtaposition exposes a certain order. Kristeva (1982) notes that this dimension of disgust involves disturbing "identity, system, order" (p. 4), and Harpham (1982) elaborates that disgust impresses us "with a remote sense that *in some other system than the one in which we normally operate, some system that is primal, prior, or 'lower,' the incongruous elements may be normative, meaningful, even sacred*" (p. 69; emphasis added). The jarring juxtaposition of elements, then, calls into question the legitimacy of a taken-for-granted category—a traditional perspective that can be fundamentally challenged (Harpham, 1982).

Consistent with this notion of disgust, both groups pointed to a clear, taken-for-granted order: the mainstream Western paradigm of pregnancy, birth, and motherhood that relies on evidence-based medicine with obstetrician practitioners. After exposing this order, participants either supported or resisted it. Interestingly, supporters directly pointed to this paradigm, while nonsupporters discussed it in subtler ways. Although both groups indicated awareness of this order, they diverged in their responses to it.

Our interviewees consistently noted that consuming or burying placentas defies typical human practices, but most importantly they signaled how consumption or burial exposes two childbirth paradigms. For this reason, we discuss how both groups operate within two worldviews that define and guide pregnancy, birthing, and postdelivery practices: mainstream Western medicine and natural childbirth. Specific practices vary, and they can overlap, yet the ways people perceive actors, places, and concepts within pregnancy and childbirth create two distinct systems and guide practices in two different ways. Ultimately, supporters and nonsupporters point to different ideological systems, embedded within each paradigm, that support particular kinds of approaches to birthing.

Mainstream medicine and placenta practices

Both supporters and nonsupporters referenced placenta practices within a mainstream, obstetric-based medical approach to childbirth. Advocates of this system argue that giving birth in hospitals with "medical professionals" is best. In discussing this mainstream mode of birthing, nonsupporters argue three points: (a) traditional Western medicine is the most rational and trusted option (and eating placentas certainly is not a part of this rational paradigm, nor is talking about the placenta); (b) humans are above animals and should not engage in "animalistic" practices, such as eating human organs; and (c) because medical researchers have not "tested" placenta use, supporters need to "prove" that these practices are beneficial.

To begin, nonsupporters argue that mainstream Western medicine is the most rational and safe option. Here, "trained" medical professionals are available in the "safest" place where birth happens—a hospital. As one nonsupporter who endorses mainstream Western medicine said: "If [childbirth] is going to be done, I'd much rather see it in the hands of some medical professionals who can guide and see." Another nonsupporter added: "Women are giving birth in their living rooms. For me, I would want every science available, just in case anything went wrong." Advocates of mainstream medicine see birth as a risky medical event, and trained professionals in hospitals are the most legitimate option.

Nonsupporters also express an understanding that, as a part of mainstream medicine, people do not talk about the placenta, much less eat, encapsulate, or bury it. Of the 16 non-supporters, only five had heard of placenta use prior to participating in the interviews. When asked what they knew about placenta practices, many replied with phrases like "barely, essentially no," and "very vaguely, yes, but very vaguely." Two nonsupporters had read an article about it. Interestingly, when many nonsupporters explained what the placenta is, they mistakenly described it as the uterus or uterine wall. Nonsupporters' lack of knowledge points to the strength of a certain kind of taboo against talking about placentas within Western medicine. These nonsupporters, then, do not challenge this taboo; they are willing to participate in an interview to discuss what they think about it, and then leave it at that.

Next, as advocates of the mainstream approach, most nonsupporters argue that humans are above animals and should not engage in "animalistic" practices such as eating human organs. As one nonsupporter noted, "This is something that animals engage in, and we as humans should hold ourselves to higher standards." One nonsupporter described the practices as "barbaric," suggesting it is uncivilized and brutish. Other terms used to describe placenta use were "animalistic," "wild," and "cannibalistic." By way of summary, one nonsupporter elaborated: "It's kind of primal, and not necessarily on a rational level. I had a visceral image of someone kind of tearing into this tissue that was a part of their body at one point. And [the placenta] came out of this very animal, bloody procedure of childbirth. It just seems very primitive." These statements reveal a belief that people should maintain a kind of superiority by not engaging in behaviors associated with lower animals.

Next, nonsupporters articulate the importance of reason and science throughout their interviews. They point to placenta use as "uneducated," "superstitious," and "irrational." One nonsupporter said, "I don't see the logic of it"; another added, "I think it's irrational, because it's what my gut tells me. It's not logical." Another participant noted how the practice "kind of hit me as outside the scientific realm and sort of cultlike." Nonsupporters, then, see these practices as defying Western medicine, science, and reason.

Last, those who subscribe to the mainstream obstetrics model employ the rhetorical strategy that we labeled "prove it." Because medical research has not "tested" placenta practices, nonsupporters want supporters to "prove" the touted benefits. As one nonsupporter said, "I prefer to have more evidence. I'm just not convinced." Distrust, then, at the lack of scientific proof was a common response for nonsupporters: "I'm not convinced it would help. If there is anecdotal evidence, that's fine, but I'm more of a numbers guy"; "If there are studies that show that there is some improvement, then I say go for it"; and "If there is a solid scientific basis for it, if the research bears that out, I can certainly see a rationale for doing it." As another nonsupporter noted: "If there was any research that there was definitely health benefits, then that would sway me and make me more supportive of the practice. If there was good scientific research done with good power that there were no benefits, then I would not be supportive of it."

Nonsupporters need confirmed scientific proof of the health benefits before they would consider supporting placenta practices. In effect, nonsupporters explicitly or implicitly back the contemporary ideologies of intensive mothering, specifically that mothers should rely on experts within mainstream medicine, including "real" medical researchers who conduct "real" medical research.

Natural childbirth and placenta practices

The second worldview is a midwifery-based natural approach, in which the placenta plays an important role in the birth cycle. In their interviews, supporters typically described birth as a normal, empowering, and beautiful life event. Of the 14 supporters, 13 had children, and all but one of these delivered at least one of their children in a birthing center (and a few at home) rather than a hospital. Within this natural model, supporters challenge the definition of "safe" birthing practices. They choose a different interpretation of birth and the place of the placenta within that experience.

In discussing natural birth, supporters argue that (a) mainstream Western medicine is damaging, and natural childbirth is the best option (one in which placentas are a normal part of childbirth); (b) humans are mammals, and therefore animals, and because most mammals eat their placentas, humans can/should too; and (c) they do not need medical proof to value placenta use; instead, supporters need only a "leap of faith" to justify consuming or burying their placentas.

First, most supporters align with a natural, midwifery approach, which they describe as a purposeful—and better—choice than mainstream "medicalized" childbirth. Supporters see natural childbirth as an alternative to—and direct interrogation of—the Western, mainstream, and largely patriarchal approach they view as problematic. In expressing this belief, one supporter noted: "There is a medicalization of birth that thinks of birth as an illness." Another supporter also referred to the "medicalization of birth," suggesting that it produces "low-quality, high-intervention births." Most of the supporters see obstetrics as a dysfunctional childbirth model that disciplines the female body and causes risk to mother and child. One supporter summarized this stance: "We've come so far from what births should be that we don't know what it is anymore. Most of OBGYNs are men; women aren't in charge of birth anymore … We don't treat birth as a normal part of life."

Supporters recognize the central, important role of the placenta in natural birth. Most mothers who practice natural childbirth do not do anything with their placentas; however, if they wish to, most medical practitioners within the midwifery model are supportive. In addition, according to several interviewees, if heavy bleeding or hemorrhaging occurs after birth, one practice that some midwives use to stop the bleeding is to cut a piece of the placenta and place it inside the new mother's mouth, between the cheek and gums. Essentially, those in the natural birthing model typically do not question the mothers' desires to use it, and sometimes health care providers even use the placenta for healing purposes.

Talking about or doing something with the placenta, therefore, is not uncommon in natural childbirth, although it largely is absent from most mainstream discussions about birth. As one interviewee affirmed, "It's not commonly discussed … When birth is talked about on TV or among people, we don't talk about the placenta part." Another supporter said that we need to "talk about it and get it out there. It's education, exposure. Most people I know, it went right to biohazard, even in my circle." Another described it as "kind of like 'don't ask, don't tell,'" and yet another said, "I think it is like miscarriages where people don't realize how common it is because we don't talk about it, and there is a lot of emotion around it." As another supporter put it, "As a practice, it's on the fringe, in the shadows. Many women in a mainstream wellness model aren't aware or willing to do it." A lack of mainstream discussion increases the tension around placenta practices, making uncomfortable responses more likely.

Next, supporters question the taken-for-granted mainstream medical model by arguing that humans are mammals (and therefore animals); because most mammals eat their placentas, humans can/should too. In contrast to nonsupporters, supporters positively compare humans and animals, acknowledging that humans *are* animals and not superior. One interviewee noted, "Of course mammals eat their placentas, and this is how you get nutrition." Another supporter echoed this sentiment, saying it "fulfilled my mammal instincts." Yet another supporter said, "It's normal and animal-like," and another said, "It's logical—all animals eat them." Supporters, then, challenge the idea of human dominance over animals by placing themselves into the animal category rather than insisting on superiority.

While nonsupporters read placenta practices literally (as disgusting, unreasonable acts), supporters often choose a more lyrical, emotional interpretation: not, as one interviewee noted, medical waste "but beautiful, poetic, and special." She elaborated: "My body made this—an organ—which is in our body for a short period of time." That the body can create an organ for one temporary purpose made the process special to her. Another supporter agreed: "I came to see the placenta as a food source made just for my baby. I couldn't imagine not treating it as this beautiful, amazing thing." Another participant also used the word "amazing" to describe the placenta as a playmate for her child: "It's an amazing organ, a tether between mother and child, a child's first playmate." Supporters find a symbolic meaning in the practice, using terms like "marvelous," "awe," and "fulfilling" to signal the transformation from a purely carnal practice to a symbolic one. Supporters celebrate the placenta's life-nourishing, mystical powers, and upon consuming or burying it, feel that a mother can capture these properties.

Last, while nonsupporters tell supporters to "prove" the benefits, supporters circumvent this in interesting ways. To increase credibility, they often evoke Chinese traditional medicine's long-standing use of the placenta as a healing agent. In addition, for backing, supporters also tap into what we label "the natural network"—a collection of peers, friends, friends of friends, birth centers, midwives, and doulas as well as online support groups and chat rooms.

Most interestingly, supporters bypass the lack of "proof" through a strategy that we label "a leap of faith." As Beacock (2012) notes, the "absence of evidence does not mean that it is not beneficial, and credible theories support placentophagy [the act of mammals eating their young's placenta] ... numerous women and midwives give narrative accounts of the benefits" (p. 468). One supporter articulated this similar sentiment—that she needs faith instead of proof: "I felt like, if it was true that it helped with PPD [postpartum depression] and milk supply and all these other things people claim, energy level, etc., what can be the harm? Even if it is a placebo effect, placebo is powerful. If it can possibly help, I don't have a problem trying it. Let's give it a shot." Here, the lack of medical research is not an issue. If it "can't hurt," and if it may just help, supporters make a leap of faith to try. As one supporter said, when explaining why she thinks people tend to do better after birth if they consume their placentas, "It can't just be a coincidence. It can't be! There's a reason why almost all animals do it. We know it is a good thing and don't have the clinical research to back it up." Another supporter agrees: "If I find something that has benefits and no harm at all, I'll try it. If it won't do harm and it makes sense, I'm willing to try."

Supporters and nonsupporters, then, go in two different directions in response to "disgusting" placenta practices. Nonsupporters do not move beyond the literal jarring elements of placenta practices; they do not challenge the systems of meaning that the juxtaposition calls into question—animalism, the Western medical system, and the "lack of proof" that placenta use works. Supporters, in contrast, make use of the juxtaposition of jarring elements to challenge the human-animal relationship, Western medicine, the taboo against talking about placentas, and the lack of scientific, medical evidence.

Step three: Reframing disgust and placenta practices

Choosing to do something with one's placenta does not just depend on whether eating an organ is disgusting. Nonsupporters end up reading placenta practices literally, and thus they reinforce their framing of disgust. Within this notion of disgust, actors see the object or experience as "no more than the sum of its synonyms—ludicrous, wildly formed, absurd, disgusting" (Harpham, 1982, p. 24). In this third step, then, nonsupporters see placenta practices as obviously strange and gross—end of story.

Supporters, on the other hand, offer a different interpretation. Rather than leaving placenta use at its literal level, they move to a place of abstraction by transforming the disparate elements into a unity. According to Prior (1997), the grotesque compels "a unique consideration of not only curiously arranged objects but of the morals, philosophies, and other such systems which are implied by these objects and their interrelations" (p. 43). This level involves more than simply an abstract understanding of two juxtaposed objects or a challenge to systems. Instead, the viewer fills in gaps in knowledge by bringing their own meanings to the object: "the opportunity is given us to bring into play our own faculty for establishing connections—for filling in the gaps left by the text itself" (p. 44).

Drawing on their own experiences and understandings of placenta practices and the larger issues implicated in placenta use, they express a new, distrustful attitude toward Western medical practices. One supporter articulated this notion: "I began to think how messed up much of our understanding of birth is ... there is an othering of women's bodies where we make everything gross—breastfeeding, menstruation, birth—it's all gross. Being around other people who were more comfortable about it started to change my beliefs. I asked myself, why am I thinking so poorly of this thing?" Another supporter similarly points to what gets framed in mainstream childbirth as dysfunctional: "People react [negatively to alternative placenta practices] because they think we have to live in a sterile environment." Supporters reject the basic tenets of Western medicine to redefine what is gross.

For supporters, then, thinking about the placenta and its role is an emotional experience: "Thinking about the placenta, I felt bad about it. It's almost like I'm not taking care of the whole experience and being respectful toward this baby and process." Another said, "I became very emotional about the idea of keeping it." Placenta practices became a way for supporters to respect themselves, their babies, their bodies, and birth—a way of "closing the loop" and "owning the whole birth process."

In addition to taking a "leap of faith" to a higher level of understanding about placenta practices, several supporters took an activist stance, directly or indirectly. Here, supporters expressed different levels of advocacy—for themselves, their babies, their partners, family and friends, or for the cause. One supporter noted: "When people bring it up, I say I did it [ate the placenta]. They then have a tangible experience with actually knowing someone who did it, which makes it more normal." Several supporters also noted the importance of advocating for alternative childbirth and the placenta cause, such as one supporter who wanted to participate in this study to "spread the word." She said, "I felt so compelled [to interview for this study]. It's so important, and I feel so strongly about birth and pregnancy care. When I saw your ad, I memorized your number and called right away."

Essentially, supporters have come to reject what Foucault (1989) called the "medical gaze," the "powerful, objective, and scientific" (Chivers & Silva, 2013, p. 410) mainstream patriarchal medicalization of birth that has given medicine power over women's bodies. In *The Birth of the Clinic*, Foucault uses the concept of the "medical gaze" to articulate how the development of Western medicine and hospitals have enabled an alienating and dehumanizing split between patients' bodies and their identities; health care professionals (mostly male doctors) in hospitals began to exert power and central authority over the body, relying on empirical observations and analyses to "treat" the body, often regardless of what patients think or want.

Instead of succumbing to the medical gaze, supporters use natural birth to step outside of Western medicine and engage in "empowered motherhood." For example, to describe placenta use, supporters employ empowerment words such as "respect," "autonomy," and "control" rather than words like "gross," "absurd," and "bizarre" (i.e., words used by nonsupporters). Supporters tap into a form of activism and social change that O'Reilly (2004) calls "empowered motherhood," circumventing or challenging patriarchal notions of mothering that make specific demands of mothers, such as spending large amounts of time with children, not working outside of the home, relying on experts, and fostering all forms of child development (Green, 2010). Regarding placenta practices, supporters resist this disciplinary medical gaze and begin to transform their sense of disgust to the patriarchal and clinical medicalization of birth itself, moving the medical establishment rather than placenta practices to the margins. The resistance to acting appropriately as per the tenants of patriarchal Western medicine and the medical gaze (e.g., give birth in a hospital, do what the obstetrician tells you, and certainly do not eat your placenta) can be empowering because mothers can exert control by doing what they want with their placentas, regardless of a "lack of proof." Moreover, they can tap into support systems to do so, and they can choose whether to tell anyone. In effect, supporters conceptualize placenta use as a form of resistance to the medical gaze, a move that particularly evokes empowered mothering.

Conclusions

In sum, supporters make additional moves to reframe what is disgusting—not placenta use, but the Western medical model of birth. Supporters describe modern rhetorics of the medicalization of birth, notably in how it disciplines and disempowers pregnant, birthing, and postpartum women and labels them dysfunctional, problematic, and harmful. Supporters reframe the meaning of disgust and redirect it toward the medical establishment to position placenta practices as a mode of empowerment. In this process, supporters' redefinition of disgust reframes mothers' relationships to their placentas as empowering. Doing something with one's placenta, then, becomes an important move to protect the birthing process from the medical gaze. In this reading of the grotesque beyond the literal—and beyond a verbal rhetoric and toward a material rhetoric—supporters bypass traditional readings and create space for new possibilities, having control over their reproductive choices, and by deciding that eating their placentas may help in their postpartum recovery.

In addition, the rhetoric of disgust, as evidenced by the supporters and nonsupporters we interviewed, reveals the different ideological systems that surround reproduction, pregnancy, and motherhood in Western contemporary culture. Supporters' redefinitions of disgust reframe mothers' relationships to their placentas and birth as special and empowering (as per natural childbirth) and not confining, dangerous, or disempowering (as per the medical gaze). Supporters construct rhetorical strategies to reframe their understandings of placenta practices as empowering to women and as a means to challenge medicalized birth.

In effect, placenta practices become a cultural intervention into medicalized, mothering, and postpartum rhetorics of sorts and not just about drinking a placenta smoothie. While supporters initially saw eating or burying their placentas as gross (and for some, this characterization does not completely disappear), engaging in postpartum placenta use is easier than putting up with what they perceive to be a dysfunctional medical model of childbirth. Supporters trust in the empowering natural model, and this approach becomes more palatable. They literally and figuratively consume empowerment as they consume or bury their placentas.

At issue is not necessarily that supporters consume the placenta but that they create a space where it is conceivable and symbolic of larger birthing and mothering possibilities. Supporters contribute to a new understanding of reproductive and mothering rhetorics, including exposing and discussing the dominance of the medical model of birth whereby by-products of birth are positioned not as "gross" waste products but as valuable nutritional and cultural material. As we discussed, the supporters represent and reproduce a particular type of woman and mothering (i.e., educated, White, financially comfortable). We also argue that consuming one's own placenta contributes to a new understanding of what the placenta is, birthing and postpartum choices, and the ways that a mother may take back her body (parts). While placenta practices may align mothers with the ideologies of intensive mothering and new momism, we argue the supporters in this study reveal that more is at stake.

How supporters have reframed their relationship to mainstream medicine has broader implications for feminist communication scholarship, notably in relation to mothering and motherhood. Clearly, those working with placentas—placenta preparers, doulas, midwives, women, and family members—may want to acknowledge the disgust factor and then move into the larger contexts of meaning in which these practices can occur. This includes moving from the personal benefits of eating the placenta to challenging childbirth practices and the medical system.

Beyond our study, other topics related to disgust circulate around reproduction, motherhood, and birth that illustrate how women challenge mainstream medical approaches. Returning to alternatives highlighted in our introduction, some women can exert choice and empowerment regarding other "disgusting" mothering-related issues. One example is breastfeeding, which has made a small comeback in some industrialized nations with some mothers. Though many practitioners, hospitals, and societal perspectives can still deem open breastfeeding in public or extended breastfeeding inappropriate or even disgusting, some mothers are engaging in what can be considered a feminist practice of doing it anyway, despite how they are criticized. The implications are that women and mothers can be empowered to operate outside of systems that they perceive as damaging to their agency, health, and empowerment, no matter what others say or think.

In our study, we have shown the significance of understanding childbirth and placenta practices as not only biological but also profoundly rhetorical practices. When tapping into a rhetoric of disgust, then, supporters reveal what they perceive to be a damaging medical ideology that isolates mothers from their own birthing experiences and subjects their bodies and children to danger. They challenge Western rhetorics of reproduction, childbirth, and mothering, and they introduce an alternative way of being by redefining disgust. Disgust becomes the rhetorical and communicative strategy that helps supporters move beyond a literal "gross" interpretation to a place for contrast, choice, and empowerment, and thus ultimately a divide between medicalized and natural ideological systems. What is considered "disgusting" becomes a chance to advocate for natural childbirth, to challenge conventional Western birthing culture, and to become empowered in the process.

Notes

1. While the terms *mainstream/Western* and *alternative/natural/midwifery* are rhetorical on some level, this language is used by interviewees, scholars, and writers in popular and research-based childbirth discussions. The "Western"/"mainstream" medical model of birth emerged over the past century as birth moved from homes into hospitals, managed mostly by Western-trained male doctors (mostly obstetricians), complete with medical interventions. The birthing body is conceptualized largely as a vessel of sorts, meant to usher a baby safely into the world (Ussher, 2006). The emphasis is on obstetricians who monitor and "deliver" babies. The birthing woman is meant to trust the professional to make informed decisions for a safe delivery, especially for the baby. Pregnancy is a medical event, complete with specific positions (lying down or semiseated), pushing routines, and interventions (labor induction, epidurals, episiotomies, and Cesarean deliveries). In contrast, "alternative"/"natural"/"midwifery" techniques have been used throughout human history. After Western medicalized births were introduced in many industrialized cultures, natural birth was less frequently practiced and even looked down on as unsafe. Over the past several decades, however, natural childbirth in industrialized countries has made a small comeback. The natural model sees birth as an empowering life event and something that pregnant women should manage in conjunction with a midwife. Medical interventions (epidurals, episiotomies, Cesarean sections) are discouraged unless necessary. Trained, predominantly female midwives assess the pregnancy and attend the birth. The birthing woman is seen as empowered and capable of ushering a baby safely into the world with limited intervention. The emphasis is on the birthing woman, who is supported by her network and other attendants (such as doulas). Women typically deliver sitting, kneeling, squatting, or standing, with several trusted people in the room.
2. Traditional Chinese medicine (TCM) practitioners have used dried human placenta for medicinal purposes (Higham, 2009), and people in various cultures have ritually buried the placenta (Cusack, 2011; Metge, 2005; Shepardson, 1978; Young & Benyshek, 2010). Some argue that humans have purposefully evolved away from eating their placentas (Feibel, 2015).
3. Some question the legality of placenta practices in the United States, where consuming a placenta is not illegal (Cusack, 2011) and policies can influence placenta use and disposal. In home births and birthing centers, providers freely give the placenta to parents when asked. In hospitals, health care providers usually ask patients to sign over their placentas, which they do, often without thinking about it, with some exceptions. Often, though, whether U.S. mothers can take home the placenta depends on hospital policies. In our research, for example, we learned of a hospital where patients' placentas are delivered to their rooms in a bucket marked "save for patient for human consumption" (personal communication, 2013). Ultimately, however, interpretations of hospital and U.S. Occupational Safety and Health Administration (OSHA) guidelines, rather than regulations or law, create an ad hoc environment around placenta disposal, use, and policy (Cusack, 2011).
4. This article involves three investigators: one in a southeastern U.S. town, one in a southwestern U.S. city, and another in Copenhagen, Denmark. Because personal experience shapes feminist scholarship (Foss & Foss, 1994), one author's personal experience is relevant. Five years ago, while she was pregnant, the author decided to encapsulate her placenta after her childbirth. The author was scheduled for a Cesarean delivery due to a breech baby, and the obstetrician told her in a presurgery meeting that she could take the placenta. However, when she arrived for the surgery, the obstetrician told her that taking the placenta violates hospital policy. The author mentioned that her midwife from a birth center would be present during the operation, and the obstetrician then spoke with the midwife, apparently agreeing to look the other way. Following the surgery, the midwife simply took the placenta, which was sitting in a plastic bag on an operating room tray, placed it in her purse, and walked out of the hospital.
5. Of the six face-to-face supporter interviews, one was in the United States and five were in Copenhagen. One U.S. author conducted all nonsupporter interviews by telephone. Our interview questions for supporters included the following: How did you first come to know about placenta practices? What was your initial response? What research, if any, did you do? Who did

the preparing/handling? Why did you choose the practice that you did? What about this is important to you? What did your health care professional think of your decision? Can you recall a memorable/significant experience regarding your placenta practice? Can you recall a conflict with someone who was critical of what you did? Why don't more people do it? Our questions for nonsupporters included: Did you know about this topic before you saw our advertisement? When was the first time you heard about this? What was your response? What do you know about the placenta, pregnancy, and birth? What do you know about placenta practices? Why do you think people do it? If a family member/friend told you they were doing this, what would you think/say/do? Would it change your impression of them? What information would change your mind? Do you think people should be allowed to do this? What about this practice deters you?

6. Interviewees who did something with their placentas reported consuming it raw (such as putting a chunk in their mouth directly after birth, or blending in a smoothie) or in capsules; burying it (under a newly planted tree, alongside varying kinds of ceremonies); and doing a lotus birth (i.e., the placenta stays attached to the baby via the umbilical cord until the cord naturally falls off). Several interviewees were professional placenta preparers who encapsulate for a small fee. In addition, several interviewees self-identified as activists, and one was particularly active in U.K. politics surrounding placenta rights.

7. To get nonsupporter interviewees, we offered, with institutional review board (IRB) approval, a monetary incentive of USD$10 or equivalent for the interview. We paid all nonsupporters $10 for their participation.

References

Beacock, M. (2012). Does eating placenta offer postpartum health benefits? *British Journal of Midwifery, 20*(7), 464–469.

Bobel, C. (2002). *The paradox of natural mothering*. Philadelphia, PA: Temple University Press.

Burke, K. (1945). *A grammar of motives*. Berkeley: University of California Press.

Burke, K. (1984). *Attitudes toward history*. Berkeley: University of California Press.

Chivers, E., & Silva, V. T. (2013). Everyday expertise, autism, and "good" mothering in the media: Discourse of Jenny McCarthy. *Communication and Critical/Cultural Studies, 10*(4), 406–426.

Cremers, G. E., & Low, K. G. (2014). Attitudes toward placentophagy: A brief report. *Health Care for Women International, 35*(2), 113–119.

Cusack, C. M. (2011). Placentophagy and embryophagy: An analysis of social deviance within gender, families, or the home. *Journal Law and Social Deviance, 1*, 112–169.

Danow, D. K. (1995). *The spirit of Carnival: Magical realism and the grotesque*. Lexington: University Press of Kentucky.

Dillard, K. N. (2015). Mompreneurs: Homemade organic baby food and the commodification of intensive mothering. In A. T. Demo, J. L. Borda, and C. H. Kroløkke (Eds.), *The motherhood business: Consumption, communication, and privilege* (pp. 151–174). Tuscaloosa: University of Alabama Press.

Douglas, S., & Michaels, M. (2004). *The mommy myth: The idealization of motherhood and how it has undermined all women*. New York, NY: Free Press.

Dworkin, S. L., & Wachs, F. L. (2009). *Body panic: Gender, health, and the selling of fitness*. New York: New York University Press.

Earle, S. (2003). "Bumps and boobs": Fatness and women's experiences of pregnancy. *Women's Studies International Forum, 26*(3), 245–252.

Ennis, L. R. (2014). *Intensive mothering: The cultural contradictions of modern motherhood*. Ontario, Canada: Demeter Press.

Feibel, C. (2015, June 28). Texas defends a woman's right to take her placenta home. *National Public Radio*. Retrieved from www.npr.org/sections/health-shots/2015/06/28/414836758/texas-defends-a-womans-right-to-take-her-placenta-home

Foss, K. A., & Foss, S. K. (1994). Personal experience as evidence in feminist scholarship. *Western Journal of Communication, 58*(1), 39–43.

Foss, S. K. (2009). *Rhetorical criticism: Exploration and practice* (4th ed.). Long Grove, IL: Waveland.

Foucault, M. (1989). *The birth of the clinic: An archaeology of medical perception.* New York, NY: Routledge.

Friess, S. (2007, July 18). Ingesting the placenta: Is it healthy for new moms?. *USA Today.* Retrieved from http://usatoday30.usatoday.com/news/health/2007-07-18-placenta-ingestion_N.htm

Frye, J., & Bruner, M. (2012). *The rhetoric of food: Discourse, materiality, and power.* New York, NY: Routledge.

Goffman, E. (1974). *Frame analysis: An essay on the organization of experience.* New York, NY: Harper Row.

Green, F. J. (2010). Empowered mothering. In A. O'Reilly (Ed.), *Encyclopedia of motherhood* (Vol. 1, pp. 347–348). Los Angeles, CA: Sage.

Harpham, G. G. (1982). *On the grotesque: Strategies of contradiction in art and literature.* Princeton, NJ: Princeton University Press.

Hayden, S., & O'Brien Hallstein, L. (2010). *Contemplating maternity in an era of choice: Explorations into discourses of reproduction.* Lanham, MD: Lexington Press.

Higham, B. (2009). Waste product or tasty treat? *The Practising Midwife, 12*(9), 33–35.

Independent Placenta Encapsulation Network. (2015). Homepage. Retrieved from https://www.placentanetwork.com/

Kayser, W. (1963). *The grotesque in art and literature* (U. Weisstein, Trans.). Bloomington: Indiana University Press.

Kristeva, J. (1982). *Powers of horror: An essay on abjection* (Leon S. Roudiez, Trans.). New York, NY: Columbia University Press.

Kuypers, J. A. (1997). *Presidential crisis rhetoric and the press in the post–cold war world.* Westport, CT: Praeger.

Mandziuk, R. M. (2014). "Grotesque and ludicrous, but yet inspiring": Depictions of Sojourner Truth and rhetorics of domination. *Quarterly Journal of Speech, 100*(4), 467–487.

Metge, J. (2005). Working in/playing with three languages: English, Te Reo Maori, and Maori body language. *Sites, 2*(2), 83–90.

Nash, M. (2012). *Making "postmodern" mothers: Pregnant embodiment, baby bumps, and body image.* New York, NY: Palgrave Macmillan.

Nussbaum, M. C. (2004). *Hiding from humanity: Disgust, shame, and the law.* Princeton, NJ: Princeton University Press.

O'Reilly, A. (2004). *Mother outlaws: Theories and practices of empowered mothering.* London, United Kingdom: The Women's Press.

Prior, T. J. (1997). *Classical and grotesque bodies: Some aspects of courtesy literature and the mid-eighteenth-century comic novel* (Doctoral thesis). University of Toronto, Toronto, Ontario, Canada.

Shepardson, M. (1978). Changes in Navajo mortuary practices and beliefs. *American Indian Quarterly, 4*(4), 383–395.

Thomson, P. (1972). *The grotesque.* London, United Kingdom: Methuen.

Ussher, J. M. (2006). *Managing the monstrous feminine: Regulating the reproductive body.* New York, NY: Routledge.

Young, S. M., & Benyshek, D. C. (2010). In search of human placentophagy: A cross-cultural survey of human placenta consumption, disposal practices, and cultural beliefs. *Ecology of Food and Nutrition, 49*(6), 467–484.

Index

ABC News interview 17–18
ADA *see* Americans with Disabilities Act (ADA)
African Americans: maternity 13, 17, 18, 19;
   motherhood 17–19; traditions 5, 12–15, 19, 24;
   women 18–20, 48, 54, 59
Afrykayn Moon 54, 59, 61, 63
Ahmed, Sara 97, 98, 103
Allers, Kimberly Seals 48, 49, 54, 61
Americans with Disabilities Act (ADA) 81
Anderson, Karrin Vasby 11
"Angry Black Woman" 23
Ann, Mary 103, 104
Applebaum, E. 83
Ashcraft, K. 82

Beacock, M. 122
The Birth of the Clinic (Foucault) 123, 124
black breastfeeding women 49, 55, 56, 57, 58
Black Mothers Breastfeeding Association
   (BMBFA) 49, 52, 54, 61, 63
Blacktavists: female breastfeeding activists 49;
   implications of 49; moments of 53; online
   activism, rhetorical analysis of 52–3; racial
   discrimination 54; rhetorical strategies of 53;
   "Stop Medolac" campaign 49; strategies of
   visibility 53; visibility strategies 49–52; white
   interests, physical needs of 56
black women's labor 49; assert agency 51; black
   nursing body 56; breastfeeding initiation 50;
   denigration of 12; economic value of 57–60;
   historical legacy of 53–7; slavery, history of 51;
   whiteness as racial category 60–2
Blum, L. M. 50
BMBFA *see* Black Mothers Breastfeeding
   Association (BMBFA)
Bobel, C. 114
Bowers, Venessa 4, 6
breastfeeding initiation rates 48, 50, 64n1
"Breastfeeding Mothers Unite" 55
Bruner, M. S. 36, 113
Buchanan, Lindal 102
Bullis, C. 71
Burke, K. 113, 114
Buzzanell, Patrice M. 4, 6, 71

Carmon, Irin 19
CASAColumbia 33–5
CDC *see* Centers for Disease Control (CDC)
Ceccarelli, Leah 14, 15, 20
Centers for Disease Control (CDC) 48, 50
CGI *see* Clinton Global Initiative (CGI)
Charmaz, K. 74
Chávez, Karma R. 4, 106
Clinton Global Initiative (CGI) 48, 62
Collins, Hill 17, 19
Collins, P. H. 18–20
"Coming to Detroit! 2015" (image framing) 56
commodify mother's milk 49
Conn, Cindy 4, 6
Coontz, S. 32
Cottle, Michelle 23
Cronenberg, David 117

Dearing, Ronda L. 102
DeLuca, Kevin M. 13
Democratic National Convention 12, 16, 18, 23
DeVault, M. L. 31, 36, 40, 42
Dickinson, Elizabeth 4, 6
Dillard, K. N. 112
Dimitriadis, G. 31
Domenici, Kathy L. 13
Donofrio, Theresa A. 94
Douglas, Mary 101
Douglas, S. J. 3, 17
Dow, Bonnie J. 23

Eating Among Teens/Project EAT 33
employment–relational rhythms 80
"empowered motherhood" 124

Fabj, Valeria 13
Fallon, Jimmy 16
familializing risk 5, 30, 32
family meal (FM): analysis, phases of 30;
   campaign model 37; "complex social event"
   36; critical concerns 35; "dying tradition"
   35; exploring experiences of 31; facilitation
   of 43; family foodwork 38; feeding risk 32;
   food industries and corporations 33–4;

INDEX

food waste, impact of 37; healthy and happy children 34; meal planning 39–40, 43n2; meals implication 40; methodological approach 30–3; neoliberal risk, mothering 32; nutritional value 38–9; provision of meals 36; pure and simple 35; retailers/manufacturers 43; rhetorical exploration of 30; risk management and miracle of 33–5; "simple family activity" 35; thinking and talking differently 36–42

"Family Meals Movement" 34

Family Medical Leave Act (FMLA) 69, 73, 80, 82, 83

feminist standpoint epistemology: maternity–disability connection 80; participants 72; procedures 72–4; research study results 74–5; standing in margin 71–2

Fessler, Ann 94, 101

Fiske, John 14

Flores, L. 56

FM *see* family meal (FM)

FMI *see* Food Marketing Institute (FMI)

Food Marketing Institute (FMI) 34

Foss, Karen A. 4, 6, 13

Foucault, M. 123

Fox, Catherine Olive-Marie 93, 105–6

Fraser, N. 51

Free to Breastfeed 57

Frye, J. 36, 113

Gallup student poll 11

Gardner, Christine J. 104–5

Gates, Henry Louis, Jr. 20

Gibson, Katie L. 13

Gilbert, J. 38, 78, 80, 81, 85

Giles, M. V. 32

Green, F. J. 53, 54, 59, 61

Green, Kidadda 61, 62, 64n11

Griffin, Cindy L. 4, 106

Hall, Meredith 95–6

Hallstein, O'Brien 1, 25n3

Hall, Stuart 14

Hammers, Michele L. 99

Harpham, G. G. 115, 118

Harris-Perry, Melissa 23

Harris, Tami Winfrey 12

Harvey, D. 31

Hayden, Sara 1, 2

Heyse, Amy L. 13

Hirshman, Linda 16

Holland, J. 73

institutional review board (IRB) 73, 127n7

intensive mothering: black women's role in 17; critique of 16–17; examinations of 112; ideology of 24, 120, 125; reverberations of 16; rhetorical contexts of 19

IRB *see* institutional review board (IRB)

Jasinski, James 12, 15

Jensen, Robin E. 14

Jones, Mary Harris 13

Jorgensen, H. 83

Kamberelis, G. 31

Kayser, W. 118

Kimball, Karen Y. 4, 6

King, Deborah K. 12, 21

Kinser, Amber E. 4, 5

Kristeva, J. 115, 118

Kr 0løkke, Charlotte 4, 6, 113

Lakoff, George 13

Lenz, B. 68

"Let's Move" campaign 23

Lewis, Robin Coste 106

Lincoln, Abraham 14

Liu, Meina 4, 6

MacIntosh, P. 39

MacKerrow, R. M. 36

Manning, Jimmie 93

Martin, Renee 18

maternity leave 6, 67–86

meal planning 39–40, 43n2

Medo, Elena 61

Medolac Laboratories 48, 51

Meisenbach, Rebecca 4, 6

Metalious, Grace 91

Michaels, M. W. 3, 17

midwifery-based natural approach 120–1

"*The momification of Michelle Obama*" (Rebecca) 12

Moms Rising 57

Moorman, Margaret 95

Morrissey, Elizabeth 4, 6

mothers' feeding activities function 32

Mother's Milk Cooperative 48

Moynihan, Daniel Patrick 17

Naples, Nancy 20

National Cattlemen's Beef Association 33

"National Family Meals Month" 34

National Occupational Employment and Wage Estimates 70

National Survey of Children's Health 35

neoliberalism 32

Nestlé's Stouffer's foods 35

New York Times 52, 53, 61

"nostalgic familialism" 23

Obama, Barack 12, 16, 23, 81

Obama, Michelle: African American history and culture 22; black women's role 17; "feminist nightmare" 23; hermeneutic depth 14; an "intensive mom" 15–17; intensive mothering, discourse of 16; low-income students 23; maternal discipline 15, 18;

INDEX

maternity, rhetorics of 13–14; metaphorical structure of 14; mothering, children of nation 21–3; multifaceted mothering contexts 23–4; othermother-in-chief 19–21; public images *vs.* private enactments 17–19; resistive reading 14; rhetorical studies, polysemy in 14–15; roles of African Americans in U.S. history 22; strategic ambiguity 14; U.S. racism, critiques of 22; white feminist critiques of 12
obstetric-based medical approach 119
Occupational Safety and Health Administration (OSHA) 126n3
Of Woman Born: Motherhood as Experience and Institution (Rich) 15
Omi, M. 53
O'Neal Parker, Lonnae 12
ontological failure 6
O'Reilly, Andrea 19, 124
OSHA *see* Occupational Safety and Health Administration (OSHA)

Palin, Sarah 13
Parker, George 58
Payne, R. 70
Peeples, Jennifer A. 13
Poirot, Kristan 12
polysemy, typology of 14
postpartum placenta practices: birthing, mainstream mode of 119; disgust cycle 118–19; ethodological approach 113–15; evidence-based medicine 119; framing placenta practices 116; juxtaposing incompatible elements 116–18; mainstream medicine 119–20; medical model 121; natural birth 120; natural childbirth 120–2; nonsupporter interviewees 114; reframing disgust 122–4; rhetoric of disgust 115–16; supporter interviews 126n5; theoretical approach 113–15
Potter, Claire Bond 95
pregnancies and maternity leaves: "business case" for 69; classist and political gender identifications 69–71; disability leave 79–82; leave as time off 75–9; leave experiences 74; medical secretary 75; middle-class mothers, consequences for 86n2; monolithic group 68; mothers' and children's health 69; organizational policies 81; pink-collar occupations 68, 74, 82; "professional stumbling block" 84; "serious health conditions" 81; sociopolitical-economic positions 73; theoretical and pragmatic implications 84–5; "time is money" conceptual metaphor 76–7
Princeton-Educated Blacks and the Black Community 21
Prior, T. J. 123

Quinn, D. 80

racial discrimination 23, 54
Ramazanoğlu, C. 73
Rand, Erin 51, 58, 104
Reid-Brinkley, Shanara Rose 14, 20
Remke, Robyn V. 4, 6
"reprosexuality," Fox's notion of 93
rhetorical ecologies 92, 104, 107n1
Rhetoric of Food (Frye) 36
Rich, Adrienne 15
Roberts, Dorothy 17, 51
Robinson, F. 72
Roe v. Wade 92, 107n2
Romano, Renee C. 95
Rosin, Hanna 19

Samek, Alyssa A. 94
Sangodele-Ayoka, Anayah 57, 63
Schell, Eileen E. 95
SDI *see* state disability insurance (SDI)
Seiler, A. 34
shame: as experienced emotion 98; and guilt 102; as ontological failure 101–5; rhetorics 92, 93, 95–8
Smith, R. C. 74
Spillers, Hortense 23
state disability insurance (SDI) 80, 83
Stearney, Lynn 13
Steiner, Leslie Morgan 23
Stout, K. 71
The Surprising Power of Family Meals (Weinstein) 34
"symbolic motherhood" 13
"symbol of American womanhood" 11

Tangney, June Price 102
Tavris, C. 82
TCM *see* Traditional Chinese medicine (TCM)
Tonn, Mari Boor 13
Traditional Chinese medicine (TCM) 126n2
Traister, Rebecca 12
Trethewey A. 84
Triece, M. E. 51
Truth, Sojourner 22
Turner, P. 74

unwed motherhood, rhetorics of: demarcation and disidentification 98–101; "logic of purity" 106; overview of 91–3; queering histories of motherhood 93–4; rhetorics of shame 92, 93, 95–8; senses and ruptures 105–6; shame as ontological failure 101–5
"urban milk donors" 48
U.S. Bureau of Labor Statistics 67–8
U.S. Census Bureau 83

The Vagina Monologues (Hammers) 99
Valenti, Jessica 12
Vogue magazine 16
von Wallmenich, L. 78, 80, 81, 85

INDEX

Wachs, F. L. 115
Waiting to Forget 102
Watson, Robert 11
Weedon, C. 70
Weinstein, M. 34
West, Isaac 13
white feminist critiques 15, 18

White House rules 18
white intensive motherhood 19
Williams, J. 82, 86n2
Williams, Patricia J. 11
Winant, H. 53
Winderman, Emily 104
Working Mother 69